Speak Irish Now

by

Patricia Delia Pugnier *and* Brian Lee Pugnier

First published 2012
by Speak Irish Now LLC
2360 Corporate Circle, Suite 400
Henderson, NV 89074-7739

Table of Contents

Introduction

Building Block Approach

The lessons in this book are short, yet powerful. Like building blocks, you can stack and rearrange the pieces to make your own sentences. At first, the range of what you can talk about will be limited, but that's okay. The advantage of building blocks is that they support and strengthen each other, and you can easily add more pieces as you learn more Irish.

With short lessons, you can practice a little every day. Learning Irish in small steps helps you remember it better. Practicing a few minutes each day is better than studying for an hour once a week.

Phonetics and Pronunciation

The aim of this book is to encourage you to speak Irish right away. Therefore, phonetics are included with all examples, and always in brackets.

They are written with the ear of an American English speaker in mind. These phonetics are a guide to get you going. They are not hard and fast rules of how each word or phrase must be pronounced. All languages have variations, and even individual speakers vary how they pronounce the same word at different times.

When you're just beginning, try your best, and you will be fine. Don't expect instant perfection; being close is good enough. Practice saying your Irish out loud. Speaking is a physical exercise. The more you hear and the more you speak out loud, the more natural your pronunciation will become.

Bonus Phrases

Many useful phrases use higher vocabulary and grammar, which are too technical to explain in beginning lessons. Rather than getting tangled up in the finer points of these phrases, they will be presented to you "as-is." We call these *"Bonus Phrases."* Although building your own Irish sentences is the primary goal of this book, these *Bonus Phrases* will give your Irish more strength, flavor, and fluency.

The Buddy System

Learning a new language with a friend or in a group is a great way to have fun and strengthen your skills. Buddies also provide support and encouragement when you're learning a challenging concept. This book can be used for self-study, but is equally effective for group-study.

When studying in a group, always have each person say every word, phrase, and sentence out loud to each other. The more voices you hear speaking Irish, the more familiar the sounds will become. Remember that conversations come in two parts: speaking *and* listening.

Invest in a Dictionary

The vocabulary in this book is focused and streamlined. Using a dictionary is the best way to broaden your vocabulary. Online Irish dictionaries can be a good alternative to a printed dictionary, and are also free.

Lesson 1 – Introductions

Most conversations start with greetings, so that's where we'll start. Greeting phrases often use higher vocabulary and grammar, which can be too technical for your first lesson. We'll be calling these kinds of phrases, "*Bonus Phrases*," and we'll just take them "as-is." You'll be learning the building blocks of Irish sentences and practice making your own sentences in the next lesson. For now, all you need to do is become familiar with these conversation starter phrases.

Greetings

When saying "hello" in Irish, you can say it in two ways, depending on how many people you're greeting. That's because Irish has both a singular "you" and a plural "you" (like "y'all" in colloquial American English). So, to greet people, you say:

"Hello."
Dia duit.
[jee-uh ghitch]

or

"Hello (y'all)."
Dia daoibh.
[jee-uh yeev]

This loosely translates as "God to you," and "God to y'all."

To respond to this greeting, rather than just repeat what has been said to you, you expand on the greeting. This is done by adding the names of holy people, starting with the Biblical Mary. Therefore, the reply to "hello" is:

"Hello (back)."
Dia 's Muire duit.
[jee-uh smwir-uh ghitch]

or

"Hello (back, y'all)."
Dia 's Muire daoibh.
[jee-uh smwir-uh yeev]

This loosely translates as "God and Mary to you," and "God and Mary to y'all."

Introductions

Another very common way to start a conversation is by introducing yourself. To say your name in Irish, you say "I am," followed by your name. To say, "I am," you say:

"I am"
is mise
[iss mih-shuh]

For example, a person named Brian would say:

"I am Brian."
Is mise Brian.
[iss mih-shuh bree-uhn]

What Is Your Name?

After introducing yourself, you'll want to know the name of the person you just started a conversation with. To ask someone's name, you say:

"What is your name?"
Cén t-ainm atá ort?
[kayn tan-um uh-taw ort]

Sometimes, you may start a conversation by introducing yourself, or the other person may ask you for your name first. If you're asking for someone else's name in return, you can change the sentence to make it more emphatic. In English, we do this by saying words more strongly. In Irish, you don't just use the tone of your voice to show emphasis. You actually change the words themselves. In this case, you can switch out the last word, "**ort**" [ort], for its *emphatic form*, which is "**ortsa**" [ort-suh].

So, to ask someone what their name is with emphasis, you say:

"What is *your* name?"
Cén t-ainm atá ortsa?
[kayn tan-um uh-taw ort-suh]

Conversation

You're ready for your first conversation in Irish! Let's practice what we've learned with a conversation between Brian and Pádraigín. In this one, we see how they meet.

Brian:
"Hello."
Dia duit.
[jee-uh ghitch]

Pádraigín:
"Hello."
Dia 's Muire duit.
[jee-uh smwir-uh ghitch]

Brian:
"What's your name?"
Cén t-ainm atá ort?
[kayn tan-um uh-taw ort]

Pádraigín:
"I'm Patricia."
Is mise Pádraigín.
[iss mih-shuh paw-druh-geen]

"What's *your* name?"
Cén t-ainm atá ortsa?
[kayn tan-um uh-taw ort-suh]

Brian:
"I'm Brian."
Is mise Brian.
[iss mih-shuh bree-uhn]

How Are You?

Now that you've said hello and introduced yourself, let's ask how the other person is doing. Just like in English, there are lots of ways to ask how someone is in Irish, but there are three common ones. All are well-known and equally acceptable.

"How are you?"
Cén chaoi a bhfuil tú?
[keh hee will too]

"How are you?"
Conas atá tú?
[kun-us uh-taw too]

"How are you?"
Cad é mar atá tú?
[kuh-jay mar uh-taw too]

Once again, these are *Bonus Phrases*, the kind that are common, but use higher vocabulary and grammar. Even though they each use different turns of phrase, they all express, "How are you?"

<u>Saying How You Are</u>

There are lots of ways to reply to "How are you?" We'll start with a simple and common reply. To say you are well, in Irish, you say:

"I am well."
Tá mé go maith.
[taw may guh mah]

This is a very basic sentence in Irish. We'll be creating a lot more sentences like this one in upcoming lessons. For now, we'll learn how to make more sentences by changing just the last two words.

When you want to describe how you are in other ways, all you have to do is switch out
"go maith" [guh mah], meaning "well," with something else. Here are some other responses you can use:

"I am well."
Tá mé go maith.
[taw may guh mah]

"I am fine."
Tá mé go breá.
[taw may guh braw]

"I am wonderful."
Tá mé go h-iontach.
[taw may guh hee-un-tahkh]

"I am bad."
Tá mé go dona.
[taw may guh dun-uh]

"I am sick."
Tá mé tinn.
[taw may tcheen]

"I am okay."
Tá mé ceart go leor.
[taw may kyart guh leeyor]

Asking Someone Else How They Are

After someone has asked about how you are, you can ask them how they are in return. You can say any of the common "How are you?" questions back, or you could choose a different one than you were asked to mix it up. You can also make your response unique by asking the question in a new way.

You may simply respond by asking, "And yourself?" The words for "and" and "self" in Irish are:

"and"
agus
[ah-gus]

"self"
féin
[fayn]

In English, we write the words for "you" and "self" together, but in Irish they stay separated. You'll notice that all of the versions of "How are you?" end with the word, "**tú**" [too]. This is the word for "you" in Irish. To say, "yourself," all you have to do is say "self," "**féin**" [fayn], after "you," "**tú**" [too]. For example:

"you" + "self" = "yourself"
tú + féin = tú féin
[too] + [fayn] = [too fayn]

So, to briefly ask how someone else is, after they've asked you, you say:

"And yourself?"
Agus tú féin?
[ah-gus too fayn]

Alternately, you can simply add "self," "**féin**" [fayn], to the end of any of the full questions:

"How's your<u>self</u>?"
Cén chaoi a bhfuil tú <u>féin</u>?
[keh hee will too fayn]

"How's your<u>self</u>?"
Conas atá tú <u>féin</u>?
[kun-us uh-taw too fayn]

"How's your<u>self</u>?"
Cad é mar atá tú <u>féin</u>?
[kuh-jay mar uh-taw too fayn]

Thank You

Now that you've exchanged pleasantries, you can thank the other person for asking about how you are. Once again, this is a *Bonus Phrase*, which is very common, but uses higher vocabulary and grammar.

To thank someone in Irish, you say:

"Thank you."
Go raibh maith agat.
[guh ruh mah ah-gut]

Loosely translated, this means "May you have good." This is a common and very useful phrase, and well worth practicing.

Conversation

Let's practice what we've learned with another conversation between Brian and Pádraigín. In this one, they're asking each other how they are.

Brian:
"Hello."
Dia duit.
[jee-uh ghitch]

Pádraigín:
"Hello."
Dia 's Muire duit.
[jee-uh smwir-uh ghitch]

Brian:
"How are you?"
Cén chaoi a bhfuil tú?
[keh hee will too]

Pádraigín:
"I am well."
Tá mé go maith.
[taw may guh mah]

"And yourself?"
Agus tú féin?
[ah-gus too fayn]

Brian:
"I am fine."
Tá mé go breá.
[taw may guh braw]

"Thank you."
Go raibh maith agat.
[guh ruh mah ah-gut]

Good-Bye

Though there are many ways to say good-bye in Irish, most of the usual ones are variations on the simplest form. The easiest way to say good-bye is:

"good-bye"
slán
[slawn]

This is a very useful phrase, and works in any situation. If you'd like to mix it up, you can use one of the common variations. Like phrases such as "bye for now" or "later," each of these depend upon the circumstances, so you can use your best judgment when choosing which to say.

When saying good-bye to someone staying behind, you can say:

slán agat
[slawn ah-gut]

When saying good-bye to many people staying behind, you can say:

slán agaibh
[slawn ah-giv]

When saying good-bye to someone going away, you can say:

slán leat
[slawn lyat]

When saying good-bye to many people going away, you can say:

slán libh
[slawn liv]

When saying good-bye for a while to one or many people, you can say:

slán tamall
[slawn tom-uhl]

When wishing a safe trip home to one or many people, you can say:

"safe home"
slán abhaile
[slawn uh-wah-lyuh]

Conversation

Now let's practice what we've learned with a full conversation between Brian and Pádraigín. In this one, they greet each other, introduce themselves, ask how each other are, and say good-bye.

Brian:
"Hello."
Dia duit.
[jee-uh ghitch]

Pádraigín:
"Hello."
Dia 's Muire duit.
[jee-uh smwir-uh ghitch]

Brian:
"I am Brian."
Is mise Brian.
[iss mih-shuh bree-uhn]

"What's *your* name?"
Cén t-ainm atá ortsa?
[kayn tan-um uh-taw ort-suh]

Pádraigín:
"I am Patricia."
Is mise Pádraigín.
[iss mih-shuh paw-druh-geen]

"How are you?"
Conas atá tú?
[kun-us uh-taw too]

Brian:
"I am well,"
Tá mé go maith,
[taw may guh mah]

"thank you."
go raibh maith agat.
[guh ruh mah ah-gut]

"And yourself?"
Agus tú féin?
[ah-gus too fayn]

Pádraigín:
"I am fine."
Tá mé go breá.
[taw may guh braw]

"Thank you."
Go raibh maith agat.
[guh ruh mah ah-gut]

Brian:
"Good-bye."
Slán agat.
[slawn ah-gut]

Pádraigín:
"Good-bye."
Slán leat.
[slawn lyat]

remember
- Cad is ainm duit
- Dómhnall is ainm dou
Ló Dónal

Lesson 2 – Making Basic Sentences

You've learned a lot, and can now have a full conversation in Irish! A lot of the greeting phrases are *Bonus Phrases,* the kind that are common, but use higher vocabulary and grammar. That's great for starters, but knowing how a sentence is made, how to break it apart, change the pieces, and put it back together, will allow you to truly express yourself in your new language.

A Basic Irish Sentence

Let's start learning how sentences are made in Irish by looking at a simple sentence you learned in Lesson 1. When answering the question, "How are you?", you can say:

"I am well."
Tá mé go maith.
[taw may guh mah]

This sentence is made like this:

tá [taw] = "am"
mé [may] = "I"
go maith [guh mah] = "well"

Notice how the *verb,* "to be," comes first in Irish. The next thing is the *pronoun,* "I." The *adjective,* "well," comes at the end. You'll see this pattern repeated a lot in Irish: a verb, a noun, then something else.

In Lesson 1, we learned how to change this sentence to describe how you are in different ways. All you have to do is switch out the adjective at the end. In this case, the descriptive part is the last two words, even though English may only translate it as one word.

Examples

Let's take a look at our sample sentence and one with a different adjective to compare:

"I am <u>well</u>."
Tá mé <u>go maith</u>.
[taw may guh mah]

"I am <u>wonderful</u>."
Tá mé <u>go h-iontach</u>.
[taw may guh hee-un-tahkh]

Here are a few more examples with different adjectives to get a better look at how this works:

"I am <u>fine</u>."
Tá mé go breá.
[taw may guh braw]

"I am <u>okay</u>."
Tá mé ceart go leor.
[taw may kyart guh leeyor]

"I am <u>bad</u>."
Tá mé go dona.
[taw may guh dun-uh]

"I am <u>sick</u>."
Tá mé tinn.
[taw may tcheen]

Pronouns

Learning how to switch out adjectives to change a sentence gives you a lot of options, but that's not the only thing you can change about this basic sentence. Sometimes, you will want to talk about how someone else is. To do that, all you have to do is switch out the *pronoun*.

A *pronoun* is a short word that can replace a noun, such as "I," "you," and "they." Here is a list of pronouns that go with sentences that use "**tá**" [taw]:

"I"
mé
[may]

"we"
muid
[mwidj]

"you"
tú
[too]

"y'all"
sibh
[shiv]

"he"
sé
[shay]

"they"
siad
[shee-ud]

"she"
sí
[shee]

You'll notice again that Irish has both a singular "you" and a plural "you" (like "y'all" in colloquial American English).

<u>Making More Sentences</u>

We've seen how you can create a new sentence by switching out the adjective. Now we'll make more sentences by switching out the pronoun.

Examples

Let's take a look at our sample sentence and one with a different pronoun to compare:

"<u>I</u> am well."
Tá <u>mé</u> go maith.
[taw may guh mah]

"<u>He</u> is well."
Tá <u>sé</u> go maith.
[taw shay guh mah]

Here are more examples with all of the pronouns:

"<u>I</u> am well."
Tá <u>mé</u> go maith.
[taw may guh mah]

"<u>You</u> are well."
Tá <u>tú</u> go maith.
[taw too guh mah]

"<u>He</u> is well."
Tá <u>sé</u> go maith.
[taw shay guh mah]

"<u>She</u> is well."
Tá <u>sí</u> go maith.
[taw shee guh mah]

"<u>We</u> are well."
Tá <u>muid</u> go maith.
[taw mwidj guh mah]

"<u>Y'all</u> are well."
Tá <u>sibh</u> go maith.
[taw shiv guh mah]

"<u>They</u> are well."
Tá <u>siad</u> go maith.
[taw shee-ud guh mah]

Notice how the verb, "tá" [taw], stayed the same in all of the sentences. In English, we change the verb to match the person, but, in Irish, the verb stays the same regardless of the person you're talking about. We'll learn more about how verbs work in upcoming lessons.

Building Even More Sentences

We've seen how you can make a new sentence by changing the adjective, and we've seen how you can make a new sentence by changing the pronoun. Now, let's combine the power of what you've learned to make even more sentences!

Examples

Let's take the sample sentence and replace both the adjective and the pronoun.

"I am *well*."
Tá mé *go maith*.
[taw may guh mah]

"She is *fine*."
Tá sí *go breá*.
[taw shee guh braw]

Use the vocabulary lists below to make more sentences. All you have to do is start with the verb "**Tá**" [taw], then pick a pronoun, and then pick an adjective. With just these three pieces, you can create forty-two unique sentences. Try them all!

Verb

"is/am/are"
tá
[taw]

Pronouns

"I"
mé
[may]

"you"
tú
[too]

"he"
sé
[shay]

"she"
sí
[shee]

"we"
muid
[mwidj]

"y'all"
sibh
[shiv]

"they"
siad
[shee-ud]

Adjectives

"good/well"
go maith
[guh mah]

"wonderful"
go h-iontach
[guh hee-un-tahkh]

"sick"
tinn
[tcheen]

"fine"
go breá
[guh braw]

"bad/not well"
go dona
[guh dun-uh]

"okay"
ceart go leor
[kyart guh leeyor]

Remember, to make a basic sentence you follow this pattern:

verb + noun (or pronoun) + adjective = sentence

For example:

Tá + muid + go h-iontach. = "We are wonderful."
[taw] + [mwidj] + [guh hee-un-tahkh] = [taw mwidj guh hee-un-tahkh]

Lesson 3 – More About "How Are You?"

In Lesson 2, we learned how to make basic sentences using different pronouns and different adjectives. Now, we will learn how to change the question "How are you?" which we learned in Lesson 1 to ask about other people.

Just like when we changed the basic sentence to talk about other people, to change the question, "How are you?", all you have to do is switch out the *pronoun*. In this question, the pronoun happens to be the last word.

Examples

Let's take a look at the basic question and the question with a different pronoun to compare:

"How are <u>you</u>?"
Cén chaoi a bhfuil <u>tú</u>?
[keh hee will too]

"How is <u>he</u>?"
Cén chaoi a bhfuil <u>sé</u>?
[keh hee will shay]

You can use any of the "How are you?" phrases we learned in Lesson 1, because they all have the pronoun at the end.

Here are more examples with all of the pronouns:

"How am <u>I</u>?"
Cén chaoi a bhfuil <u>mé</u>?
[keh hee will may]

"How are <u>you</u>?"
Cén chaoi a bhfuil <u>tú</u>?
[keh hee will too]

"How is <u>he</u>?"
Cén chaoi a bhfuil <u>sé</u>?
[keh hee will shay]

"How is <u>she</u>?"
Cén chaoi a bhfuil <u>sí</u>?
[keh hee will shee]

"How are <u>we</u>?"
Cén chaoi a bhfuil <u>muid</u>?
[keh hee will mwidj]

"How are <u>y'all</u>?"
Cén chaoi a bhfuil <u>sibh</u>?
[keh hee will shiv]

"How are <u>they</u>?"
Cén chaoi a bhfuil <u>siad</u>?
[keh hee will shee-ud]

To answer these questions, you can use the sentences we practiced in Lesson 2. For example:

"How is <u>she</u>?"
Cén chaoi a bhfuil <u>sí</u>?
[keh hee will shee]

"<u>She</u> is well."
Tá <u>sí</u> go maith.
[taw shee guh mah]

When you're being asked about other people, just remember to answer using the correct pronoun in response. For example:

"How are <u>y'all</u>?"
Cén chaoi a bhfuil <u>sibh</u>?
[keh hee will shiv]

"<u>We</u> are well."
Tá <u>muid</u> go maith.
[taw mwidj guh mah]

Asking About People By Name

Often times, when you ask about how someone else is, you will refer to them by name. To ask the question "How are you?" using a name, you simply switch the *pronoun* for the name.

For example, if you wanted to ask about someone named Brian, you could say:

"How is <u>he</u>?"
Cén chaoi a bhfuil <u>sé</u>?   or
[keh hee will shay]

"How is <u>Brian</u>?"
Cén chaoi a bhfuil <u>Brian</u>?
[keh hee will bree-uhn]

If you want to ask about more than one person, you can use the word "and" in between the names. The word "and" in Irish is:

"and"
agus
[ah-gus]

So, for example, if you want to ask about two people named Brian and Patricia, you could say:

"How are <u>they</u>?"   "How are <u>Brian</u> *and* <u>Patricia</u>?"
Cén chaoi a bhfuil <u>siad</u>?   or   **Cén chaoi a bhfuil <u>Brian</u> *agus* <u>Pádraigín</u>?**
[keh hee will shee-ud]   [keh hee will bree-uhn ah-gus paw-druh-geen]

Conversation

Let's see how this works in action through a conversation between Brian and Pádraigín. Notice how they greet each other with the phrases we learned in Lesson 1.

Brian:
"Hello."
Dia duit.
[jee-uh ghitch]

Pádraigín:
"Hello."
Dia 's Muire duit.
[jee-uh smwir-uh ghitch]

Brian:
"How is Liam?"
Cén chaoi a bhfuil Liam?
[keh hee will lee-um]

Pádraigín:
"He's fine."
Tá sé go breá.
[taw shay guh braw]

Brian:
"How is Noreen?"
Cén chaoi a bhfuil Noirín?
[keh hee will nor-een]

Pádraigín:
"She's okay."
Tá sí ceart go leor.
[taw shee kyart guh leeyor]

Conversation

Now we'll see a complete conversation between Brian and Pádraigín. This one uses more phrases from Lesson 1.

Pádraigín:
"Hello."
Dia duit.
[jee-uh ghitch]

Brian:
"Hello."
Dia 's Muire duit.
[jee-uh smwir-uh ghitch]

Pádraigín:
"How are you?"
Conas atá tú?
[kun-us uh-taw too]

Brian:
"I'm fine,"
Tá mé go breá,
[taw may guh braw]

"thank you."
go raibh maith agat.
[guh ruh mah ah-gut]

"And yourself?"
Agus tú féin?
[ah-gus too fayn]

Pádraigín:
"I am okay."
Tá mé ceart go leor.
[taw may kyart guh leeyor]

"Thank you."
Go raibh maith agat.
[guh ruh mah ah-gut]

Brian:
"How are Liam and Noreen?"
Cén chaoi a bhfuil Liam agus Noirín?
[keh hee will lee-um ah-gus nor-een]

Pádraigín:
"They're wonderful."
Tá siad go h-iontach.
[taw shee-ud guh hee-un-tahkh]

Brian:
"Good-bye."
Slán agat.
[slawn ah-gut]

Pádraigín:
"Good-bye."
Slán leat.
[slawn lyat]

Lesson 4 – The Negative of "Tá"

So far, we've been answering the question "How are you?" with positive statements. But what if you wanted to use a negative statement? You could answer "How are you?" with "I'm well," or "I'm not bad."

The Negative Form of "Tá"

We saw before that verbs in Irish don't change based on the person you're talking about. However, the verb does change to show that what you're talking about is positive or negative. The *negative form* of "**tá**" [taw] is "**níl**" [neel]. So, to turn a positive statement into a negative statement, you simply switch the word "**tá**" [taw] with "**níl**" [neel]. For example:

"I <u>am</u> bad."
Tá mé go dona.
[taw may guh dun-uh]

"I <u>am not</u> bad."
Níl mé go dona.
[neel may guh dun-uh]

We saw in the sentences in Lesson 2 that the verb, "**tá**" [taw], stayed the same for all persons when you switched the pronoun. That's also the way it works for the negative form, and, as you'll see in upcoming lessons, for the question forms, too.

Examples

Here are samples of negative statements using all of the pronouns, as well as names.

"I <u>am not</u> bad."
Níl mé go dona.
[neel may guh dun-uh]

"You <u>are not</u> bad."
Níl tú go dona.
[neel too guh dun-uh]

"He <u>is not</u> bad."
Níl sé go dona.
[neel shay guh dun-uh]

"She <u>is not</u> bad."
Níl sí go dona.
[neel shee guh dun-uh]

"We <u>are not</u> bad."
<u>Níl</u> muid go dona.
[neel mwidj guh dun-uh]

"Y'all <u>are not</u> bad."
<u>Níl</u> sibh go dona.
[neel shiv guh dun-uh]

"They <u>are not</u> bad."
<u>Níl</u> siad go dona.
[neel shee-ud guh dun-uh]

"Brian <u>is not</u> bad."
<u>Níl</u> Brian go dona.
[neel bree-uhn guh dun-uh]

Use the vocabulary lists below to make more sentences. All you have to do is start with the verb "**Níl**" [neel], then pick a pronoun, and then pick an adjective. Try saying each of the forty-two unique sentences you can create with these words below.

Verb

"is not/am not/are not"
níl
[neel]

Pronouns

"I"
mé
[may]

"you"
tú
[too]

"he"
sé
[shay]

"she"
sí
[shee]

"we"
muid
[mwidj]

"y'all"
sibh
[shiv]

"they"
siad
[shee-ud]

Adjectives

"good/well"
go maith
[guh mah]

"wonderful"
go h-iontach
[guh hee-un-tahkh]

"sick"
tinn
[tcheen]

"fine"
go breá
[guh braw]

"bad/not well"
go dona
[guh dun-uh]

"okay"
ceart go leor
[kyart guh leeyor]

Conversation

Let's see this form in practice with a conversation between Brian and Pádraigín. Notice how they start with the greetings we learned in Lesson 1.

Pádraigín:
"Hello."
Dia duit.
[jee-uh ghitch]

Brian:
"Hello."
Dia 's Muire duit.
[jee-uh smwir-uh ghitch]

Pádraigín:
"How are you?"
Cén chaoi a bhfuil tú?
[keh hee will too]

Brian:
"I'm not bad."
Níl mé go dona.
[neel may guh dun-uh]

"And yourself?"
Agus tú féin?
[ah-gus too fayn]

Pádraigín:
"I'm wonderful!"
Tá mé go h-iontach!
[taw may guh hee-un-tahkh]

"Thank you."
Go raibh maith agat.
[guh ruh mah ah-gut]

Brian:
"How is Noreen?"
Cén chaoi a bhfuil Noirín?
[keh hee will nor-een]

Pádraigín:
"She's not well."
Níl sí go maith.
[neel shee guh mah]

Lesson 5 – The Question Forms of "Tá"

You've learned how to say "**tá**" [taw] to make a positive statement, and "**níl**" [neel] to make a negative statement. Now we'll learn how to ask questions using this verb.

In English, you move the verb to the front of the sentence to indicate a question. In a basic Irish sentence, the verb comes first. This is true for positive and negative statements, as well as positive and negative questions.

Positive Questions

Positive questions ask about how something is. To turn a positive statement into a positive question, you simply switch the word "**tá**" [taw] with its *question form*, which is "**an bhfuil**" [un will]. For example:

"He <u>is</u> well."
Tá sé go maith.
[taw shay guh mah]

"<u>Is</u> he well?"
An bhfuil sé go maith?
[un will shay guh mah]

Notice that the verb in both Irish sentences is in the front.

Examples

Here are samples of positive questions using all of the pronouns, as well as names.

"<u>Am</u> I fine?"
An bhfuil mé go breá?
[un will may guh braw]

"<u>Are</u> you fine?"
An bhfuil tú go breá?
[un will too guh braw]

"<u>Is</u> he fine?"
An bhfuil sé go breá?
[un will shay guh braw]

"<u>Is</u> she fine?"
An bhfuil sí go breá?
[un will shee guh braw]

"<u>Are</u> we fine?"
An bhfuil muid go breá?
[un will mwidj guh braw]

"<u>Are</u> y'all fine?"
An bhfuil sibh go breá?
[un will shiv guh braw]

"<u>Are</u> they fine?"
An bhfuil siad go breá?
[un will shee-ud guh braw]

"<u>Is</u> Brian fine?"
An bhfuil Brian go breá?
[un will bree-uhn guh braw]

Use the vocabulary lists below to make positive questions. Start with the verb, "**An bhfuil**" [un will], then pick a pronoun, and then pick an adjective. Try saying each of the forty-two unique sentences you can create with these words below.

<u>Verb</u>

"is?/am?/are?"
an bhfuil?
[un will]

<u>Pronouns</u>

"I"
mé
[may]

"we"
muid
[mwidj]

"you"
tú
[too]

"y'all"
sibh
[shiv]

"he"
sé
[shay]

"they"
siad
[shee-ud]

"she"
sí
[shee]

Adjectives

"good/well"	"wonderful"	"sick"
go maith	**go h-iontach**	**tinn**
[guh mah]	[guh hee-un-tahkh]	[tcheen]
"fine"	"bad/not well"	"okay"
go breá	**go dona**	**ceart go leor**
[guh braw]	[guh dun-uh]	[kyart guh leeyor]

Negative Questions

Negative questions ask about how something isn't, like "*Isn't* it a nice day?" or "*Aren't* they here yet?" To turn a positive statement into a negative question, you simply switch the word "**tá**" [taw] with its negative question form, which is "**nach bhfuil**" [nahkh will]. For example:

"He <u>is</u> well."
<u>Tá</u> sé go maith.
[taw shay guh mah]

"<u>Isn't</u> he well?"
<u>Nach bhfuil</u> sé go maith?
[nahkh will shay guh mah]

Examples

Here are samples of negative questions using all of the pronouns, as well as names.

"<u>Am</u> I <u>not</u> wonderful?"
<u>Nach bhfuil</u> mé go h-iontach?
[nahkh will may guh hee-un-tahkh]

"<u>Aren't</u> you wonderful?"
<u>Nach bhfuil</u> tú go h-iontach?
[nahkh will too guh hee-un-tahkh]

"<u>Isn't</u> he wonderful?"
<u>Nach bhfuil</u> sé go h-iontach?
[nahkh will shay guh hee-un-tahkh]

"<u>Isn't</u> she wonderful?
<u>Nach bhfuil</u> sí go h-iontach?
[nahkh will shee guh hee-un-tahkh]

"Aren't we wonderful?"
<u>Nach bhfuil</u> muid go h-iontach?
[nahkh will mwidj guh hee-un-tahkh]

"Aren't y'all wonderful?"
<u>Nach bhfuil</u> sibh go h-iontach?
[nahkh will shiv guh hee-un-tahkh]

"Aren't they wonderful?"
<u>Nach bhfuil</u> siad go h-iontach?
[nahkh will shee-ud guh hee-un-tahkh]

"Isn't Brian wonderful?"
<u>Nach bhfuil</u> Brian go h-iontach?
[nahkh will bree-uhn guh hee-un-tahkh]

Use the vocabulary lists below to make negative questions. Start with the verb, "**Nach bhfuil**" [nahkh will], then pick a pronoun, and then pick an adjective. Try saying each of the forty-two unique sentences you can create with these words below.

Verb

"isn't?/am not?/aren't?"
nach bhfuil?
[nahkh will]

Pronouns

"I"
mé
[may]

"we"
muid
[mwidj]

"you"
tú
[too]

"y'all"
sibh
[shiv]

"he"
sé
[shay]

"they"
siad
[shee-ud]

"she"
sí
[shee]

Adjectives

"good/well"
go maith
[guh mah]

"wonderful"
go h-iontach
[guh hee-un-tahkh]

"sick"
tinn
[tcheen]

"fine"
go breá
[guh braw]

"bad/not well"
go dona
[guh dun-uh]

"okay"
ceart go leor
[kyart guh leeyor]

Lesson 6 – Answering Questions

Now that you've learned how to ask questions using the verb "**tá**" [taw], "to be," the next logical step is to learn how to answer questions.

Irish has no single word for "yes" or "no." Instead, you reply by repeating the *positive form* or the *negative form* of the verb that was in the question. That means that we have to pay attention to what's being asked; we can't just nod our heads and say "yes" or "no" blindly.

Answering "Yes" or "No" to a "Tá" Question

If you are asked a question using "**an bhfuil**" [un will] or "**nach bhfuil**" [nahkh will], this is how you answer:

"Yes."	"No."
Tá.	**Níl.**
[taw]	[neel]

Notice that the "yes" and "no" answers basically mean "is" and "is not," or, loosely, "it is so" and "it is not so."

Examples

Let's look at some sample questions with simple "yes" and "no" answers.

"Is Patricia okay?"
An bhfuil Pádraigín ceart go leor?
[un will paw-druh-geen kyart guh leeyor]

"Yes."	"No."
Tá.	**Níl.**
[taw]	[neel]

"Isn't Brian sick?"
Nach bhfuil Brian tinn?
[nahkh will bree-uhn tcheen]

"Yes."	"No."
Tá.	**Níl.**
[taw]	[neel]

Lesson 7 – Full Answers After "Yes" and "No"

Though the simple answers are perfectly fine, sometimes you'll want to follow a "yes" or "no" with a full sentence, like "Yes, *he is*." Since Irish echoes the verb for "yes" and "no," you *repeat the verb* in order to answer with a complete sentence.

Examples

Let's look at some sample questions with full "yes" and "no" answers.

"Is Patricia okay?"
An bhfuil Pádraigín ceart go leor?
[un will paw-druh-geen kyart guh leeyor]

"Yes, she is okay."
Tá. Tá sí ceart go leor.
[taw. taw shee kyart guh leeyor]

"No, she is not okay."
Níl. Níl sí ceart go leor.
[neel. neel shee kyart guh leeyor]

"Isn't Brian sick?"
Nach bhfuil Brian tinn?
[nahkh will bree-uhn tcheen]

"Yes, he is sick."
Tá. Tá sé tinn.
[taw. taw shay tcheen]

"No, he isn't sick."
Níl. Níl sé tinn.
[neel. neel shay tcheen]

This may feel strange to a native English speaker at first, but you'll get used to it over time. It's a good idea to practice repeating the verb when you answer questions, so that it will become a motor habit more quickly.

Also, keep in mind that it's not advisable to omit the repeated verb. You can do so, but it sounds curt. If you say the verb only once, then it's like answering "Is she okay?" with an abrupt "She's okay," rather than "Yes, she's okay."

TIP! While you're learning, try to always answer with complete sentences. Not only will this help you remember to repeat the verb for "yes" and "no," but it will also reinforce the full sentences, too!

Conversation

Now we'll see a brief conversation between Brian and Pádraigín that uses some questions and answers.

Brian:
"Hello."
Dia duit.
[jee-uh ghitch]

Pádraigín:
"Hello."
Dia 's Muire duit.
[jee-uh smwir-uh ghitch]

Brian:
"Aren't you well?"
Nach bhfuil tú go maith?
[nahkh will too guh mah]

Pádraigín:
"No, I'm not well."
Níl. Níl mé go maith.
[neel. neel may guh mah]

Brian:
"Are you sick?"
An bhuil tú tinn?
[un will too tcheen]

Pádraigín:
"Yes, I'm sick."
Tá. Tá mé tinn.
[taw. taw may tcheen]

Lesson 8 – Mixing Positives and Negatives

When answering questions, the full sentence you may want to follow "yes" or "no" with doesn t necessarily have to match the positive or the negative answer. For example, you could answer "Is Patricia okay?" with "*No*, she *is* bad." That's a negative answer followed by a positive statement.

Examples

Let's see some sample questions and answers that mix positives and negatives.

"Is Patricia okay?"
An bhfuil Pádraigín ceart go leor?
[un will paw-druh-geen kyart guh leeyor]

"No, she is sick."
Níl, tá sí tinn.
[neel, taw shee tcheen]

"Isn't Brian sick?"
Nach bhfuil Brian tinn?
[nahkh will bree-uhn tcheen]

"No, he is well."
Níl, tá sé go maith.
[neel, taw shay guh mah]

Conversation

Let's see some questions and answers in practice with a conversation between Brian and Pádraigín. Notice how they still use many of the phrases we learned in Lesson 1.

Pádraigín:
"Hello."
Dia duit.
[jee-uh ghitch]

Brian:
"Hello."
Dia 's Muire duit.
[jee-uh smwir-uh ghitch]

Pádraigín:
"How are you?"
Cén chaoi a bhfuil tú?
[keh hee will too]

Brian:
"I'm not bad."
Níl mé go dona.
[neel may guh dun-uh]

"And yourself?"
Agus tú féin?
[ah-gus too fayn]

Pádraigín:
"I'm wonderful!"
Tá mé go h-iontach!
[taw may guh hee-un-tahkh]

"Thank you."
Go raibh maith agat.
[guh ruh mah ah-gut]

Brian:
"Is Noreen well?"
An bhfuil Noirín go maith?
[un will nor-een guh mah]

Pádraigín:
"Yes, she's well."
Tá, tá sí go maith.
[taw, taw shee guh mah]

Brian:
"Is Liam well?"
An bhfuil Liam go maith?
[un will lee-um guh mah]

Pádraigín:
"Yes."
Tá.
[taw]

Brian:
"Isn't Liam sick?"
Nach bhfuil Liam tinn?
[nahkh will lee-um tcheen]

Pádraigín:
"No, he's fine."
Níl, tá sé go breá.
[neel, taw shay guh braw]

Lesson 9 – Describing People

We've learned how to describe how people are doing, but, sometimes, you'll want to describe what people are like. With our basic sentence, you can use any kind of adjective at the end.

Vocabulary

Here are a few more words you can use to describe people:

"big"	"old"	"beautiful"	"smart, clever"
mór	**sean**	**go h-álainn**	**cliste**
[mor]	[shan]	[guh haw-ling]	[klish-tuh]

"small"	"young"	"handsome"	
beag	**óg**	**dathúil**	
[bayug]	[oeg]	[dah-hool]	

Examples

Let's see some sample sentences that use these adjectives:

"I am big."
Tá mé mór.
[taw may mor]

"You aren't small."
Níl tú beag.
[neel too bayug]

"Is he old?"
An bhfuil sé sean?
[un will shay shan]

"Isn't she young?"
Nach bhfuil sí óg?
[nahkh will shee oeg]

"We are beautiful!"
Tá muid go h-álainn!
[taw mwidj guh haw-ling]

"Are y'all handsome?"
An bhfuil sibh dathúil?
[un will shiv dah-hool]

"Aren't they <u>clever</u>?"
Nach bhfuil siad <u>cliste</u>?
[nahkh will shee-ud klish-tuh]

"Patricia is <u>beautiful</u>."
Tá Pádraigín <u>go h-álainn</u>.
[taw paw-druh-geen guh haw-ling]

Lesson 10 – Showing Emphasis with Pronouns

As we learned in Lesson 1, Irish doesn't just use tone of voice to show emphasis; the words themselves change. When words change like this, this is called their *emphatic form*. Pronouns are commonly used this way, so you see their emphatic forms a lot.

Vocabulary

Here is a list of emphatic pronouns that go with sentences that use "**tá**" [taw]:

"I!"
mise
[mih-shuh]

"we!"
muide
[mwidj-uh]

"you!"
tusa
[tuh-suh]

"y'all!"
sibhse
[shiv-shuh]

"he!"
seisean
[shesh-in]

"they!"
siadsan
[shee-ud-sun]

"she!"
sise
[shih-shuh]

Examples

Let's see some sample sentences that use these emphatic pronouns:

"*I* am small."
Tá mise beag.
[taw mih-shuh bayug]

"*You* aren't old."
Níl tusa sean.
[neel tuh-suh shan]

"Is *he* young?"
An bhfuil seisean óg?
[un will shesh-in oeg]

"Isn't *she* beautiful?"
Nach bhfuil <u>sise</u> go h-álainn?
[nahkh will shih-shuh guh haw-ling]

"*We* are handsome!"
Tá <u>muide</u> dathúil!
[taw mwidj-uh dah-hool]

"Are *y'all* clever?"
An bhfuil <u>sibhse</u> cliste?
[un will shiv-shuh klish-tuh]

"Aren't *they* big?"
Nach bhfuil <u>siadsan</u> mór?
[nahkh will shee-ud-sun mor]

Lesson 11 – Using Emphatic Pronouns to Compare

Many times, emphatic pronouns are used to contrast with something that was just said. Therefore, you often see sentences with an emphatic pronoun following sentences without any emphatic pronouns.

Examples

Let's take a look at some sentences with regular pronouns and then with emphatic pronouns to compare:

"I am clever."
Tá <u>mé</u> cliste.
[taw may klish-tuh]

"I am clever."
Tá <u>mise</u> cliste.
[taw mih-shuh klish-tuh]

"You are not small."
Níl <u>tú</u> beag.
[neel too bayug]

"You are not small."
Níl <u>tusa</u> beag.
[neel tuh-suh bayug]

Conversation

Let's see emphatic pronouns used to compare people in a brief conversation.

Pádraigín:
"I'm old."
Tá mé sean.
[taw may shan]

Brian:
"No. You're not old."
Níl. Níl tú sean.
[neel. neel too shan]

"You are young. I'm old."
Tá túsa óg. Tá mise sean.
[taw tuh-suh oeg. taw mih-shuh shan]

Pádraigín:
"No. *We* are wonderful!"
Níl. Tá muide go h-iontach!
[neel. taw mwidj-uh guh hee-un-tahkh]

Me, Too

When you're being emphatic, lots of times you may want add the word "too" to show just how much something applies to you, too. The word "too," or "also," in Irish is:

"too, also"
freisin
[fresh-in]

Examples

If someone describes something, and you want to say that it's the same for someone else, you can use an emphatic pronoun, and simply add the word "too," "**freisin**" [fresh-in], at the end of the sentence.

"I am clever."
Tá mé cliste.
[taw may klish-tuh]

"*I* am clever, <u>too</u>."
Tá mise cliste, <u>freisin</u>.
[taw mih-shuh klish-tuh, fresh-in]

This can work with any emphatic pronoun, as well as a person's name.

"They are big."
Tá siad mór.
[taw shee-ud mor]

"*She* is big, too."
Tá sise mór, freisin.
[taw shih-shuh mor, fresh-in]

"Brian is big, too."
Tá Brian mór, freisin.
[taw bree-uhn mor, fresh-in]

You can even make your sentence short and sweet by just saying the emphatic pronoun and "too," **"freisin"** [fresh-in].

"I'm wonderful."
Tá mé go h-iontach.
[taw may guh hee-un-tahkh]

"*Me*, too!"
Mise, freisin!
[mih-shuh, fresh-in]

Conversation

Let's practice what we've learned with a conversation using some emphatic pronouns.

Pádraigín:
"Hello."
Dia duit.
[jee-uh ghitch]

Brian:
"Hello."
Dia 's Muire duit.
[jee-uh smwir-uh ghitch]

"How is Liam?"
Cén chaoi a bhfuil Liam?
[keh hee will lee-um]

Pádraigín:
"He's sick."
Tá sé tinn.
[taw shay tcheen]

Brian:
"How is Noreen?"
Cén chaoi a bhfuil Noirín?
[keh hee will nor-een]

"Is *she* is sick, too?"
An bhfuil sise tinn, freisin?
[un will shih-shuh tcheen, fresh-in]

Pádraigín:
"No. She's fine."
Níl. Tá sí go breá.
[neel. taw shee guh braw]

Brian:
"And how are *you*?"
Agus cén chaoi a bhfuil tusa?
[ah-gus keh hee will tuh-suh]

Pádraigín:
"I'm well."
Tá mé go maith.
[taw may guh mah]

Brian:
"*Me*, too."
Mise, freisin.
[mih-shuh, fresh-in]

Lesson 12 – Talking About the Weather

You can use what you learned from talking about people to talk about a lot of other things, too. One thing that's always around to discuss is the weather.

To make a sentence about the weather, all you have to do is switch out the pronoun or person's name with "the weather." We'll also use the words for "the day" and "the night," so we can get more practice.

Vocabulary

"the weather"
an aimsir
[un am-sheer]

"the day"
an lá
[un law]

"the night"
an oíche
[un ee-khuh]

Examples

Let's make some sentences that describe the weather:

"The weather is fine."
Tá an aimsir go breá.
[taw un am-sheer guh braw]

"The day is wonderful."
Tá an lá go h-iontach.
[taw un law guh hee-un-tahkh]

"The night is beautiful."
Tá an oíche go h-álainn.
[taw un ee-khuh guh haw-ling]

"The weather isn't bad."
Níl an aimsir go dona.
[neel un am-sheer guh dun-uh]

Vocabulary

Here are some new words that you can use to describe things, especially the weather:

"cold"
fuar
[foo-uhr]

"wet"
fliuch
[flyukh]

"cloudy"
scamallach
[skom-uh-lahkh]

"hot"
te
[tcheh]

"dry"
tirim
[tchih-ruhm]

"sunny"
grianmhar
[gree-un-wer]

Examples

Now, let's make more sentences about the weather using our new words:

"The night is cold."
Tá an oíche fuar.
[taw un ee-khuh foo-uhr]

"The day is hot."
Tá an lá te.
[taw un law tcheh]

"The weather is wet."
Tá an aimsir fliuch.
[taw un am-sheer flyukh]

"The day isn't dry."
Níl an lá tirim.
[neel un law tchih-ruhm]

"The night isn't cloudy."
Níl an oíche scamallach.
[neel un ee-khuh skom-uh-lahkh]

"The weather isn't sunny."
Níl an aimsir grianmhar.
[neel un am-sheer gree-un-wer]

Vocabulary

To make your sentences more interesting, you can also add words to the end of your sentence that describe when something is happening.

"today"
inniu
[in-yoo]

"tonight"
anocht
[uh-nahkht]

Examples

"The weather isn't hot today."
Níl an aimsir te inniu.
[neel un am-sheer tcheh in-yoo]

"The night is cold tonight."
Tá an oíche fuar anocht.
[taw un ee-khuh foo-uhr uh-nahkht]

Lesson 13 – Asking About the Weather

When you want to ask questions about the weather, all you have to do is take a weather statement and switch the word "**tá**" [taw] with one of the question forms of "**tá**" [taw] that we learned in Lesson 5. For a positive question you say, "**an bhfuil**" [un will], and for a negative question you say, "**nach bhfuil**" [nahkh will].

Examples

Let's take a look at some statements and questions about the weather to compare.

"The day <u>is</u> sunny."
Tá an lá grianmhar.
[taw un law gree-un-wer]

"<u>Is</u> the day sunny?"
An bhfuil an lá grianmhar?
[un will un law gree-un-wer]

"The night <u>is</u> cold."
Tá an oíche fuar.
[taw un ee-khuh foo-uhr]

"<u>Isn't</u> the night cold?"
Nach bhfuil an oíche fuar?
[nahkh will un ee-khuh foo-uhr]

"The weather <u>is</u> hot today."
Tá an aimsir te inniu.
[taw un am-sheer tcheh in-yoo]

"<u>Is</u> the weather hot today?"
An bhfuil an aimsir te inniu?
[un will un am-sheer tcheh in-yoo]

Answering Questions About the Weather

As we learned before, you answer a question in Irish with the positive or negative form of the verb you were asked. So, to answer a descriptive question about the weather, you do the same as you did for answering about a person.

Examples

"Is the weather cloudy?"
An bhfuil an aimsir scamallach?
[un will un am-sheer skom-uh-lahkh]

"Yes, the weather is cloudy."
Tá. Tá an aimsir scamallach.
[taw. taw un am-sheer skom-uh-lahkh]

"Is the day hot today?"
An bhfuil an lá te inniu?
[un will un law tcheh in-yoo]

"No, the day is not hot today."
Níl. Níl an lá te inniu.
[neel. neel un law tcheh in-yoo]

"Is the night wet?"
An bhfuil an oíche fliuch?
[un will un ee-khuh flyukh]

"No. The night is dry."
Níl. Tá an oíche tirim.
[neel. taw un ee-khuh tchih-ruhm]

"Isn't the weather beautiful?"
Nach bhfuil an aimsir go h-álainn?
[nahkh will un am-sheer guh haw-ling]

"Yes, the weather is beautiful."
Tá. Tá an aimsir go h-álainn.
[taw. taw un am-sheer guh haw-ling]

Lesson 14 – Asking "How Is the Weather?"

Oftentimes, you simply want to ask how the weather is, rather that asking about a specific kind of weather. To ask, "How is the weather?" in Irish, you can say:

"How is the weather?"
Cén chaoi a bhfuil an aimsir?
[keh hee will un am-sheer]

Notice that this is a *Bonus Phrase*, very much like the question, "How are you?" "**Cén chaoi a bhfuil tú?**" [keh hee will too], which we learned in Lesson 1. Just like we did when asking about other people, all you do is switch out the last word, "you," "**tú**" [too], with the words for "the weather," "**an aimsir**" [un am-sheer].

Examples

You can use any of these *Bonus Phrases* to ask about the weather.

"How is the weather?"
Conas atá an aimsir?
[kun-us uh-taw un am-sheer]

"How is the weather?"
Cad é mar atá an aimsir?
[kuh-jay mar uh-taw un am-sheer]

"How is the weather?"
Cén chaoi a bhfuil an aimsir?
[keh hee will un am-sheer]

Answering Questions About the Weather

To answer one of these questions, you just say a statement about the weather.

Examples

"How is the weather?"
Conas atá an aimsir?
[kun-us uh-taw un am-sheer]

"The weather is fine."
Tá an aimsir go breá.
[taw un am-sheer guh braw]

"How is the weather?"
Cad é mar atá an aimsir?
[kuh-jay mar uh-taw un am-sheer]

"The weather isn't bad."
Níl an aimsir go dona.
[neel un am-sheer guh dun-uh]

"How is the weather?"
Cén chaoi a bhfuil an aimsir?
[keh hee will un am-sheer]

"The weather is cold."
Tá an aimsir fuar.
[taw un am-sheer foo-uhr]

"How is the weather?"
Conas atá an aimsir?
[kun-us uh-taw un am-sheer]

"The weather isn't good."
Níl an aimsir go maith.
[neel un am-sheer guh mah]

Conversation

Let's practice what we've learned with a conversation about the weather.

Pádraigín:
"Hello."
Dia duit.
[jee-uh ghitch]

Brian:
"Hello."
Dia 's Muire duit.
[jee-uh smwir-uh ghitch]

"How is the weather?"
Cén chaoi a bhfuil an aimsir?
[keh hee will un am-sheer]

Pádraigín:
"The weather is beautiful!"
Tá an aimsir go h-álainn!
[taw un am-sheer guh haw-ling]

Brian:
"Is the day sunny?"
An bhfuil an lá grianmhar?
[un will un law gree-un-wer]

Pádraigín:
"Yes."
Tá.
[taw]

Brian:
"Aren't you hot?"
Nach bhfuil tú te?
[nahkh will too tcheh]

Pádraigín:
"No. *I'm* fine."
Níl. Tá mise go breá.
[neel. taw mih-shuh guh braw]

Lesson 15 – A Bit About Nouns

Nouns are a big part of any language, and there are lots of interesting things about them and how they work.

We won't go into all of the finer points here, but we will take a look at some of the most common aspects of nouns in Irish. We'll learn more through practice in the upcoming lessons.

Genders

Like many languages, nouns in Irish have what's called *grammatical gender*. This means that you refer to some things as "he," and some things as "she," because the nouns for them are considered grammatically *masculine* or *feminine*. In English, we only use this for poetic reasons, as in "She's a good ship," and so forth. However, in Irish, as in many other languages, nouns are categorized by gender.

Unlike natural gender, there's no single way to figure out if a noun is masculine or feminine. At this stage, the best thing you can do is make a mental note of the gender as you learn new words, and try to practice referring to them as "he" or "she" as much as you can.

If you can't remember a noun's gender, or simply haven't learned it yet, you can default to "he" and still be understood. Things that have natural gender, like people or animals, are always referred to by their actual gender.

Definite and Indefinite Articles

No Need to Say "A" or "An"

There is no *indefinite article* in Irish, like "a" or "an" in English. When you want to talk about "a thing," you just say "thing," and the "a" is implied. It's understood that you mean an indefinite thing.

"The" Definite Article

Irish does have a *definite article*, like "the" in English. In fact, Irish has two of them: one for singular nouns, and one for plural nouns. The singular "the" is "**an**" [un], and the plural "the" is "**na**" [nuh].

Softening

An interesting feature of Irish is that the beginnings of words change sometimes. Usually, the start of a word will change because of a word that comes in front of it.

One of the ways a word can change in Irish is for the first sound to become *softer*. This is called "**séimhiú**" [shay-voo], or *softening*. A good way to think of it is as if the hard edge of a consonant is being said more softly. To represent this softer sound, Irish puts an "**h**" after the letter to show that it's being changed.

We can take a look at a few words in English to see how this works. Imagine that you see a pay phone on a pole. If we look at the words "pay," "phone," and "pole," we see that they are all "p" words, but one of them is said like it starts with an "f." If you take a hard "p" sound and soften it by putting some air into it, it pretty much makes an "f" sound. That's how *softening* works.

Most consonants can be softened, but some never soften. We'll learn more about softening through practicing phrases and sentences in upcoming lessons. For a list of which letters do and do not soften, see the Appendix.

Lesson 16 – "The" with Feminine Nouns

We learned before that sometimes a word will change in Irish because of a word that comes in front of it. The singular "the" is one of those words that can cause a change to occur.

The singular "the," "**an**" [un], will *soften* the word that comes after it if it's a *feminine noun*. If a *feminine noun* starts with a vowel, there's no change. We actually saw this before when talking about the weather. The words for "weather," "**aimsir**" [am-sheer], and "night," "**oíche**" [ee-khuh], are both *feminine*, but, since they start with vowels, they didn't change after "**an**" [un], "the."

Examples

Let's take a look at a few *feminine nouns* with and without the word "the" to compare:

"a chair"
cathaoir (f.)
[kah-heer]

"the chair"
an chathaoir
[un khah-heer]

"a window"
fuinneog (f.)
[fwin-yoeg]

"the window"
an fhuinneog
[un in-yoeg]

"a key"
eochair (f.)
[ukh-er]

"the key"
an eochair
[un ukh-er]

Lesson 17 – "The" with Masculine Nouns

The singular "the," "**an**" [un], doesn't soften *masculine nouns*. However, if a *masculine noun* begins with a vowel, then the singular "the," "**an**" [un], will add a "**t-**" in front of it.

Examples

Let's take a look at a few *masculine nouns* with and without the word "the" to compare:

"a table"
bord (m.)
[bord]

"the table"
an bord
[un bord]

"a door"
doras (m.)
[dor-us]

"the door"
an doras
[un dor-us]

"a floor"
urlár (m.)
[oor-lawr]

"the floor"
an t-urlár
[un toor-lawr]

Lesson 18 – Describing Things

We can use the basic "**tá**" [taw] sentences we've learned to talk about all kinds of things. As we learned in Lesson 15, there are two definite articles: one for a singular noun and one for a plural noun. The singular "the" is "**an**" [un]. We'll start by practicing with only singular nouns for now.

Remember, a basic Irish sentence is formed like this:

verb + noun + adjective

Vocabulary

Here are some nouns we've seen before with the definite article:

"the chair"
an chathaoir (f.)
[un khah-heer]

"the window"
an fhuinneog (f.)
[un in-yoeg]

"the key"
an eochair (f.)
[un ukh-er]

"the table"
an bord (m.)
[un bord]

"the door"
an doras (m.)
[un dor-us]

"the floor"
an t-urlár (m.)
[un toor-lawr]

Vocabulary

Here are some adjectives we've seen before, along with a few new ones:

"big"
mór
[mor]

"small"
beag
[bayug]

"old"
sean
[shan]

"new"
nua
[noo-uh]

"clean"
glan
[glon]

"dirty"
salach
[sahl-ahkh]

Examples

"The chair is big."
Tá an chathaoir mór.
[taw un khah-heer mor]

"The window isn't small."
Níl an fhuinneog beag.
[neel un in-yoeg bayug]

"The key is old."
Tá an eochair sean.
[taw un ukh-er shan]

"The table isn't new."
Níl an bord nua.
[neel un bord noo-uh]

"The door is clean."
Tá an doras glan.
[taw un dor-us glon]

"The floor isn't dirty."
Níl an t-urlár salach.
[neel un toor-lawr sahl-ahkh]

Lesson 19 – A Look at Plural Nouns

When you want to talk about more than one of a thing, you use the *plural* form of the noun. There are many ways to pluralize nouns in Irish, just as there are in English.

Some plural nouns look a lot like their singular form, and others look more different. Nouns in Irish are categorized into groups called *declensions*. That means that nouns from one group follow different patterns than nouns from other groups. In Irish, there are five noun groups, and then some nouns that fall into the irregular group.

We won't go into all of the details about noun groups here. When you're just beginning, it's best to simply learn the plurals along with the singular forms. Practicing them together also helps you remember them, so that, when you speak, they just come out naturally, and you don't have to stop in the middle of your sentence to "figure out" what the plural is.

Vocabulary

Let's take a look at a few nouns in the *singular* and in the *plural* to compare.

"a chair"
cathaoir (f.)
[kah-heer]

"a key"
eochair (f.)
[ukh-er]

"a door"
doras (m.)
[dor-us]

"chairs"
cathaoireacha
[kah-heer-ih-khuh]

"keys"
eochracha
[ukh-rukh-uh]

"doors"
doirse
[deer-shuh]

"a window"
fuinneog (f.)
[fwin-yoeg]

"a table"
bord (m.)
[bord]

"a floor"
urlár (m.)
[oor-lawr]

"windows"
fuinneoga
[fwin-yoeg-uh]

"tables"
boird
[bweerj]

"floors"
urláir
[oor-lawyer]

Once again, we won't go into all of the details about how each noun group forms plurals. Learning and practicing the singular and plural forms together will help you remember them better.

Lesson 20 – Describing Many Things

As we learned in Lesson 15, there are two definite articles: one for singular nouns and one for plural nouns. The plural "the" is "**na**" [nuh], and it doesn't soften the word that comes after it.

However, if the noun starts with a vowel, "**na**" [nuh] adds an "**h-**" to the front of nouns after it, regardless of gender. This is done to make it easier to say, since one word ends in a vowel sound, and the next one begins with a vowel sound.

Vocabulary

Let's take a look at a few nouns in the *singular* and the *plural* with the word "the" to compare.

"the chair"
an chathaoir (f.)
[un khah-heer]

"the key"
an eochair (f.)
[un ukh-er]

"the door"
an doras (m.)
[un dor-us]

"the chairs"
na cathaoireacha
[nuh kah-heer-ih-khuh]

"the keys"
na h-eochracha
[nuh hukh-rukh-uh]

"the doors"
na doirse
[nuh deer-shuh]

"the window"
an fhuinneog (f.)
[un in-yoeg]

"the table"
an bord (m.)
[un bord]

"the floor"
an t-urlár (m.)
[un toor-lawr]

"the windows"
na fuinneoga
[nuh fwin-yoeg-uh]

"the tables"
na boird
[nuh bweerj]

"the floors"
na h-urláir
[nuh hoor-lawyer]

Examples

"The chairs are old."
Tá na cathaoireacha sean.
[taw nuh kah-heer-ih-khuh shan]

"The windows aren't new."
Níl na fuinneoga nua.
[neel nuh fwin-yoeg-uh noo-uh]

"The keys are small."
Tá na h-eochracha beag.
[taw nuh hukh-rukh-uh bayug]

"The tables aren't big."
Níl na boird mór.
[neel nuh bweerj mor]

"The doors are dirty."
Tá na doirse salach.
[taw nuh deer-shuh sahl-ahkh]

"The floors aren't clean."
Níl na h-urláir glan.
[neel nuh hoor-lawyer glon]

Lesson 21 – Asking and Answering About Things

We can ask and answer questions about things just like we did with people. All you have to do is put the noun in between the form of "**tá**" [taw] you want and the adjective. If you're using the definite article, just remember to use the patterns we learned about how they work.

When you're answering a question about a noun, you don't have to say the noun in the answer. You can refer to it with a pronoun. For masculine nouns, you'll use "**sé**" [shay], "he," for feminine nouns, you'll use "**sí**" [shee], "she," and for plural nouns, you'll use "**siad**" [shee-ud], "they."

Examples

"Is the floor clean?"
An bhfuil an t-urlár glan?
[un will un toor-lawr glon]

"Yes, the floor is clean."
Tá. Tá an t-urlár glan.
[taw. taw un toor-lawr glon]

"No, the floor isn't clean."
Níl. Níl an t-urlár glan.
[neel. neel un toor-lawr glon]

"No, the floor is dirty."
Níl. Tá an t-urlár salach.
[neel. taw un toor-lawr sahl-ahkh]

"Isn't the key small?"
Nach bhfuil an eochair beag?
[nahkh will un ukh-er bayug]

"Yes, it's small."
Tá. Tá sí beag.
[taw. taw shee bayug]

"No, it isn't small."
Níl. Níl sí beag.
[neel. neel shee bayug]

"No, it's big."
Níl. Tá sí mór.
[neel. taw shee mor]

Conversation

Let's practice what we've learned about nouns with a conversation.

Brian:
"Are the tables new?"
An bhfuil na boird nua?
[un will nuh bweerj noo-uh]

Pádraigín:
"Yes, they're new."
Tá. Tá siad nua.
[taw. taw shee-ud noo-uh]

"Aren't they clean?"
Nach bhfuil siad glan?
[nahkh will shee-ud glon]

Brian:
"No. The tables are dirty."
Níl. Tá na boird salach.
[neel. taw nuh bweerj sahl-ahkh]

Pádraigín:
"Is the floor dirty, too?"
An bhfuil an t-urlár salach, freisin?
[un will un toor-lawr sahl-ahkh, fresh-in]

Brian:
"No. It's clean."
Níl. Tá sé glan.
[neel. taw shay glon]

Pádraigín:
"And is the window clean?"
Agus an bhfuil an fhuinneog glan?
[ah-gus un will un in-yoeg glon]

Brian:
"Yes, it's clean."
Tá. Tá sí glan.
[taw. taw shee glon]

Lesson 22 – Some Exceptions When Softening

The letter "**s**" sometimes plays by its own rules in Irish. When a feminine noun that starts with "**s**" follows the definite article "**an**" [un], instead of being *softened*, the letter "**t**" is placed in front of it.

Vocabulary

"a street"
sráid (f.)
[sroyj]

"streets"
sráideanna
[sroy-jin-uh]

"the street"
an tsráid
[un troyj]

"the streets"
na sráideanna
[nuh sroy-jin-uh]

However, when a feminine noun begins with the letters "**sc**," "**sf**," "**sm**," "**sp**," or "**st**," it does not soften or get a "**t**" in front of it when said after the definite article "**an**" [un].

Vocabulary

"a knife"
scian (f.)
[shkee-un]

"a spoon"
spúnóg (f.)
[spoo-noeg]

"the knife"
an scian
[un shkee-un]

"the spoon"
an spúnóg
[un spoo-noeg]

"knives"
sceana
[shkyah-nuh]

"spoons"
spúnóga
[spoo-noeg-uh]

"the knives"
na sceana
[nuh shkyah-nuh]

"the spoons"
na spúnóga
[nuh spoo-noeg-uh]

Other Special Cases

When a word that causes softening ends in the letter "**n**," and the word after it begins with the letter "**d**" or "**t**," the "**d**" or the "**t**" *does not get softened*. Saying a softened "**d**" or a softened "**t**" right after an "**n**" is awkward, so Irish makes an exception in these cases.

Vocabulary

Let's take a look at some nouns that start with "**d**" or "**t**" with and without the definite articles to compare.

"a land"
tír (f.)
[tcheer]

"the land"
an tír
[un tcheer]

"lands"
tíortha
[tcheer-huh]

"the lands"
na tíortha
[nuh tcheer-huh]

"a drink"
deoch (f.)
[jawkh]

"the drink"
an deoch
[un jawkh]

"drinks"
deochanna
[jawkh-uh-nuh]

"the drinks"
na deochanna
[nuh jawkh-uh-nuh]

Examples

"The street is small."
Tá an tsráid beag.
[taw un troyj bayug]

"The knife is not dirty."
Níl an scian salach.
[neel un shkee-un sahl-ahkh]

"The spoon is clean."
Tá an spúnóg glan.
[taw un spoo-noeg glon]

"The land is big."
Tá an tír mór.
[taw un tcheer mor]

"The drink is not hot."
Níl an deoch te.
[neel un jawkh tcheh]

Lesson 23 – Addressing People

We've seen how the word "**an**" [un] can soften the word after it. Softening occurs in other situations, too. One very useful situation is when you're addressing someone.

When you speak to someone directly, it's different than when you're just talking about them to someone else. In Irish, when addressing a person, you say the word "**a**" [uh] before their name, then soften their name. This is called the *vocative case*. English has this case, too, but it's no longer used, except poetically. For example, if a girl named Juliet wanted to talk to a boy named Romeo, she would put the word "o" before his name when addressing him in English.

While this sounds very old-fashioned in English, it's perfectly ordinary to address people this way in Irish. It might even be considered rude if you don't use the *vocative* when speaking to someone directly. Also, the *vocative* is used in both formal and casual situations.

Examples

Let's take a look at some names with and without the *vocative* "**a**" [uh] in front of them to compare. To remind us which one is used when addressing the person, we'll also use the *vocative* "o" in the English translations.

"Kathleen"	"Patricia"	"Patrick"
Caitlín	**Pádraigín**	**Pádraig**
[katch-leen]	[paw-druh-geen]	[paw-drig]
"O Kathleen"	"O Patricia"	"O Patrick"
a Chaitlín	**a Phádraigín**	**a Phádraig**
[uh khatch-leen]	[uh faw-druh-geen]	[uh faw-drig]
"Mary"	"Sheila"	
Máire	**Síle**	
[moy-ruh]	[shee-luh]	
"O Mary"	"O Sheila"	
a Mháire	**a Shíle**	
[uh woy-ruh]	[uh hee-luh]	

Slenderizing Men's Names

Aside from softening, there is another thing that happens when you address people by name in Irish. If you're using a man's name, sometimes the end of it changes a little, usually by adding an "**i**" before the last letter to make the sound more slender. If a man's name already has an "**i**" at or just before the end, then no changes occur, and you just soften the beginning.

Examples

"Brian"
Brian
[bree-uhn]

"John"
Seán
[shawn]

"Paul"
Pól
[poel]

"O Brian"
a Bhriain
[uh vree-in]

"O John"
a Sheáin
[uh hyah-een]

"Paul"
a Phóil
[uh foe-il]

"James"
Séamas
[shay-muss]

"Michael"
Mícheál
[mee-hawl]

"O James"
a Shéamais
[uh hey-mish]

"O Michael"
a Mhíchíl
[uh vee-heel]

Names That Don't Change

If the name starts with a letter that can't be softened, then you just say the *vocative* "**a**" [uh] followed by the person's name. This is also the case when a name uses letters or sounds that are not native to Irish.

"Liam"
Liam
[lee-um]

"Rory"
Rúairí
[roo-ree]

"O Liam"
a Liam
[uh lee-um]

"O Rory"
a Rúairí
[uh roo-ree]

"Noreen"
Noirín
[nor-een]

"Xavier"
Xavier
[zay-vee-er]

"O Noreen"
a Noirín
[uh nor-een]

"O Xavier"
a Xavier
[uh zay-vee-er]

Conversation

Very often, when you address someone by name, it's right after you greet them. We'll practice using the *vocative case* by using it in a brief conversation using the greetings we learned in Lesson 1.

Pádraigín:
"I'm Patricia."
Is mise Pádraigín.
[iss mih-shuh paw-druh-geen]

Brian:
"Hello, Patricia."
Dia duit, a Phádraigín.
[jee-uh ghitch, uh faw-druh-geen]

"I'm Brian."
Is mise Brian.
[iss mih-shuh bree-uhn]

Pádraigín:
"Hello, Brian."
Dia 's Muire duit, a Bhriain.
[jee-uh smwir-uh ghitch, uh vree-in]

Lesson 24 – More About Initial Changes to Words

We learned about how Irish changes the beginning of a word sometimes, and that this usually happens because of a word that comes in front of it. One of the ways words can change is by *softening* them. Now we'll learn about another way Irish can change the beginning of a word.

Eclipsis

Another way words change in Irish is when one sound is *eclipsed* by another sound. This is called "**urú**" [uh-roo], or *eclipsis*. This is when a new letter is put at the beginning of the word, and takes over for the original letter.

A good way to think of it is like when the moon eclipses the sun. The sun is still there, but all you can see is the moon. Likewise, the original first letter of the word remains; there's just another letter in front of it, which you say instead.

TIP!   If you see a word that you can't find in the dictionary, try looking it up by the second letter instead of the first; it might be getting *eclipsed*.

Some consonants cannot be *eclipsed*, but those that can be are *eclipsed* by a specific letter. We'll learn more about *eclipsis* through practicing phrases and sentences in upcoming lessons. For a list of which letters *eclipse* which, and letters that do not *eclipse* at all, see the Appendix.

Just to note, this may look like what we've seen before when you add a "**t-**" or an "**h-**" in front of a word that starts with a vowel. Those changes are a little different, because you still say the sound of the vowel, so vowels doesn't actually get *eclipsed*. Also, the new letter doesn't even touch the original letter, as it's separated by a hyphen. (Sometimes, though, people might leave the hyphen out, so keep the above tip about trying to find words in the dictionary by the second letter in mind.)

Also, as we saw in Lesson 22, the letter "**t**" is put in front of some words that begin with "**s**." Even though this sounds like *eclipsis*, it is not considered *eclipsis* because this generally happens when the "**s**" word should be *softened*.

Lesson 25 – Possessives

Words that stand for nouns, such as "I," "you," and "they," are called *pronouns*. Words that show possession or ownership, such as "my," "your," and "their," are called *possessive pronouns*. In Irish, possessive pronouns will change the word after them. Some of them will *soften* the next word, and some of them will *eclipse* the next word.

Vocabulary

Here is a list of possessive pronouns, along with a note as to whether they *soften* or *eclipse* the word after them:

"my"
mo
[muh]
softens

"your"
do
[duh]
softens

"his"
a
[uh]
softens

"her"
a
[uh]
no change

"our"
ár
[awr]
eclipses

"your" ("y'all's")
bhur
[woor]
eclipses

"their"
a
[uh]
eclipses

Notice how the first three *soften*, the middle one makes *no change*, and the last three *eclipse*.

You'll also notice that three of the possessive pronouns look the same. The words for the third-person possessives, "his," "her," and "their," are all "**a**" [uh]. The clue to telling them apart is how they change the next word. The "**a**" [uh] for "his" *softens*, the "**a**" [uh] for "her" makes *no change*, and the "**a**" [uh] for "their" *eclipses*.

Examples

Let's take a sample word that can both *soften* and *eclipse* to see how the *possessive pronouns* work. We'll use the word "box," "**bosca**" [bus-kuh], which is masculine (m.).

"my box"
mo bhosca
[muh wuhss-kuh]

"your box"
do bhosca
[duh wuhss-kuh]

"his box"
a bhosca
[uh wuhss-kuh]

"her box"
a bosca
[uh bus-kuh]

"our box"
ár mbosca
[awr muss-kuh]

"y'all's box"
bhur mbosca
[woor muss-kuh]

"their box"
a mbosca
[uh muss-kuh]

Lesson 26 – Possessives with Vowels

When you're using *possessive pronouns* with words that start with a vowel sound, they act a little differently. This goes for both nouns that start with a vowel, and nouns that start with the letter "**f**" which, when *softened*, becomes silent. Once again, within the list there are some patterns, so we'll take a look at them in small groups.

"My" and "Your"

The first two possessive pronouns, "my," "**mo**" [muh] and "your" (singular), "**do**" [duh], both end in a vowel. When they are followed by a word that begins with a vowel, you run the words together. When you write them, you put an "**m'**" (m+apostrophe) or a "**d'**" (d+apostrophe) directly in front of the noun.

Examples

Let's take two sample words and see how they combine with "**mo**" [muh] and "**do**" [duh]. One starts with a vowel and one starts with a vowel sound when *softened*.

"apple"
úll (m.)
[ool]

"my apple"
m'úll
[mool]

"your apple"
d'úll
[dool]

"ring"
fáinne (m.)
[faw-nyuh]

"my ring"
m'fháinne
[maw-nyuh]

"your ring"
d'fháinne
[daw-nyuh]

"His"

The next possessive pronoun, "his," "**a**" [uh], causes *no change* to a word that starts with a vowel, and still *softens* a word that starts with a consonant.

Examples

"apple"
úll
[col]

"his apple"
a úll
[uh ool]

"ring"
fáinne
[faw-nyuh]

"his ring"
a fháinne
[uh aw-nyuh]

"Her"

The next possessive pronoun, "her," "**a**" [uh], adds an "**h-**" to the beginnings of words that start with a vowel, and still makes *no change* to words that start with a consonant.

Examples

"apple"
úll
[ool]

"her apple"
a h-úll
[uh hool]

"ring"
fáinne
[faw-nyuh]

"her ring"
a fáinne
[uh faw-nyuh]

"Our," "Your," and "Their"

The last three possessive pronouns, "our," "**ár**" [awr], "your" (plural), "**bhur**" [woor], and "their," "**a**" [uh], add an "**n-**" to the beginnings of words that start with a vowel, and still *eclipse* words that start with a consonant.

Examples

"apple"
úll
[ool]

"our apple"
ár n-úll
[awr nool]

"y'all's apple"
bhur n-úll
[woor nool]

"their apple"
a n-úll
[uh nool]

"ring"
fáinne
[faw-nyuh]

"our ring"
ár bhfáinne
[awr wah-nyuh]

"y'all's ring"
bhur bhfáinne
[woor wah-nyuh]

"their ring"
a bhfáinne
[uh wah-nyuh]

Lesson 27 – Using Possessives in a Sentence

Using possessives in a sentence is like using pronouns in a sentence. You simply say the possessive and its noun after the verb and before the adjective.

Examples

Let's look at some sentences that use simple pronouns and possessive pronouns to compare.

"It is big."
Tá sé mór.
[taw shay mor]

"My table is big."
Tá mo bhord mór.
[taw muh word (rhymes with "board") mor]

"It isn't small."
Níl sé beag.
[neel shay bayug]

"Your apple isn't small."
Níl d'úll beag.
[neel dool bayug]

Examples

Now we'll look at sample sentences using the possessive pronouns.

"Is my window clean?"
An bhfuil m'fhuinneog glan?
[un will min-yoeg glon]

"Yes. Your window is clean."
Tá, tá d'fhuinneog glan.
[taw, taw din-yoeg glon]

"Isn't your drink hot?"
Nach bhfuil do dheoch te?
[nahkh will duh yawkh tcheh]

"No, my drink is cold."
Níl. Tá mo dheoch fuar.
[neel. taw muh yawkh foo-uhr]

"Is his table wet?"
An bhfuil a bhord fliuch?
[un will uh word (rhymes with "board") flyukh]

"No, his table is not wet."
Níl, níl a bhord fliuch.
[neel, neel uh word (rhymes with "board") flyukh]

"Isn't her ring new?"
Nach bhfuil a fáinne nua?
[nahkh will uh faw-nyuh noo-uh]

"Yes, her ring is new."
Tá. Tá a fáinne nua.
[taw. taw uh faw-nyuh noo-uh]

"Is our box okay?"
An bhfuil ár mbosca ceart go leor?
[un will awr muss-kuh kyart guh leeyor]

"Yes, y'all's box is okay."
Tá, tá bhur mbosca ceart go leor.
[taw, taw woor muss-kuh kyart guh leeyor]

"Aren't y'all's knives clean?"
Nach bhfuil bhur sceana glan?
[nahkh will woor shkyah-nuh glon]

"No. Our knives are dirty."
Níl. Tá ár sceana salach.
[neel. taw awr shkyah-nuh sahl-ahkh]

"Are their chairs fine?"
An bhfuil a gcathaoireacha go breá?
[un will uh gah-heer-ih-khuh guh braw]

"Yes. Their chairs are fine."
Tá. Tá a gcathaoireacha go breá.
[taw. taw uh gah-heer-ih-khuh guh braw]

Conversation

Now we'll practice what we've learned about possessive pronouns with a conversation.

Brian:
"Hello, Patricia."
Dia duit, a Phádraigín.
[jee-uh ghitch, uh faw-druh-geen]

Pádraigín:
"Hello, Brian."
Dia 's Muire duit, a Bhriain.
[jee-uh smwir-uh ghitch, uh vree-in]

Brian:
"Is your table small?"
An bhfuil do mhord beag?
[un will duh word (rhymes with "board") bayug]

Pádraigín:
"Yes, my table is small."
Tá. Tá mo mhord beag.
[taw. taw muh word (rhymes with "board") bayug]

Brian:
"Is your chair small, too?"
An bhfuil do chathaoir beag, freisin?
[un will duh khah-heer bayug, fresh-in]

Pádraigín:
"No. My chair is big."
Níl. Tá mo chathaoir mór.
[neel. taw muh khah-heer mor]

"Are their tables okay?"
An bhfuil a mboird ceart go leor?
[un will uh mweerj kyart guh leeyor]

Brian:
"No. Their tables and their chairs are wet."
Níl. Tá a mboird agus a gcathaoireacha fliuch.
[neel. taw uh mweerj ah-gus uh gah-heer-ih-khuh flyukh]

Lesson 28 – Expressing "To Have"

We've seen how to express possession in Irish using the possessive pronouns, but you can also say that you "have" something. Irish doesn't use an exclusive verb for this concept. Instead, you say that something is "at" you. The word for "at" in Irish is "**ag**" [ehg].

Making a Simple Sentence Using the "Have" Construction

Sentences about "having" begin just like the basic sentences we've been working with. You start with the verb "**tá**" [taw], then say the thing that's being had, and finally who has the thing.

For the moment, we'll only use this construction with names, so that you can get used to how this turn of phrase works. To name the person who has something, all you have to do is say the word "**ag**" [ehg], "at," and then the person's name.

Examples

"Brian has a ring."
Tá fáinne ag Brian.
[taw faw-nyuh ehg bree-uhn]

"Patricia doesn't have a spoon."
Níl spúnóg ag Pádraigín.
[neel spoo-noeg ehg paw-druh-geen]

"Does Liam have the box?"
An bhfuil an bosca ag Liam?
[un will un bus-kuh ehg lee-um]

"Doesn't Noreen have the keys?"
Nach bhfuil na h-eochracha ag Noirín?
[nahkh will nuh hukh-rukh-uh ehg nor-een]

"Patricia and Brian have the drinks."
Tá na deochanna ag Pádraigín agus Brian.
[taw nuh jawkh-uh-nuh ehg paw-druh-geen ah-gus bree-uhn]

"Liam and Noreen don't have a table."
Níl bord ag Liam agus Noirín.
[neel bord ehg lee-um ah-gus nor-een]

Lesson 29 – Saying "Have" with Pronouns

As we learned in Lesson 28, you can say that somebody has something by simply putting their name after the word "**ag**" [ehg], "at." The word "at" is a *preposition*. Prepositions are words that show a noun's relationship to some other thing in the sentence, like "in," "for," "with," etc.

In Irish, when *prepositions* (like "at") and *pronouns* (like "I") come together, they combine into one word. This is called a *prepositional pronoun*. (Think: preposition + pronoun = prepositional pronoun.)

We've learned before that the words for "at" and "I" are "**ag**" [ehg] and "**mé**" [may]. Let's see how they combine to make a new word for "at me."

"at" + "me" = "at me"
ag + **mé** = **agam**
[ehg] + [may] = [ah-gum]

Vocabulary

Here are all the prepositional pronoun forms for the preposition "**ag**" [ehg]:

"at me"
agam
[ah-gum]

"at you"
agat
[ah-gut]

"at him"
aige
[ehg-uh]

"at her"
aici
[ehk-ee]

"at us"
againn
[ah-geen]

"at y'all"
agaibh
[ah-giv]

"at them"
acu
[ah-kuh]

Lesson 30 – Making "Have" Sentences with Pronouns

Making a "have" sentence using a prepositional pronoun is a lot like making one using a name. All you have to do is switch out the last two words, "**ag**" [ehg], and the person's name, for one of the prepositional pronoun forms of "**ag**" [ehg].

Examples

Let's take a look at some "have" sentences that use names, and compare them to some that use prepositional pronouns.

"Brian has a box."
Tá bosca ag Brian.
[taw bus-kuh ehg bree-uhn]

"He has a box."
Tá bosca aige.
[taw bus-kuh ehg-uh]

"Does Patricia have the key?"
An bhfuil an eochair ag Pádraigín?
[un will un ukh-er ehg paw-druh-geen]

"Does she have the key?"
An bhfuil an eochair aici?
[un will un ukh-er ehk-ee]

Examples

Let's take a look at sample sentences that use each of the prepositional pronoun forms for "**ag**" [ehg].

"I have a box."
Tá bosca agam.
[taw bus-kuh ah-gum]

"You have a box."
Tá bosca agat.
[taw bus-kuh ah-gut]

"He has a box."
Tá bosca aige.
[taw bus-kuh ehg-uh]

"She has a box."
Tá bosca aici.
[taw bus-kuh ehk-ee]

"We have a box."
Tá bosca againn.
[taw bus-kuh ah-geen]

"Y'all have a box."
Tá bosca agaibh.
[taw bus-kuh ah-giv]

"They have a box."
Tá bosca acu.
[taw bus-kuh ah-kuh]

Lesson 31 – Answering "Have" Questions

When answering questions, remember that Irish doesn't have a single word for "yes" or "no." You use the positive statement or negative statement form of the same verb. To answer "yes" or "no" to an "**an bhfuil**" [un will] or "**nach bhfuil**" [nahkh will] question, you say "**tá**" [taw] for "yes," or "**níl**" [neel] for "no."

If you're asked about a specific thing, something that uses the definite article, "the," you can choose to repeat the noun in your response, or use the appropriate pronoun in its place. For example, if you're asked, "Do you have the box?", you can answer, "Yes, I have *the box*," or, "Yes, I have *it*."

Examples

Let's look at some sample questions with answers using both nouns and pronouns.

"Do you have a key?"
An bhfuil eochair agat?
[un will ukh-er ah-gut]

"Yes, I have a key."
Tá. Tá eochair agam.
[taw, taw ukh-er ah-gum]

"Does she have the ring?"
An bhfuil an fáinne aici?
[un will un faw-nyuh ehk-ee]

"No, she doesn't have the ring."
Níl. Níl an fáinne aici.
[neel. neel un faw-nyuh ehk-ee]

"No, she doesn't have it."
Níl. Níl sé aici.
[neel. neel shay ehk-ee]

"Don't y'all have the spoons?"
Nach bhfuil na spúnóga agaibh?
[nahkh will nuh spoo-noeg-uh ah-giv]

"Yes, we have the spoons."
Tá. Tá na spúnóga againn.
[taw. taw nuh spoo-noeg-uh ah-geen]

"Yes, we have them."
Tá. Tá siad againn.
[taw. taw shee-ud ah-geen]

Conversation

Now we'll practice asking and answering "have" questions with a conversation.

Pádraigín:
"Hello, Brian."
Dia duit, a Bhriain.
[jee-uh ghitch, uh vree-in]

Brian:
"Hello, Patricia."
Dia 's Muire duit, a Phádraigín.
[jee-uh smwir-uh ghitch, uh faw-druh-geen]

Pádraigín:
"I have an apple."
Tá úll agam.
[taw ool ah-gum]

"Do you have a knife?"
An bhfuil scian agat?
[un will shkee-un ah-gut]

Brian:
"No, I don't have a knife."
Níl. Níl scian agam.
[neel. neel shkee-un ah-gum]

Pádraigín:
"Does Liam have a knife?"
An bhfuil scian ag Liam?
[un will shkee-un ehg lee-um]

Brian:
"No. He has a spoon."
Níl. Tá spúnóg aige.
[neel. taw spoo-noeg ehg-uh]

Pádraigín:
"Doesn't Noreen have a knife?"
Nach bhfuil scian ag Noirín?
[nahkh will shkee-un ehg nor-een]

Brian:
"No. They don't have knives."
Níl. Níl sceana acu.
[neel. neel shkyah-nuh ah-kuh]

Lesson 32 – Having More Things

Let's take a look at more nouns, so we can talk about having more things. Learning these new words with the "have" construction will not only expand your vocabulary, but will help you practice prepositional pronouns, too.

Vocabulary

Here are some common nouns. Their grammatical gender has been noted beside each one, so you can learn them as you go.

"a bag"
mála (m.)
[maw-luh]

"the bag"
an mála
[un maw-luh]

"a bicycle"
rothar (m.)
[ruh-her]

"the bicycle"
an rothar
[un ruh-her]

"a book"
leabhar (m.)
[lyow-er]

"the book"
an leabhar
[un lyow-er]

"a fork"
gabhlóg (f.)
[gow-loeg]

"the fork"
an ghabhlóg
[un ghow-loeg]

"a glass"
gloine (f.)
[glih-nyuh]

"the glass"
an ghloine
[un ghlih-nyuh]

"a pen"
peann (m.)
[pyawn]

"the pen"
an peann
[un pyawn]

Examples

Let's take a look at some sample sentences using our new vocabulary.

"I have a bag."
Tá mála agam.
[taw maw-luh ah-gum]

"You don't have a bicycle."
Níl rothar agat.
[neel ruh-her ah-gut]

"Does he have the book?"
An bhfuil an leabhar aige?
[un will un lyow-er ehg-uh]

"Doesn't she have a fork?"
Nach bhfuil gabhlóg aici?
[nahkh will gow-loeg ehk-ee]

"We have the glass."
Tá an ghloine againn.
[taw un ghlih-nyuh ah-geen]

"Y'all don't have a pen."
Níl peann agaibh.
[neel pyawn ah-giv]

"Do they have the bag?"
Ar bhfuil an mála acu?
[un will un maw-luh ah-kuh]

"Doesn't Brian have the book?"
Nach bhfuil an leabhar ag Brian?
[nahkh will un lyow-er ehg bree-uhn]

Conversation

Now we'll practice some of our new vocabulary with a conversation.

Brian:
"Hello, Patricia."
Dia duit, a Phádraigín.
[jee-uh ghitch, uh faw-druh-geen]

Pádraigín:
"Hello, Brian."
Dia 's Muire duit, a Bhriain.
[jee-uh smwir-uh ghitch, uh vree-in]

Brian:

"Does Liam have the bag?"

An bhfuil an mála ag Liam?

[un will un maw-luh ehg lee-um]

Pádraigín:

"Yes, he has it."

Tá. Tá sé aige.

[taw. taw shay ehg-uh]

Brian:

"Does he have the book and the pen, too?

An bhfuil an leabhar agus an peann aige, freisin?

[un will un lyow-er ah-gus un pyawn ehg-uh, fresh-in]

Pádraigín:

"No, he doesn't have them."

Níl. Níl siad aige.

[neel. neel shee-ud ehg-uh]

Lesson 33 – Doing Things

Irish makes great use of prepositions to express all sorts of concepts. We've seen how possession can be expressed using "**ag**" [ehg], "at." This preposition can also be used to say what you're doing.

When you talk about what someone is doing right now, that's called the *progressive tense*, because the action is *progressing* as we speak. In English, we put the ending "-ing" on a word in order to express this, like "walk*ing*". In Irish, we put the preposition "**ag**" [ehg] before a noun to express this. When a noun comes after "**ag**" [ehg] like this, it's called a *verbal noun*.

For example, the word for "a walk" in Irish is "**siúl**" [shool], which is masculine (m.). To say, "Patricia is walking," you express it by saying that "Patricia is at a walk," "**Tá Pádraigín ag siúl**," [taw paw-druh-geen ehg shool].

This has a different feel than the English expression, but you'll get used to it over time. Just try to think that "**ag** + something" phrases are like "-ing" words.

Making a Simple Sentence Using Verbal Nouns

To make a sentence using this turn of phrase, you begin the same way you do with a basic sentence. You start by saying the verb, "**tá**" [taw], "is," then you say who is doing the action (a noun or a pronoun, like "Patricia," or "she"), and then you say the "-ing" expression.

Examples

Let's take a look at this expression using a name and all of the pronouns.

"Patricia is <u>walking</u>."
Tá Pádraigín <u>ag siúl</u>.
[taw paw-druh-geen ehg shool]

"I am walking."
Tá mé ag siúl.
[taw may ehg shool]

"You are walking."
Tá tú ag siúl.
[taw too ehg shool]

"He is walking."
Tá sé ag siúl.
[taw shay ehg shool]

"She is walking."
Tá sí ag siúl.
[taw shee ehg shool]

"We are walking."
Tá muid ag siúl.
[taw mwidj ehg shool]

"Y'all are walking."
Tá sibh ag siúl.
[taw shiv ehg shool]

"They are walking."
Tá siad ag siúl.
[taw shee-ud ehg shool]

Lesson 34 – Making More Progressive Sentences

People often talk about what's happening now, so the progressive tense gets used a lot in both English and Irish. We'll learn a few more verbal noun phrases (which correspond to "-ing" words in English), so we can talk about doing even more things.

Vocabulary

Here are some common verbal noun phrases:

"learning"
ag foghlaim
[ehg foe-lum]

"laughing"
ag gáire
[ehg goy-ruh]

"eating"
ag ithe
[ehg ih-huh]

"working"
ag obair
[ehg uh-ber]

"talking"
ag caint
[ehg kyintch]

"running"
ag rith
[ehg rih]

"drinking"
ag ól
[ehg oel]

Examples

"I am learning."
Tá mé ag foghlaim.
[taw may ehg foe-lum]

"You are not talking."
Níl tú ag caint.
[neel too ehg kyintch]

"Is he laughing?"
An bhfuil sé ag gáire?
[un will shay ehg goy-ruh]

"Isn't she running?"
Nach bhfuil sí ag rith?
[nahkh will shee ehg rih]

"We are eating."
Tá muid ag ithe.
[taw mwidj ehg ih-huh]

"Are y'all drinking?"
An bhfuil sibh ag ól?
[un will shiv ehg oel]

"Aren't they working?"
Nach bhfuil siad ag obair?
[nahkh will shee-ud ehg uh-ber]

Lesson 35 – Answering Progressive Questions

When answering questions, remember that Irish doesn't have a single word for "yes" or "no." You use the positive statement form of the verb to say "yes," or the negative statement form of the verb to say "no." To answer "yes" or "no" to an "**an bhfuil**" [un will] or "**nach bhfuil**" [nahkh will] question, you say "**tá**" [taw] for "yes," or "**níl**" [neel] for "no."

Examples

"Are we learning?"
An bhfuil muid ag foghlaim?
[un will mwidj ehg foe-lum]

"Yes, we are learning!"
Tá, tá muid ag foghlaim!
[taw, taw mwidj ehg foe-lum]

"Is Brian walking?"
An bhfuil Brian ag siúl?
[un will bree-uhn ehg shool]

"No, he is running."
Níl, tá sé ag rith.
[neel, taw shay ehg rih]

"Aren't they working?"
Nach bhfuil siad ag obair?
[nahkh will shee-ud ehg uh-ber]

"Yes, they are working."
Tá, tá siad ag obair.
[taw, taw shee-ud ehg uh-ber]

"Isn't she laughing?"
Nach bhfuil sí ag gáire?
[nahkh will shee ehg goy-ruh]

"No, she isn't laughing."
Níl, níl sí ag gáire.
[neel, neel shee ehg goy-ruh]

Conversation

Now we'll practice speaking in the progressive tense with a conversation.

Pádraigín:
"Is Liam eating?"
An bhfuil Liam ag ithe?
[un will lee-um ehg ih-huh]

Brian:
"No, he's running."
Níl. Tá sé ag rith.
[neel. taw shay ehg rih]

Pádraigín:
"Is Noreen eating?"
An bhfuil Noirín ag ithe?
[un will nor-een ehg ih-huh]

Brian:
"No, she's working."
Níl. Tá sí ag obair.
[neel. taw shee ehg uh-ber]

Pádraigín:
"Are *you* working, too?"
An bhfuil tusa ag obair, freisin?
[un will tuh-suh ehg uh-ber, fresh-in]

Brian:
"No. I'm talking."
Níl Tá mé ag caint.
[neel. taw may ehg kyintch]

Pádraigín:
"Yes! *We* are talking!"
Tá! Tá muide ag caint!
[taw! taw mwidj-uh ehg kyintch]

Brian:
"And we're learning."
Agus tá muid ag foghlaim.
[ah-gus taw mwidj ehg foe-lum]

Pádraigín:
"Yes, we're talking, learning, and laughing!"
Tá. Tá muid ag caint, ag foghlaim, agus ag gáire!
[taw. taw mwidj ehg kyintch, ehg foe-lum, ah-gus ehg goy-ruh]

Lesson 36 – Doing More Things

We're going to take a look at a few more verbal noun phrases (which correspond to "-ing" words in English), so we can not only expand our vocabulary, but also practice these types of sentences.

Vocabulary

Here are a few more common verbal noun phrases:

"coming"
ag teacht
[ehg tchakht]

"reading"
ag léamh
[ehg lay-uv]

"listening"
ag éisteacht
[ehg aysh-tahkht]

"waiting, staying"
ag fanacht
[ehg faw-nahkht]

Examples

"I'm coming!"
Tá mé ag teacht!
[taw may ehg tchakht]

"Are you listening?"
An bhfuil tú ag éisteacht?
[un will too ehg aysh-tahkht]

"Aren't they reading?"
Nach bhfuil siad ag léamh?
[nahkh will shee-ud ehg lay-uv]

"She isn't staying."
Níl sí ag fanacht.
[neel shee ehg faw-nahkht]

"He's waiting."
Tá sé ag fanacht.
[taw shay ehg faw-nahkht]

Lesson 37 – What Are You Doing?

Now that you know how to talk about doing so many things, you may want to ask someone what they are doing. Like the *Bonus Phrases* we learned in Lesson 1, you don't need to worry about the construction of this question for now. Just learn it as is, and you'll be fine.

To ask, "What are you doing?" in Irish, you say:

"What are you doing?"
Céard atá tú ag déanamh?
[kayrd uh-taw too ehg jay-nuv]

Notice how the word "**tú**" [too], "you," appears in the middle of the sentence. You can switch out this pronoun for any other pronoun, a name, or a noun. For example, if you wanted to ask what Brian is doing, you would say:

"What is <u>Brian</u> doing?"
Céard atá <u>Brian</u> ag déanamh?
[kayrd uh-taw bree-uhn ehg jay-nuv]

or

"What is <u>he</u> doing?"
Céard atá <u>sé</u> ag déanamh?
[kayrd uh-taw shay ehg jay-nuv]

Examples

Let's look at this *Bonus Phrase* question with all the pronouns.

"What am <u>I</u> doing?"
Céard atá <u>mé</u> ag déanamh?
[kayrd uh-taw may ehg jay-nuv]

"What are <u>you</u> doing?"
Céard atá <u>tú</u> ag déanamh?
[kayrd uh-taw too ehg jay-nuv]

"What is <u>he</u> doing?"
Céard atá <u>sé</u> ag déanamh?
[kayrd uh-taw shay ehg jay-nuv]

"What is <u>she</u> doing?"
Céard atá <u>sí</u> ag déanamh?
[kayrd uh-taw shee ehg jay-nuv]

"What are <u>we</u> doing?"
Céard atá <u>muid</u> ag déanamh?
[kayrd uh-taw mwidj ehg jay-nuv]

"What are <u>y'all</u> doing?"
Céard atá <u>sibh</u> ag déanamh?
[kayrd uh-taw shiv ehg jay-nuv]

"What are <u>they</u> doing?"
Céard atá <u>siad</u> ag déanamh?
[kayrd uh-taw shee-ud ehg jay-nuv]

Conversation

Brian:
"Hello, Patricia."
Dia duit, a Phádraigín.
[jee-uh ghitch, uh faw-druh-geen]

Pádraigín:
"Hello, Brian."
Dia 's Muire duit, a Bhriain.
[jee-uh smwir-uh ghitch, uh vree-in]

"How are you?"
Cén chaoi a bhfuil tú?
[keh hee will too]

Brian:
"I'm well, thanks."
Tá mé go maith, go raibh maith agat.
[taw may guh mah, guh ruh mah ah-gut]

"How's yourself?"
Conas atá tú féin?
[kun-us uh-taw too fayn]

Pádraigín:
"I am fine, thanks."
Tá mé go breá, go raibh maith agat.
[taw may guh braw, guh ruh mah ah-gut]

Brian:
"What are you doing?"
Céard atá tú ag déanamh?
[kayrd uh-taw too ehg jay-nuv]

Pádraigín:
"I'm reading."
Tá mé ag leamh.
[taw may ehg lay-uv]

"What are *you* doing?"
Céard atá tusa ag déanamh?
[kayrd uh-taw tuh-suh ehg jay-nuv]

Brian:
"I'm waiting."
Tá mé ag fanacht.
[taw may ehg faw-nahkht]

"What are Noreen and Liam doing?"
Céard atá Noirín agus Liam ag déanamh?
[kayrd uh-taw nor-een ah-gus lee-um ehg jay-nuv]

Pádraigín:
"They're coming."
Tá siad ag teacht.
[taw shee-ud ehg tchakht]

Lesson 38 – Where Is It?

There are many kinds of questions you can ask in Irish. One handy question is "Where is it?" This is a *Bonus Phrase*, so we'll learn it as is.

To ask, "Where is it?" in Irish, you say:

"Where is it?"
Cá bhfuil sé?
[kaw will shay]

Notice that the *masculine* "it," "**sé**" [shay], is used at the end of the sentence. If you don't know the gender of a particular noun you're asking about, it's okay to default to the *masculine* "it." If you do know the gender of the noun you're asking about, make sure to use the appropriate *masculine* or *feminine* "it." Not only is this correct, but it's good practice, too!

Remember that you can switch out a pronoun for any other pronoun, a name, or a noun. For example, if you wanted to ask where Patricia is, you would say:

"Where is <u>Patricia</u>?"   "Where is <u>she</u>?"
Cá bhfuil <u>Pádraigín</u>?   or   **Cá bhfuil <u>sí</u>?**
[kaw will paw-druh-geen]   [kaw will shee]

You can also use this question to ask about where things are. For example:

"Where is <u>the book</u>?"
Cá bhfuil <u>an leabhar</u>?
[kaw will un lyow-er]

"Where are <u>the keys</u>?"
Cá bhfuil <u>na h-eochracha</u>?
[kaw will nuh hukh-rukh-uh]

An especially useful thing to ask for is the location of the bathroom. The word for "bathroom" in Irish is "**leithreas**" [leh-hruss], which is masculine (m.). To ask where the bathroom is, you say:

"Where is the bathroom?"
Cá bhfuil an leithreas?
[kaw will un leh-hruss]

We'll be learning how to answer a "where is" question in the next lesson. In the mean time, if you need to ask where the bathroom is in Irish, hopefully, the person answering you will be pointing, as well as speaking.

Lesson 39 – Saying Where It Is

Answering a "where" question is easy, because you can use a basic "**tá**" [taw] sentence. There are a lot of places things can be, but we'll just practice with a few general places.

Vocabulary

"here"	"there"	"inside"	"outside"
anseo	**ansin**	**istigh**	**amuigh**
[un-shuh]	[un-shin]	[iss-tchih]	[uh-muh]

Examples

You can use these location words the same way you would use a descriptive word in a "**tá**" [taw] sentence.

"Where is the bathroom?"
Cá bhfuil an leithreas?
[kaw will un leh-hruss]

"It is here."
Tá sé anseo.
[taw shay un-shuh]

"It is there."
Tá sé ansin.
[taw shay un-shin]

"It is inside."
Tá sé istigh.
[taw shay iss-tchih]

"It is outside."
Tá sé amuigh.
[taw shay uh-muh]

Remember that you can use the negative form of "**tá**" [taw] to answer location questions, too.

"Where is the bathroom?"
Cá bhfuil an leithreas?
[kaw will un leh-hruss]

"It's not here."
Níl sé anseo.
[neel shay un-shuh]

Lesson 40 – Speaking Vaguely About Where It Is

Sometimes when you talk about where something is, you're not actually being very specific, even when you say the word "there." In Irish, "**anseo**" [un-shuh], "here," and "**ansin**" [un-shin], "there," refer to a specific "here" and "there," a place you could point to. When you want to say that something is "there," meaning that it's "around," or in "a general area," you use a different word.

Vocabulary

To say "there" when talking about a vague location, you say:

> "there"
> **ann**
> [on]

EXAMPLES

Let's take a look at two sentences that use "there" in English to compare:

"It's <u>there</u>." (in that specific place)
Tá sé <u>ansin</u>.
[taw shay un-shin]

"It's <u>there</u>." (somewhere)
Tá sé <u>ann</u>.
[taw shay on]

Though both sentences look the same in English, the two Irish sentences are distinct. The first one, using "**ansin**" [un-shin], is referring to a specific location, and the second one, using "**ann**" [on], is talking about a general location.

Lesson 41 – Going Places

Now that we've learned about where things are, let's learn about going places. To say "going" in Irish, you say:

"going"
ag dul
[ehg dull]

When you're saying that someone "is going," you usually say *where* they're going. In English, we'll often leave the place we're talking about implied. In Irish, a word for the place is always included, even if it's only the vague "there," "**ann**" [on].

Examples

Let's take a look at a few sentences that use the vague "there" to describe where people are going:

"She's going there."
Tá sí ag dul ann.
[taw shee ehg dull on]

"Is he going?"
An bhfuil sé ag dul ann?
[un will shay ehg dull on]

"I'm not going."
Níl mise ag dul ann.
[neel mih-shuh ehg dull on]

Notice that, in the last two sentences, the word "there" doesn't appear in the English translation. Once again, in Irish, you can't just leave the concept of "going" hanging. You always mention some kind of place, even if it's simply "**ann**" [on].

Usually, though, when you're talking about going places, you'll say the place someone's going to. In Irish, you can be very clear about the kind of places you can go, because Irish uses different words for "to" based on the circumstances.

Going to a Place

When you're going to a place you're referring to using the *indefinite article*, "a" or "an," you use the simplest form of "to," which is "**go**" [guh]. If the place you're going to begins with a vowel, you add an "**h-**" to the front of the noun after "**go**" [guh] to make it easier to say.

Vocabulary

Here are some nouns for places:

"a beach"
trá (f.)
[traw]

"a restaurant"
bialann (f.)
[bee-uh-luhn]

"a hotel"
óstán (m.)
[oess-tawn]

"a store"
siopa (m.)
[shuhp-uh]

"a park"
páirc (f.)
[pawrk]

Examples

"They're going to a beach."
Tá siad ag dul go trá.
[taw shee-ud ehg dull guh traw]

"He's not going to a hotel."
Níl sé ag dul go h-óstán.
[neel shay ehg dull guh hoess-tawn]

"Are y'all going to a park?"
An bhfuil sibh ag dul go páirc?
[un will shiv ehg dull guh pawrk]

"Aren't we going to a restaurant?"
Nach bhfuil muid ag dul go bialann?
[nahkh will mwidj ehg dull guh bee-uh-luhn]

"She's going to a store."
Tá sí ag dul go siopa.
[taw shee ehg dull guh shuhp-uh]

Lesson 42 – Going to the Place

When you're going to "the" place, a place you're referring to using the *definite article*, you add a word after the simple "to," making it "**go dtí**" [guh jee].

Vocabulary

Here are the nouns for places we learned in the last lesson with the definite article:

"the beach"
an trá (f.)
[un traw]

"the restaurant"
an bhialann (f.)
[un vee-uh-luhn]

"the hotel"
an t-óstán (m.)
[un toess-tawn]

"the store"
an siopa (m.)
[un shuhp-uh]

"the park"
an pháirc (f.)
[un fawrk]

Examples

"They're going to the beach."
Tá siad ag dul go dtí an trá.
[taw shee-ud ehg dull guh jee un traw]

"He's not going to the hotel."
Níl sé ag dul go dtí an t-óstán.
[neel shay ehg dull guh jee un toess-tawn]

"Are y'all going to the park?"
An bhfuil sibh ag dul go dtí an pháirc?
[un will shiv ehg dull guh jee un fawrk]

"Aren't we going to the restaurant?"
Nach bhfuil muid ag dul go dtí an bhialann?
[nahkh will mwidj ehg dull guh jee un vee-uh-luhn]

"She's going to the store."
Tá sí ag dul go dtí an siopa.
[taw shee ehg dull guh jee un shuhp-uh]

Lesson 43 – Going to an Event

There's a difference between going to a place and going to an event. When it's more important *what* is happening rather than *where* it's happening, you use a special word for "to," which is "**chuig**" [khig]. This can be used for any kind of event, from a party, to a showing of a movie, to a doctor's appointment.

Vocabulary

Here are some nouns for events:

"a movie"
scannán (m.)
[skuh-nawn]

"a wedding"
bainis (f.)
[ban-ish]

"a meeting"
cruinniú (m.)
[krin-nyew]

"a party"
cóisir (f.)
[koe-sher]

"a doctor"
dochtúir (m.)
[dokh-toor]

Examples

"We are going to a movie."
Tá muid ag dul chuig scannán.
[taw mwidj ehg dull khig skuh-nawn]

"They aren't going to a party."
Níl siad ag dul chuig cóisir.
[neel shee-ud ehg dull khig koe-sher]

"Are y'all going to a wedding?"
An bhfuil sibh ag dul chuig bainis?
[un will shiv ehg dull khig ban-ish]

"Isn't he going to a doctor?" (an appointment is implied)
Nach bhfuil sé ag dul chuig dochtúir?
[nahkh will shay ehg dull khig dokh-toor]

"I am going to a meeting."
Tá mé ag dul chuig cruinniú.
[taw may ehg dull khig krin-nyew]

Lesson 44 – Going to the Event

By itself, "**chuig**" [khig] doesn't change the word after it. When you use it with the definite article "**an**" [un], it *eclipses* the word after it, unless that word begins with "**d**" or "**t**". This overrides how the definite article by itself changes the word that follows it.

Vocabulary

Here are the nouns for events we learned in the last lesson with the definite article:

"the movie"
an scannán (m.)
[un skuh-nawn]

"the wedding"
an bhainis (f.)
[un wan-ish]

"the meeting"
an cruinniú (m.)
[un krin-nyew]

"the party"
an chóisir (f.)
[un khoe-sher]

"the doctor"
an dochtúir (m.)
[un dokh-toor]

Examples

Now we'll look at sentences using these event nouns with the definite article. Notice that when you use "**chuig an**" [khig un] it *eclipses* the noun (except words that start with "**d**" or "**t**"), even though "**an**" [un] by itself may change the noun differently or not at all.

"We are going to the movie."
Tá muid ag dul chuig an scannán.
[taw mwidj ehg dull khig un skuh-nawn]

"They aren't going to the party."
Níl siad ag dul chuig an gcóisir.
[neel shee-ud ehg dull khig un goe-sher]

"Are y'all going to the wedding?"
An bhfuil sibh ag dul chuig an mbainis?
[un will shiv ehg dull khig un man-ish]

"Isn't he going to the doctor?" (an appointment is implied)
Nach bhfuil sé ag dul chuig an dochtúir?
[nahkh will shay ehg dull khig un dokh-toor]

"I am going to the meeting."
Tá mé ag dul chuig an gcruinniú.
[taw may ehg dull khig un grin-nyew]

Lesson 45 – Going Home

Of all the places you can go, there's no place like home. When you're just talking about home, you use the simple word for "home," "**baile**" [ball-yeh], which is masculine (m.). However, when you say that you're "going home," you say "**abhaile**" [uh-wah-lyuh]. There's no need to use any form of "to" with this, because "**abhaile**" [uh-wah-lyuh] means "homeward," which implies that you're going "to home."

Examples

"I am going home."
Tá mé ag dul abhaile.
[taw may ehg dull uh-wah-lyuh]

"They aren't going home."
Níl siad ag dul abhaile.
[neel shee-ud ehg dull uh-wah-lyuh]

"Are we going home?"
An bhfuil muid ag dul abhaile?
[un will mwidj ehg dull uh-wah-lyuh]

"Aren't you going home?"
Nach bhfuil tú ag dul abhaile?
[nahkh will too ehg dull uh-wah-lyuh]

Lesson 46 – Going In and Out

We've learned the words for "inside" and "outside" when talking about where someone or something is. When you talk about where someone is going, you use a special form of these words that implies movement "inward" or "outward."

"in" (with movement)
isteach
[iss-tchahkh]

"out" (with movement)
amach
[uh-mahkh]

These terms are relative to the speaker, just as they are in English. When you say that someone is moving inward or outward, which of these words you choose depends on where you are compared to the person that's moving.

Examples

"She is going in."
Tá sí ag dul isteach.
[taw shee ehg dull iss-tchahkh]

"She is going out."
Tá sí ag dul amach.
[taw shee ehg dull uh-mahkh]

"Is he coming in?"
An bhfuil sé ag teacht isteach?
[un will shay ehg tchakht iss-tchahkh]

"Is he coming out?"
An bhfuil sé ag teacht amach?
[un will shay ehg tchakht uh-mahkh]

Lesson 47 – Where are You Going?

When you're talking about going places, you may want to ask someone where they're going. To ask where someone is going, you say:

"Where are you going?"
Cá bhfuil tú ag dul?
[kaw will too ehg dull]

You can use any of the ways to say where someone is going to answer this question. You can also use a different pronoun or a name in the question to ask where other people are going.

Examples

"Where are you going?"
Cá bhfuil tú ag dul?
[kaw will too ehg dull]

"I'm going to a restaurant."
Tá mé ag dul go bialann.
[taw may ehg dull guh bee-uh-luhn]

"Where is Patricia going?"
Cá bhfuil Pádraigín ag dul?
[kaw will paw-druh-geen ehg dull]

"She is going to the beach."
Tá sí ag dul go dtí an trá.
[taw shee ehg dull guh jee un traw]

"Where are y'all going?"
Cá bhfuil sibh ag dul?
[kaw will shiv ehg dull]

"We are going to a party."
Tá muid ag dul chuig cóisir.
[taw mwidj ehg dull khig koe-sher]

"Where are they going?"
Cá bhfuil siad ag dul?
[kaw will shee-ud ehg dull]

"They are going home."
Tá siad ag dul abhaile.
[taw shee-ud ehg dull uh-wah-lyuh]

"Where is he going?"
Cá bhfuil sé ag dul?
[kaw will shay ehg dull]

"He is going in."
Tá sé ag dul isteach.
[taw shay ehg dull iss-tchahkh]

"Where is she going?"
Cá bhfuil sí ag dul?
[kaw will shee ehg dull]

"She is going out."
Tá sí ag dul amach.
[taw shee ehg dull uh-mahkh]

Conversation

Now we'll practice what we've learned about going places with a conversation.

Pádraigín:
"Hello, Brian."
Dia duit, a Bhriain.
[jee-uh ghitch, uh vree-in]

Brian:
"Hello, Patricia."
Dia 's Muire duit, a Phádraigín.
[jee-uh smwir-uh ghitch, uh faw-druh-geen]

Pádraigín:
"Where are you going?"
Cá bhfuil tú ag dul?
[kaw will too ehg dull]

Brian:
"I'm going to the restaurant."
Tá mé ag dul go dtí an bhialann.
[taw may ehg dull guh jee un vee-uh-luhn]

Pádraigín:
"Is Liam going, too?"
An bhfuil Liam ag dul ann, freisin?
[un will lee-um ehg dull on, fresh-in]

Brian:
"No. He's going to a meeting."
Níl. Tá sé ag dul chuig cruinniú.
[neel. taw shay ehg dull khig krin-nyew]

Pádraigín:
"Isn't Noreen going to the meeting?"
Nach bhfuil Noirín ag dul chuig an gcruinniú?
[nahkh will nor-een ehg dull khig un grin-nyew]

Brian:
"No. She's going home."
Níl. Tá sí ag dul abhaile.
[neel. taw shee ehg dull uh-wah-lyuh]

"Where are *you* going?"
Cá bhfuil tusa ag dul?
[kaw will tuh-suh ehg dull]

Pádraigín:
"I'm going to the park."
Tá mé ag dul go dtí an pháirc.
[taw may ehg dull guh jee un fawrk]

"Bye!"
Slán leat!
[slawn lyat]

Brian:
"Good-bye!"
Slán leat!
[slawn lyat]

Lesson 48 – Basic Numbers

There are several number systems in Irish, just as there are in English. For example, if you wanted to count something, you would say, "*one* thing," but if you wanted to describe the order of something, you would say, "the *first* thing."

We'll start by learning the basic numbers in Irish. These are the numbers used for numbering things, like phone numbers, house numbers, bus numbers, and such. These are also the numbers used to tell the hours of the day.

Numbers from Zero to Ten

When you use the numbers from zero to ten for simple numbering, you put a helper word, "**a**" [uh], in front the number. This is just like when you hear a musician using a helper word to start counting a beat: "a one, a two, a three..." If the number starts with a vowel, you add an "**h-**" to the beginning of it.

Vocabulary

Here are the basic numbers in Irish from zero to ten. These numbers can be used without their helper, but we'll learn them with the "**a**" [uh] in front for practice.

"zero"	"three"	"six"	"nine"
a náid	**a trí**	**a sé**	**a naoi**
[uh noyj]	[uh tree]	[uh shay]	[uh nee]

"one"	"four"	"seven"	"ten"
a h-aon	**a ceathair**	**a seacht**	**a deich**
[uh hayn]	[uh kya-her]	[uh shakht]	[uh jeh]

"two"	"five"	"eight"	
a dó	**a cúig**	**a h-ocht**	
[uh doe]	[uh kooig]	[uh hawkht]	

Numbers from Eleven to Twenty

When you're numbering between eleven and twenty, the word for "ten" is used, but it changes a little, like we see with "teen" in English. This word for "ten" is "**déag**" [jayug], and it stays as a separate word from the smaller, single-digit number. In the number "twelve," the word for "two," "**dó**" [doe], will *soften* the word "**déag**" [jayug].

Vocabulary

Here are the basic numbers in Irish from eleven to twenty:

"eleven" **a h-aon déag** [uh hayn jayug]	"fourteen" **a ceathair déag** [uh kya-her jayug]	"seventeen" **a seacht déag** [uh shakht jayug]	"twenty" **fiche** [fih-huh]
"twelve" **a dó dhéag** [uh doe yayug]	"fifteen" **a cúig déag** [uh kooig jayug]	"eighteen" **a h-ocht déag** [uh hawkht jayug]	
"thirteen" **a trí déag** [uh tree jayug]	"sixteen" **a sé déag** [uh shay jayug]	"nineteen" **a naoi déag** [uh nee jayug]	

Notice that the word "**fiche**" [fih-huh], "twenty," doesn't have the word, "**a**" [uh], in front of it. After ten itself, the multiples of ten don't use the helper word in front of them.

Numbers Above Twenty

After twenty, the basic numbers start following a pattern. From twenty onward, you say the multiple of ten, and then the small, single-digit number with its helper, "**a**" [uh].

Vocabulary

Here are the basic numbers in Irish from twenty-one to thirty:

"twenty-one" **fiche a h-aon** [fih-huh uh hayn]	"twenty-four" **fiche a ceathair** [fih-huh uh kya-her]	"twenty-seven" **fiche a seacht** [fih-huh uh shakht]	"thirty" **tríocha** [tree-khuh]
"twenty-two" **fiche a dó** [fih-huh uh doe]	"twenty-five" **fiche a cúig** [fih-huh uh kooig]	"twenty-eight" **fiche a h-ocht** [fih-huh uh hawkht]	
"twenty-three" **fiche a trí** [fih-huh uh tree]	"twenty-six" **fiche a sé** [fih-huh uh shay]	"twenty-nine" **fiche a naoi** [fih-huh uh nee]	

Vocabulary

Here is a list of other numbers above thirty that are good to know in Irish:

"forty"
daichead
[dah-khayd]

"seventy"
seachtó
[shakh-toe]

"hundred"
céad
[kayud]

"fifty"
caoga
[kay-guh]

"eighty"
ochtó
[awkh-toe]

"thousand"
míle
[mee-luh]

"sixty"
seasca
[shas-kuh]

"ninety"
nócha
[no-khuh]

"million"
milliún
[mil-yoon]

Lesson 49 – Talking About Time

When talking about time in Irish, you start with a form of "**tá**" [taw], then the word "it," "**sé**" [shay], and then you say the basic number, followed by "**a chlog**" [uh khluhg], meaning "o'clock."

Vocabulary

Here are the hours of the day in Irish. Notice that you still use the helper "**a**" [uh] before the hour number.

"one o'clock" **a h-aon a chlog** [uh hayn uh khluhg]	"five o'clock" **a cúig a chlog** [uh kooig uh khluhg]	"nine o'clock" **a naoi a chlog** [uh nee uh khluhg]
"two o'clock" **a dó a chlog** [uh doe uh khluhg]	"six o'clock" **a sé a chlog** [uh shay uh khluhg]	"ten o'clock" **a deich a chlog** [uh jeh uh khluhg]
"three o'clock" **a trí a chlog** [uh tree uh khluhg]	"seven o'clock" **a seacht a chlog** [uh shakht uh khluhg]	"eleven o'clock" **a h-aon déag a chlog** [uh hayn jayug uh khluhg]
"four o'clock" **a ceathair a chlog** [uh kya-her uh khluhg]	"eight o'clock" **a h-ocht a chlog** [uh hawkht uh khluhg]	"twelve o'clock" **a dó dhéag a chlog** [uh doe yayug uh khluhg]

Examples

"It is one o'clock."
Tá sé a h-aon a chlog.
[taw shay uh hayn uh khluhg]

"It isn't seven o'clock."
Níl sé a seacht a chlog.
[neel shay uh shakht uh khluhg]

"Is it twelve o'clock?"
An bhfuil sé a dó dhéag a chlog?
[un will shay uh doe yayug uh khluhg]

"Isn't it six o'clock?"
Nach bhfuil sé a sé a chlog?
[nahkh will shay uh shay uh khluhg]

Lesson 50 – More About Telling Time

Sometimes, you want to be more precise when telling the time, such as when you want to be clear about whether you mean eight o'clock in the morning or eight o'clock at night. There are lots of phrases you can add at the end of these time-telling sentences to expand on what you're saying.

Vocabulary

Here are some useful phrases that specify a time:

"now"
anois
[uh-nish]

"in the morning"
ar maidin
[air ma-jin]

"at night"
san oíche
[sun ee-khuh]

"right now"
anois díreach
[uh-nish jee-rahkh]

"in the afternoon"
sa tráthnóna
[suh traw-no-nuh]

Examples

These time phrases are simply added on to the end of a time-telling sentence.

"It is four o'clock now."
Tá sé a ceathair a chlog anois.
[taw shay uh kya-her uh khluhg uh-nish]

"It is eleven o'clock right now."
Tá sé a h-aon déag a chlog anois díreach.
[taw shay uh hayn jayug uh khluhg uh-nish jee-rahkh]

"It is five o'clock in the morning."
Tá sé a cúig a chlog ar maidin.
[taw shay uh kooig uh khluhg air ma-jin]

"It is two o'clock in the afternoon."
Tá sé a dó a chlog sa tráthnóna.
[taw shay uh doe uh khluhg suh traw-no-nuh]

"It is ten o'clock at night."
Tá sé a deich a chlog san oíche.
[taw shay uh jeh uh khluhg sun ee-khuh]

Lesson 51 – Using Parts of Hours

When you're telling the time, it won't always be the top of the hour. This is where phrases like, "a half past," or "a quarter till," come in handy. These phrases are actually made of two parts: the fraction and whether it's before or after the hour. We'll learn these pieces separately, so you can mix and match them.

Vocabulary

"a quarter" "before"
ceathrú (f.) **roimh**
[kya-hroo] [riv]

"a half (of an hour)" "after"
leathuair (f.) **tar éis**
[lah-hooir] [tar aysh]

Examples

Let's look at all the combinations for these parts of the hour.

"a quarter till"
ceathrú roimh
[kya-hroo riv]

"a quarter past"
ceathrú tar éis
[kya-hroo tar aysh]

"a half (of an hour) till"
leathuair roimh
[lah-hooir riv]

"a half (of an hour) past"
leathuair tar éis
[lah-hooir tar aysh]

Examples

These partial time phrases are inserted between the "it," and the hour.

"It is a quarter till one o'clock."
Tá sé ceathrú roimh a h-aon a chlog.
[taw shay kya-hroo riv uh hayn uh khluhg]

"It is a quarter past three o'clock."
Tá sé ceathrú tar éis a trí a chlog.
[taw shay kya-hroo tar aysh uh tree uh khluhg]

"It is half till five o'clock."
Tá sé leathuair roimh a cúig a chlog.
[taw shay lah-hooir riv uh kooig uh khluhg]

"It is half past seven o'clock."
Tá sé leathuair tar éis a seacht a chlog.
[taw shay lah-hooir tar aysh uh shakht uh khluhg]

"It isn't a quarter till two o'clock."
Níl sé ceathrú roimh a dó a chlog.
[neel shay kya-hroo riv uh doe uh khluhg]

"It isn't half till four o'clock."
Níl sé leathuair roimh a ceathair a chlog.
[neel shay lah-hooir riv uh kya-her uh khluhg]

"Is it a quarter past ten o'clock?"
An bhfuil sé ceathrú tar éis a deich a chlog?
[un will shay kya-hroo tar aysh uh jeh uh khluhg]

"Is it half past twelve o'clock?"
An bhfuil sé leathuair tar éis a dó dhéag a chlog?
[un will shay lah-hooir tar aysh uh doe yayug uh khluhg]

"Isn't it a quarter past eight o'clock?"
Nach bhfuil sé ceathrú tar éis a h-ocht a chlog?
[nahkh will shay kya-hroo tar aysh uh hawkht uh khluhg]

"Isn't it half till nine o'clock?"
Nach bhfuil sé leathuair roimh a naoi a chlog?
[nahkh will shay lah-hooir riv uh nee uh khluhg]

Lesson 52 – "What Time Is It?" and Being Polite

When you want to know what time it is, you can ask:

"What time is it?"
Cén t-am é?
[kayn tom ay]

Polite Bonus Phrases

Before you ask someone a question, it's polite to get their attention by excusing yourself first. To do this in Irish, you can say:

"Excuse me."
Gabh mo leithscéal.
[guhv muh leh-shkayl]

It's also polite to say "please" when asking for something. Here are two *Bonus Phrases* you can use to say "please" to one person or to many people:

"Please." (to one person)   "Please." (to many people)
Le do thoil.   or   **Le bhur dtoil.**
[leh duh hull]   [leh woor dull]

These phrases translate as "with your will" or "with y'all's will." Notice that the possessive pronouns match the number of people you're talking to.

Of course, it's also polite to thank someone when they answer your questions or give you something. Here are two *Bonus Phrases* you can use to say "thank you" to one person or to many people:

"Thank you." (to one person)   "Thank you." (to many people)
Go raibh maith agat.   or   **Go raibh maith agaibh.**
[guh ruh mah ah-gut]   [guh ruh mah ah-giv]

Notice that the prepositional pronouns "**agat**" [ah-gut] and "**agaibh**" [ah-giv] match the number of people you're thanking.

Finally, you can use these *Bonus Phrases* after one or many people thank you:

"You're welcome." (to one person)   "You're welcome." (to many people)
Tá fáilte romhat.   or   **Tá fáilte romhaibh.**
[taw fawl-tchuh roet]   [taw fawl-tchuh roe-ihv]

These *Bonus Phrases* use the prepositional pronouns "**romhat**" [roet] and "**romhaibh**" [roe-ihv], which match the number of people you're welcoming.

Conversation

Let's practice what we've learned about telling time with a conversation.

Pádraigín:
"Excuse me."
Gabh mo leithscéal.
[guhv muh leh-shkayl]

"What time is it, please?"
Cén t-am é, le do thoil?
[kayn tom ay, leh duh hull]

Brian:
"It's a quarter till eight o'clock."
Tá sé ceathrú roimh a h-ocht a chlog.
[taw shay kya-hroo riv uh hawkht uh khluhg]

Pádraigín:
"Isn't it half past seven o'clock?"
Nach bhfuil sé leathuair tar éis a seacht a chlog?
[nahkh will shay lah-hooir tar aysh uh shakht uh khluhg]

Brian:
"No. It's a quarter till eight o'clock right now."
Níl. Tá sé ceathrú roimh a h-ocht a chlog anois díreach.
[neel. taw shay kya-hroo riv uh hawkht uh khluhg uh-nish jee-rahkh]

Pádraigín:
"Thank you."
Go raibh maith agat.
[guh ruh mah ah-gut]

Brian:
"You're welcome."
Tá fáilte romhat.
[taw fawl-tchuh roet]

Pádraigín:
"Good-bye!"
Slán agat!
[slawn ah-gut]

Brian:
"Bye."
Slán leat.
[slawn lyat]

Lesson 53 – Counting Things

When you're just numbering things, like the hours of the day, you use the *basic numbers* in Irish. When you're counting things, you use a different set of numbers. We'll start by learning how to count things up to ten.

When you want to count things in Irish, you say the *counting number* followed by the noun you're counting. Also, you use the *singular* form of the noun, even when you're counting more than one thing.

The counting numbers are words which will change the word that comes after them. Some of them will *soften* the next word, and others will *eclipse* the next word.

If the noun you're counting starts with a vowel, you can't soften it, so there's no change. For the counting numbers that eclipse, you add an "**n-**" in front of nouns that start with a vowel.

When you're counting only one thing, you must add the word "alone," "**amháin**" [uh-woyn], after the noun, so you're really saying, "one thing alone." You can even leave out the counting number for "one," and say simply "thing alone." Also, if the word following "one," "**aon**" [ayn], starts with "**d**", "**t**", or "**s**", you don't soften it.

Vocabulary

Here is a list of the numbers used for counting things from one to ten, along with a note as to whether they *soften* or *eclipse* the word after them:

"one"	"four"	"seven"	"ten"
aon	**ceithre**	**seacht**	**deich**
[ayn]	[keh-ruh]	[shakht]	[jeh]
softens	*softens*	*eclipses*	*eclipses*

"two"	"five"	"eight"	"alone"
dhá	**cúig**	**ocht**	**amháin**
[ghaw]	[kooig]	[awkht]	[uh-woyn]
softens	*softens*	*eclipses*	

"three"	"six"	"nine"
trí	**sé**	**naoi**
[tree]	[shay]	[nee]
softens	*softens*	*eclipses*

Examples

Let's take a sample word that can both soften and eclipse to see how the counting numbers work.

"one box alone"
aon bhosca amháin
[ayn wuhss-kuh uh-woyn]

"two boxes"
dhá bhosca
[ghaw wuhss-kuh]

"three boxes"
trí bhosca
[tree wuhss-kuh]

"four boxes"
ceithre bhosca
[keh-ruh wuhss-kuh]

"five boxes"
cúig bhosca
[kooig wuhss-kuh]

"six boxes"
sé bhosca
[shay wuhss-kuh]

"seven boxes"
seacht mbosca
[shakht muss-kuh]

"eight boxes"
ocht mbosca
[awkht muss-kuh]

"nine boxes"
naoi mbosca
[nee muss-kuh]

"ten boxes"
deich mbosca
[jeh muss-kuh]

Lesson 54 – Counting More Things

We'll practice counting by using a few more nouns. Most of these are ones you've seen before, with a few notable extras. We'll learn the word for "thing," which is very useful when you want to talk about something, but haven't learned the word for it yet.

We'll also learn the word for "minute," which will let you tell the time using the exact time. You use the same phrase for the partial hours we learned in Lesson 51, but replace the fraction with the counting number followed by "minute."

Vocabulary

Here are some nouns you can count. Some of these we've seen before, and some are new.

"a thing"	"a key"	"a chair"	"a cup"
rud (m.)	**eochair** (f.)	**cathaoir** (f.)	**cupán** (m.)
[ruhd]	[ukh-er]	[kah-heer]	[kuh-pawn]

"a minute"	"a car"	"a table"	"a glass"
nóiméad (m.)	**carr** (m.)	**bord** (m.)	**gloine** (f.)
[no-mayd]	[kahr]	[bord]	[glih-nyuh]

Examples

Let's take several kinds of sentences you've learned before and use counting numbers in them.

"She has three things."
Tá trí rud aici.
[taw tree ruhd ehk-ee]

"It's four minutes past four o'clock."
Tá sé ceithre nóiméad tar éis a ceathair a chlog.
[taw shay keh-ruh no-mayd tar aysh uh kya-her uh khluhg]

"Aren't there seven keys inside?"
Nach bhfuil seacht n-eochair istigh?
[nahkh will shakht nukh-er iss-tchih]

"They have one car."
Tá aon charr amháin acu.
[taw ayn khahr uh-woyn ah-kuh]

"There are nine chairs here."
Tá naoi gcathaoir anseo.
[taw nee gah-heer un-shuh]

"Aren't five tables outside?"
Nach bhfuil cúig bhord amuigh?
[nahkh will kooig word (rhymes with "board") uh-muh]

"We have eight cups."
Tá ocht gcupán againn.
[taw awkht guh-pawn ah-geen]

"Are there six glasses?"
An bhfuil sé ghloine ann?
[un will shay ghlih-nyuh on]

Lesson 55 – Counting Without Naming a Thing

Sometimes when you're counting, you don't want to say the name of the things as you're counting them. In English, we just say the number without the noun, but, in Irish, you use a placeholder for the noun instead.

This placeholder word is "**ceann**" [kyawn], which is masculine (m.). This literally means "head." English actually uses this in some rare cases, too, as when you're counting "head of cattle," but even then it's not absolutely necessary to include the word "head." In Irish, however, you always have to be counting something, so you use "**ceann**" [kyawn], "head," when you're not using another noun.

You use the *singular* form, "**ceann**" [kyawn], when you're counting one thing, two things, or multiples of ten starting with 20. However, when you're counting all other numbers, you use the *plural* form of "head," which is "**cinn**" [keen], "heads." Also, you don't *soften* "**cinn**" [keen]. Otherwise, the patterns we learned before for *softening* or *eclipsing* still apply.

Vocabulary

"a head"	"heads"
ceann (m.)	**cinn**
[kyawn]	[keen]

Examples

Let's take a look at counting non-specific things from one to ten:

"one (thing) alone"
aon cheann amháin
[ayn khyawn uh-woyn]

"two (things)"
dhá cheann
[ghaw khyawn]

"three (things)"
trí cinn
[tree keen]

"four (things)"
ceithre cinn
[keh-ruh keen]

"five (things)"
cúig cinn
[kooig keen]

"six (things)"
sé cinn
[shay keen]

"seven (things)"
seacht gcinn
[shakht geen]

"eight (things)"
ocht gcinn
[awkht geen]

"nine (things)"
naoi gcinn
[nee geen]

"ten (things)"
deich gcinn
[jeh geen]

Examples

Now let's look at some sentences using the word "**ceann**" [kyawn] to count unspecified things:

"There are two here."
Tá dhá cheann anseo.
[taw ghaw khyawn un-shuh]

"Aren't there four outside?"
Nach bhfuil ceithre cinn amuigh?
[nahkh will keh-ruh keen uh-muh]

"He has six."
Tá sé cinn aige.
[taw shay keen ehg-uh]

"Do y'all have seven?"
An bhfuil seacht gcinn agaibh?
[un will shakht geen ah-giv]

Conversation

Now we'll practice what we've learned about counting things with a conversation.

Brian:
"Do you have five cups?"
An bhfuil cúig chupán agat?
[un will kooig khuh-pawn ah-gut]

Pádraigín:
"No. I have five boxes."
Níl. Tá cúig bhosca agam.
[neel. taw kooig wuhss-kuh ah-gum]

"Aren't there eight cups inside?
Nach bhfuil ocht gcupán istigh?
[nahkh will awkht guh-pawn iss-tchih]

Brian:
"No. There are eight glasses."
Níl. Tá ocht ngloine ann.
[neel. taw awkht nglih-nyuh on]

"Do you have two spoons?"
An bhfuil dhá spúnóg agat?
[un will ghaw spoo-noeg ah-gut]

Pádraigín:
"Yes, I have two."
Tá. Tá dhá cheann agam.
[taw. taw ghaw khyawn ah-gum]

Brian:
"Wonderful!"
Go h-iontach!
[guh hee-un-tahkh]

Lesson 56 – Counting from Ten to Twenty

When you start counting things above ten in Irish, you say the thing you're counting in between the number words. For example, in English you say, "fifteen boxes," and in Irish you say, "five box ten." You say the small number first, then the thing you're counting, and then the bigger number (ten, twenty, thirty, etc.) at the end.

As the noun comes after the small number, the patterns we learned before for *softening* or *eclipsing* after the counting number still apply.

Examples

Let's take a sample word to see how the counting numbers between ten to twenty work.

"eleven boxes"
aon bhosca déag
[ayn wuhss-kuh jayug]

"twelve boxes"
dhá bhosca déag
[ghaw wuhss-kuh jayug]

"thirteen boxes"
trí bhosca déag
[tree wuhss-kuh jayug]

"fourteen boxes"
ceithre bhosca déag
[keh-ruh wuhss-kuh jayug]

"fifteen boxes"
cúig bhosca déag
[kooig wuhss-kuh jayug]

"sixteen boxes"
sé bhosca déag
[shay wuhss-kuh jayug]

"seventeen boxes"
seacht mbosca déag
[shakht muss-kuh jayug]

"eighteen boxes"
ocht mbosca déag
[awkht muss-kuh jayug]

"nineteen boxes"
naoi mbosca déag
[nee muss-kuh jayug]

"twenty boxes"
fiche bosca
[fih-huh bus-kuh]

Notice that the word for "twenty" didn't change the noun after it. Aside from ten itself, any multiple of ten makes no change to the noun after it.

Examples

Here are some full sentences counting things between ten and twenty.

"There are eleven tables here."
Tá aon bhord déag anseo.
[taw ayn word (rhymes with "board") jayug un-shuh]

"Do they have fourteen glasses?"
An bhfuil ceithre ghloine déag acu?
[un will keh-ruh ghlih-nyuh jayug ah-kuh]

"There are sixteen cars outside."
Tá sé charr déag amuigh.
[taw shay khahr jayug uh-muh]

"It's seventeen minutes after one o'clock."
Tá sé seacht nóiméad déag tar éis a h-aon a chlog.
[taw shay shakht no-mayd jayug tar aysh uh hayn uh khluhg]

"Brian has twenty."
Tá fiche ceann ag Brian.
[taw fih-huh kyawn ehg bree-uhn]

Lesson 57 – Counting Above Twenty

From twenty to ninety-nine, the counting numbers follow a pattern similar to counting the teens, only you include the word "and," "**agus**" [ah-gus], in the phrase. For example, for "fifteen boxes," you say, "five box ten," and for "twenty five boxes," you say, "five box *and* twenty."

Things that are said a lot tend to get shortened, so, instead of saying the full word "**agus**" [ah-gus] when counting, you usually just say the "s" sound at the end, which is written "**'s**" (apostrophe+s) [iss].

TIP! Note that you may sometimes see this short form written as "**is**" [iss], which looks like a completely different word in Irish. If you're trying to figure out a sentence in Irish that has a word spelled "**is**" [iss] in it, be mindful that it might, in truth, be a short form of "**agus**" [ah-gus].

When you count any multiple of ten, aside from ten itself, you simply say the counting number, and then the noun with no changes. Once again, when a noun comes after the single-digit number, the patterns we learned before for *softening* or *eclipsing* after the counting number still apply.

Examples

Let's take a sample word to see how the counting numbers above twenty work.

"twenty-one boxes"
aon bhosca 's fiche
[ayn wuhss-kuh iss fih-huh]

"twenty-two boxes"
dhá bhosca 's fiche
[ghaw wuhss-kuh iss fih-huh]

"twenty-three boxes"
trí bhosca 's fiche
[tree wuhss-kuh iss fih-huh]

"twenty-four boxes"
ceithre bhosca 's fiche
[keh-ruh wuhss-kuh iss fih-huh]

"twenty-five boxes"
cúig bhosca 's fiche
[kooig wuhss-kuh iss fih-huh]

"twenty-six boxes"
sé bhosca 's fiche
[shay wuhss-kuh iss fih-huh]

"twenty-seven boxes"
seacht mbosca 's fiche
[shakht muss-kuh iss fih-huh]

"twenty-eight boxes"
ocht mbosca 's fiche
[awkht muss-kuh iss fih-huh]

"twenty-nine boxes"
naoi mbosca 's fiche
[nee muss-kuh iss fih-huh]

"thirty boxes"
tríocha bosca
[tree-khuh bus-kuh]

TIP!   You now know enough Irish to tell the time of day, no matter what time it is! Practice saying the time throughout your day. You'll find that the more you practice telling time, the faster you'll become.

Examples

Here are some full sentences counting things above twenty.

"It's twenty-four minutes after six o'clock."
Tá sé ceithre nóiméad 's fiche tar éis a sé a chlog.
[taw shay keh-ruh no-mayd iss fih-huh tar aysh uh shay uh khluhg]

"Do we have thirty glasses?"
An bhfuil tríocha gloine againn?
[un will tree-khuh glih-nyuh ah-geen]

"Aren't there sixty-five chairs inside?"
Nach bhfuil cúig chathaoir 's seasca istigh?
[nahkh will kooig khah-heer iss shas-kuh iss-tchih]

"There are ninety-nine things there."
Tá naoi rud 's nócha ann.
[taw nee ruhd iss no-khuh on]

Lesson 58 – How Many Are There?

When you want to ask how many things there are, you use this *Bonus Phrase*:

"How many are there?"
Cé mhéad atá ann?
[kay vay-ud uh-taw on]

Notice how the vague "there," "**ann**" [on], is used. You could switch it out with any other location word, if you wanted to ask how many things there are in a specific place.

To answer a "how many" question, you can use any kind of "there are" statement with the counting number. You can even just use the counting number and noun by themselves to answer, if you like. Remember, though, when you're learning, it's best to use full sentences to answer. That way, you give yourself more practice and reinforce all of your skills.

Examples

Let's take a look at a "how many" question with some possible answers.

"How many are there?"
Cé mhéad atá ann?
[kay vay-ud uh-taw on]

"There are seven boxes."
Tá seacht mbosca ann.
[taw shakht muss-kuh on]

"There are seven."
Tá seacht gcinn ann.
[taw shakht geen on]

"Seven."
Seacht gcinn.
[shakht geen]

Lesson 59 – Asking and Answering "How Many" with Nouns

When you ask how many things there are, you're also likely to name the thing you're asking about. To use a noun in a "how many" question, all you have to do is say the noun in the middle of the question.

The first two words of the "how many" question, "**Cé mhéad**" [kay vay-ud], is the part that means, "how many." So, you say the noun after the first two words, and before the last two words, "**atá ann**" [uh-taw on]. Also, you use the singular form of the noun in the question, just like you do when answering.

Examples

"How many <u>boxes</u> are there?"
Cé mhéad <u>bosca</u> atá ann?
[kay vay-ud bus-kuh uh-taw on]

"How many <u>cups</u> are there?"
Cé mhéad <u>cupán</u> atá ann?
[kay vay-ud kuh-pawn uh-taw on]

Answering "How Many" with Nouns

You can answer a "how many" question that uses a noun in any of the ways we've learned before. Let's take a look at a few questions with some possible answers.

Examples

"How many chairs are there?"
Cé mhéad cathaoir atá ann?
[kay vay-ud kah-heer uh-taw on]

"There are three chairs."
Tá trí chathaoir ann.
[taw tree khah-heer on]

"There are three."
Tá trí cinn ann.
[taw tree keen on]

"Three."
Trí cinn.
[tree keen]

"How many glasses are there?"
Cé mhéad gloine atá ann?
[kay vay-ud glih-nyuh uh-taw on]

"There are fifteen glasses."
Tá cúig ghloine déag ann.
[taw kooig ghlih-nyuh jayug on]

"There are fifteen."
Tá cúig cinn déag ann.
[taw kooig keen jayug on]

"Fifteen."
Cúig cinn déag.
[kooig keen jayug]

"How many keys are there?"
Cé mhéad eochair atá ann?
[kay vay-ud ukh-er uh-taw on]

"There are thirty-seven keys."
Tá seacht n-eochair 's tríocha ann.
[taw shakht nukh-er iss tree-khuh on]

"There are thirty-seven."
Tá seacht gcinn 's tríocha ann.
[taw shakht geen iss tree-khuh on]

"Thirty-seven."
Seacht gcinn 's tríocha.
[shakht geen iss tree-khuh]

"How many cars are there?"
Cé mhéad carr atá ann?
[kay vay-ud kahr uh-taw on]

"There are two cars."
Tá dhá charr ann.
[taw ghaw khahr on]

"There are two."
Tá dhá cheann ann.
[taw ghaw khyawn on]

"Two."
Dhá cheann.
[ghaw khyawn]

Lesson 60 – How Many Do You Have?

The "how many" *Bonus Phrase* question can be used with the expression for "to have," as well. You can make a lot of useful sentences by combining the counting numbers with having things.

To ask how many things someone has, you use the same question for how many things there are, only you use a phrase with a form of "**ag**" [ehg] at the end, instead of the vague "there."

Examples

"How many boxes do <u>you have</u>?"
Cé mhéad bosca <u>atá agat</u>?
[kay vay-ud bus-kuh uh-taw ah-gut]

To answer this question, all you have to do is use a "have" statement with a counting number.

"I have two boxes."
Tá dhá bhosca agam.
[taw ghaw wuhss-kuh ah-gum]

"I have two."
Tá dhá cheann agam.
[taw ghaw khyawn ah-gum]

"Two."
Dhá cheann.
[ghaw khyawn]

You can even ask if someone has a specific number of things by using the "have" expression. Instead of using the "how many" question, you just use one of the question forms of "**tá**" [taw], a counted noun, and then a form of "**ag**" [ehg]. When answering these types of questions, don't forget to repeat the verb.

"Do you have two boxes?
An bhfuil dhá bhosca agat?
[un will ghaw wuhss-kuh ah-gut]

"Yes, I have two."
Tá, tá dhá cheann agam.
[taw, taw ghaw khyawn ah-gum]

"Doesn't Patricia have eight boxes?"
Nach bhfuil ocht mbosca ag Pádraigín?
[nahkh will awkht muss-kuh ehg paw-druh-geen]

"No. She has four."
Níl. Tá ceithre cinn aici.
[neel. taw keh-ruh keen ehk-ee]

Conversation

Let's practice asking how many things there are with a conversation.

Pádraigín:
"How many books are there?"
Cé mhéad leabhar atá ann?
[kay vay-ud lyow-er uh-taw on]

Brian:
"There are twenty-five books.
Tá cúig leabhar 's fiche ann.
[taw kooig lyow-er iss fih-huh on]

Pádraigín:
"And how many pens do you have?"
Agus cé mhéad peann atá agat?
[ah-gus kay vay-ud pyawn uh-taw ah-gut]

Brian:
"I have twenty-five pens."
Tá cúig pheann 's fiche agam.
[taw kooig fyawn iss fih-huh ah-gum]

Pádraigín:
"Do you have twenty-five bags, too?"
An bhfuil cúig mhála 's fiche agat, freisin?
[un will kooig wah-luh iss fih-huh ah-gut, fresh-in]

Brian:
"No. I have seventeen bags."
Níl. Tá seacht mála déag agam.
[neel. taw shakht maw-luh jayug ah-gum]

Pádraigín:
"How many boxes does Liam have?"
Cé mhéad bosca atá ag Liam?
[kay vay-ud bus-kuh uh-taw ehg lee-um]

Brian:
"Ten."
Deich gcinn.
[jeh geen]

Lesson 61 – Counting People

Just as you don't treat people like things, you don't count them like things, either. When you're counting people, you use a different set of numbers. These numbers for people are like the English words "duo," "trio," "quartet," etc., so you can use the people counting numbers all by themselves, without naming any nouns.

You can use nouns for people with these numbers, too, but that causes other changes, so we won't go over those concepts here. The only time you have to use a noun is when you're counting one person. The noun comes between "**aon**" [ayn], "one," and "**amháin**" [uh-woyn], "alone." Though you can use many nouns for people, we'll just use the general word, "person," "**duine**" [din-uh], which is masculine (m.).

Vocabulary

Here are the numbers used for counting people from one to ten:

"one person" **aon duine amháin** [ayn din-uh uh-woyn]	"four (people)" **ceathrar** [kya-hrer]	"seven (people)" **seachtar** [shakh-tur]	"ten (people)" **deichniúr** [jeh-noor]
"two (people)" **beirt** [baertch]	"five (people)" **cúigear** [kooih-gur]	"eight (people)" **ochtar** [awkh-tur]	
"three (people)" **triúr** [troo-ihr]	"six (people)" **seisear** [shesh-er]	"nine (people)" **naonúr** [nee-noor]	

Notice that, even though "one," "**aon**" [ayn], softens the following word, the word "**duine**" [din-uh] did not get softened. That's because this is one of those special cases we learned about in Lesson 22: a "**d**" or a "**t**" cannot be softened right after an "**n**."

Examples

Let's take a look at several kinds of sentences using the counting numbers for people.

"There is one person."
Tá aon duine amháin ann.
[taw ayn din-uh uh-woyn on]

"There are two people here."
Tá beirt anseo.
[taw baertch un-shuh]

"Three people are there."
Tá triúr ansin.
[taw troo-ihr un-shin]

"There are four people inside."
Tá ceathrar istigh.
[taw kya-hrer iss-tchih]

"Five people are outside."
Tá cúigear amuigh.
[taw kooih-gur uh-muh]

"There are six people coming."
Tá seisear ag teacht ann.
[taw shesh-er ehg tchakht on]

"Seven people are going."
Tá seachtar ag dul ann.
[taw shakh-tur ehg dull on]

"There are eight people going to the party."
Tá ochtar ag dul chuig an gcóisir.
[taw awkh-tur ehg dull khig un goe-sher]

"Nine people are cold."
Tá naonúr fuar.
[taw nee-noor foo-uhr]

"There are ten people laughing."
Tá deichniúr ag gáire.
[taw jeh-noor ehg goy-ruh]

Notice that these sentences are built the same way in Irish, but can be translated in more than one way in English. You can choose to use the phrase "there are" to start the English translation, or just start with the number.

Lesson 62 – How Many People Are There?

Asking about how many people there are is just like asking how many things there are. To ask how many people there are, you say:

"How many people are there?"
Cé mhéad duine atá ann?
[kay vay-ud din-uh uh-taw on]

Examples

Let's look at a "how many people" question with some possible answers.

"How many people are there?"
Cé mhéad duine atá ann?
[kay vay-ud din-uh uh-taw on]

"There are three."
Tá triúr ann.
[taw troo-ihr on]

"Three."
Triúr.
[troo-ihr]

"How many people are there?"
Cé mhéad duine atá ann?
[kay vay-ud din-uh uh-taw on]

"There is one person."
Tá aon duine amháin ann.
[taw ayn din-uh uh-woyn on]

"One."
Aon duine amháin.
[ayn din-uh uh-woyn]

Conversation

Let's practice using the people counting numbers with a conversation.

Brian:
"Hello, Patricia."
Dia duit, a Phádraigín.
[jee-uh ghitch, uh faw-druh-geen]

Pádraigín:
"Hello, Brian."
Dia 's Muire duit, a Bhriain.
[jee-uh smwir-uh ghitch, uh vree-in]

"Are you going to the restaurant?"
An bhfuil tú ag dul go dtí an bhialann?
[un will too ehg dull guh jee un vee-uh-luhn]

Brian:
"Yes, I'm going."
Tá. Tá mé ag dul ann.
[taw. taw may ehg dull on]

Pádraigín:
"How many people are going?"
Cé mhéad duine atá ag dul ann?
[kay vay-ud din-uh uh-taw ehg dull on]

Brian:
"There are ten going."
Tá deichniúr ag dul ann.
[taw jeh-noor ehg dull on]

"How many people are there now?"
Cé mhéad duine atá ann anois?
[kay vay-ud din-uh uh-taw on uh-nish]

Pádraigín:
"Four."
Ceathrar.
[kya-hrer]

Lesson 63 – Someone and Something

To say "someone" or "something" in Irish, all you have to do is add the word "some," "**éigin**" [ay-gihn], after the word for "person" or "thing." This word can also be added to any noun to indicate some indefinite one of those things.

Vocabulary

"some"
éigin
[ay-gihn]

"a person"
duine (m.)
[din-uh]

"a thing"
rud (m.)
[ruhd]

"a box"
bosca (m.)
[bus-kuh]

"someone"
duine éigin
[din-uh ay-gihn]

"something"
rud éigin
[ruhd ay-gihn]

"some box"
bosca éigin
[bus-kuh ay-gihn]

Examples

Let's take a look at a few sentences that use the word "some."

"There's someone there."
Tá duine éigin ann.
[taw din-uh ay-gihn on]

"Something is coming."
Tá rud éigin ag teacht.
[taw ruhd ay-gihn ehg tchakht]

"There is some box outside."
Tá bosca éigin amuigh.
[taw bus-kuh ay-gihn uh-muh]

Lesson 64 – Anyone and Anything

To say "anyone" or "anything" in Irish, all you have to do is add the word "any" before the word for "person" or "thing." This word can also be added to any noun, singular or plural, to indicate any indefinite one, or ones, of those things.

The word for "any" in Irish is "**aon**" [ayn], which is also the word for "one." As we saw before when counting things, "**aon**" [ayn] will soften the word that comes after it, if it can be softened.

Vocabulary

Below are some examples of using "**aon**" [ayn] before a noun to mean "any." Remember what we learned in Lesson 22 about special cases when softening: when a word that causes softening ends in the letter "**n**," and the word after it begins with the letter "**d**" or "**t**," the "**d**" or the "**t**" *does not get softened.*

"a person"	"a thing"	"a box"
duine (m.)	**rud** (m.)	**bosca** (m.)
[din-uh]	[ruhd]	[bus-kuh]
"anyone"	"anything"	"any box"
aon duine	**aon rud**	**aon bhosca**
[ayn din-uh]	[ayn ruhd]	[ayn wuhss-kuh]
"people"	"things"	"boxes"
daoine	**rudaí**	**boscaí**
[dee-nuh]	[ruh-dee]	[bus-kee]
"any people"	"any things"	"any boxes"
aon daoine	**aon rudaí**	**aon bhoscaí**
[ayn dee-nuh]	[ayn ruh-dee]	[ayn wuhss-kee]

Examples

Let's take a look at some sentences that use "any."

"There isn't anyone there."
Níl aon duine ann.
[neel ayn din-uh on]

"Do you have anything?"
An bhfuil aon rud agat?
[un will ayn ruhd ah-gut]

"Aren't there any boxes outside?"
Nach bhfuil aon bhoscaí amuigh?
[nahkh will ayn wuhss-kee uh-muh]

Lesson 65 – No One and Nothing

In Irish, to express that there is none of a thing, you say that there isn't any of it. That means that you use a negative form of the verb when you want to say "no one" or "nothing."

When you use "**aon**" [ayn] in its sense of "any" in a negative statement in Irish, you could translate it into English as either "is not any" or "is no." For example:

"There <u>isn't anyone</u> there."
Níl aon duine ann.
[neel ayn din-uh on]

or

"There <u>is no one</u> there."
Níl aon duine ann.
[neel ayn din-uh on]

Notice that the Irish sentences are the same, even though they can be translated in more than one way in English.

Examples

Let's take a look at some negative sentences that use "**aon**" [ayn] to mean "not any."

"There isn't anyone inside." (or "There is no one inside.")
Níl aon duine istigh.
[neel ayn din-uh iss-tchih]

"They don't have anything." (or "They have nothing.")
Níl aon rud acu.
[neel ayn ruhd ah-kuh]

"There aren't any boxes here." (or "There are no boxes here.")
Níl aon bhoscaí anseo.
[neel ayn wuhss-kee un-shuh]

Lesson 66 – "At All"

Another way you can express "any" in Irish, is by saying the phrase "**ar bith**" [air bih], which means "at all," after the noun. This also means "not any at all" or "none at all" when used in negative statements. Also, you usually use "**ar bith**" [air bih] with the singular form of the noun, meaning that there isn't one quantity of the noun at all.

Examples

Let's take a look at some sentences that use the phrase "**ar bith**" [air bih].

"Is anyone here?"
An bhfuil duine ar bith anseo?
[un will din-uh air bih un-shuh]

"There isn't anyone here." (or "No one is here.")
Níl duine ar bith anseo.
[neel din-uh air bih un-shuh]

"Is there anything inside?"
An bhfuil rud ar bith istigh?
[un will ruhd air bih iss-tchih]

"There isn't anything inside." (or "There is nothing inside.")
Níl rud ar bith istigh.
[neel ruhd air bih iss-tchih]

"Aren't there any boxes outside?"
Nach bhfuil bosca ar bith amuigh?
[nahkh will bus-kuh air bih uh-muh]

"I don't have any boxes." (or "I have no boxes.")
Níl bosca ar bith agam.
[neel bus-kuh air bih ah-gum]

Notice again that some of these sentences can be translated in more than one way in English. You can choose to translate them by saying that there "is no" or there "isn't any." In Irish, they all use the phrase "**ar bith**" [air bih] to express "at all".

Being More Emphatic

If you like, you can mix things up by adding the word "**aon**" [ayn], "any," in front of the noun, as well as using "**ar bith**" [air bih]. This emphasizes the concept that you're talking about "*any* noun *at all*." Just remember to soften the noun after "**aon**" [ayn], if it can be softened.

Examples

"Is anyone here at all?"
An bhfuil aon duine ar bith anseo?
[un will ayn din-uh air bih un-shuh]

"There isn't anyone at all here."
Níl aon duine ar bith anseo.
[neel ayn din-uh air bih un-shuh]

"Aren't there any boxes at all outside?"
Nach bhfuil aon bhosca ar bith amuigh?
[nahkh will ayn wuhss-kuh air bih uh-muh]

"I don't have anything at all."
Níl aon rud ar bith agam.
[neel ayn ruhd air bih ah-gum]

Lesson 67 – Only

When you want to say that there is "only" one of something, you use a turn of phrase, rather than a single word. In Irish, "only one" is expressed by saying, "not but one." Also, as you're really saying "not but one thing," you use a counting number with the noun. This way, you can express "only" for any number of things: only one person, only two things, only fifty boxes, etc.

To say "only," you use a negative statement or a negative question, and put the word "but," "**ach**" [akh], before the noun with its counting number. Keep in mind that you use different counting numbers for things than you use for people.

Vocabulary

Below are some samples of using "**ach**" [akh], "but," before a noun to mean "only." As the verb contains the negative part of the sentence, the word "**níl**" [neel], "is not," has been included in these samples.

"only one person"
níl ach duine amháin
[neel akh din-uh uh-woyn]

"only one box"
níl ach aon bhosca amháin
[neel akh ayn wuhss-kuh uh-woyn]

"only two people"
níl ach beirt
[neel akh baertch]

"only two boxes"
níl ach dhá bhosca
[neel akh ghaw wuhss-kuh]

"only one thing"
níl ach aon rud amháin
[neel akh ayn ruhd uh-woyn]

"only two things"
níl ach dhá rud
[neel akh ghaw ruhd]

Examples

Let's take a look at a few sentences that use "only." As this turn of phrase only works with negative sentences, we'll only use examples with negative statements and negative questions.

"There are only three people inside."
Níl ach triúr istigh.
[neel akh troo-ihr iss-tchih]

"Aren't there only two boxes?"
Nach bhfuil ach dhá bhosca ann?
[nahkh will akh ghaw wuhss-kuh on]

"She only has twenty-seven things."
Níl ach seacht rud 's fiche aici.
[neel akh shakht ruhd iss fih-huh ehk-ee]

Conversation

Let's practice using the phrases for "some," "any," none," and "only," in a conversation.

Pádraigín:
"Do you have any forks?"
An bhfuil aon ghabhlóg agat?
[un will ayn ghow-loeg ah-gut]

Brian:
"No. I have no forks."
Níl. Níl gabhlóg ar bith agam.
[neel. neel gow-loeg air bih ah-gum]

"Is there something inside?"
An bhfuil rud éigin istigh?
[un will ruhd ay-gihn iss-tchih]

Pádraigín:
"There are only two knives there."
Níl ach dhá scian ann.
[neel akh ghaw shkee-un on]

Brian:
"Are there any forks at all here?"
An bhfuil aon ghabhlóg ar bith anseo?
[un will ayn ghow-loeg air bih un-shuh]

Pádraigín:
"No. We don't have any forks."
Níl. Níl gabhlóg ar bith againn.
[neel. neel gow-loeg air bih ah-geen]

Lesson 68 – Very

When you describe a noun, you may want to say that it's "very" something, as in "It's very big." To do so, you add "very," "an-" [on], directly to the front of the adjective. "An-" [on] will soften the word it gets attached to, if it can be softened, unless the word start with "d," "s," or "t."

Vocabulary

Here are some examples using "an-" [on], "very," added to the front of an adjective.

"very big"	"very cold"	"very old"
an-mhór	**an-fhuar**	**an-sean**
[on wor]	[on oo-uhr]	[on shan]

"very small"	"very hot"	"very young"
an-bheag	**an-te**	**an-óg**
[on vayug]	[on tcheh]	[on oeg]

Examples

Let's take a look at some sentences that use "very."

"It is very big."
Tá sé an-mhór.
[taw shay on wor]

"They are not very small."
Níl siad an-bheag.
[neel shee-ud on vayug]

"Is it very cold?"
An bhfuil sé an-fhuar?
[un will shay on oo-uhr]

"Isn't the day very hot?"
Nach bhfuil an lá an-te?
[nahkh will un law on tcheh]

"The car is very old."
Tá an carr an-sean.
[taw un kahr on shan]

"Isn't she very young?"
Nach bhfuil sí an-óg?
[nahkh will shee on oeg]

Adding Emphasis

If you want to be more emphatic when saying that a thing is "very" something, you can add the phrase "**ar fad**" [air fahd] after the adjective. This loosely translates into English as "on length," but, in Irish, it has the feeling of saying "really," as in "It's *really* cold."

Examples

"It's really big!"
Tá sé an-mhór ar fad!
[taw shay on wor air fahd]

"Isn't he really young?"
Nach bhfuil sé an-óg ar fad?
[nahkh will shay on oeg air fahd]

"Is the drink really hot?"
An bhfuil an deoch an-te ar fad?
[un will un jawkh on tcheh air fahd]

"The bicycle isn't really old."
Níl an rothar an-sean ar fad.
[neel un ruh-her on shan air fahd]

"It's really cloudy today."
Tá sé an-scamallach ar fad inniu.
[taw shay on skom-uh-lahkh air fahd in-yoo]

"Patricia is really smart."
Tá Pádraigín an-chliste ar fad.
[taw paw-druh-geen on khlish-tuh air fahd]

Lesson 69 – Too

You can describe a noun as being "too" something. Similar to what we saw with "very," to say "too" in Irish, you add "ró-" [roe] directly to the front of the adjective. "Ró-" [roe] will soften the word it attaches to, if it can be softened.

Vocabulary

Here are some examples using "ró-" [roe], "too," added to the front of an adjective.

"too big"	"too cold"	"too old"
ró-mhór	**ró-fhuar**	**ró-shean**
[roe wor]	[roe oo-uhr]	[roe hyan]

"too small"	"too hot"	"too young"
ró-bheag	**ró-the**	**ró-óg**
[roe vayug]	[roe heh]	[roe oeg]

Examples

Let's take a look at some sentences that use "too."

"It's too big."
Tá sé ró-mhór.
[taw shay roe wor]

"Isn't the window too small?"
Nach bhfuil an fhuinneog ró-bheag?
[nahkh will un in-yoeg roe vayug]

"It isn't too cold today."
Níl sé ró-fhuar inniu.
[neel shay roe oo-uhr in-yoo]

"The weather is too hot."
Tá an aimsir ró-the.
[taw un am-sheer roe heh]

"You're not too old."
Níl tú ró-shean.
[neel too roe hyan]

"Aren't they too young?"
Nach bhfuil siad ró-óg?
[nahkh will shee-ud roe oeg]

Adding Emphasis

As with "very," if you want to be more emphatic when saying that a thing is "too" something, you can use "**ró-**" [roe] and add the phrase "**ar fad**" [air fahd] after the adjective.

"It's way too big!"
Tá sé ró-mhór ar fad!
[taw shay roe wor air fahd]

"The ring isn't way too small."
Níl an fáinne ró-bheag ar fad.
[neel un faw-nyuh roe vayug air fahd]

"Isn't it way too cold tonight?"
Nach bhfuil sé ró-fhuar ar fad anocht?
[nahkh will shay roe oo-uhr air fahd uh-nahkht]

"Is the drink way too hot?"
An bhfuil an deoch ró-the ar fad?
[un will un jawkh roe heh air fahd]

Conversation

Let's practice using "very" and "too" in a conversation.

Brian:
"The weather is very sunny today."
Tá an aimsir an-ghrianmhar inniu.
[taw un am-sheer on ghree-un-wer in-yoo]

Pádraigín:
"Yes. It's not too cloudy now."
Tá. Níl sé ró-scamallach anois.
[taw. neel shay roe skom-uh-lahkh uh-nish]

Brian:
"Aren't you hot?"
Nach bhfuil tú te?
[nahkh will too tcheh]

Pádraigín:
"No. I'm not too hot."
Níl. Níl mé ró-the.
[neel. neel may roe heh]

"Are *you* hot?"
An bhfuil tusa te?
[un will tuh-suh tcheh]

Brian:
"I'm way too hot!"
Tá mé ró-the ar fad!
[taw may roe heh air fahd]

"And my drink isn't very cold."
Agus níl mo dheoch an-fhuar.
[ah-gus neel muh yawkh on oo-uhr]

Pádraigín:
"I'm going to the restaurant."
Tá mé ag dul go dtí an bhialann.
[taw may ehg dull guh jee un vee-uh-luhn]

"Their drinks are really cold."
Tá a ndeochanna an-fhuar ar fad.
[taw uh nyawkh-uh-nuh on oo-uhr air fahd]

Brian:
"You're too clever!"
Tá tú ró-chliste!
[taw too roe khlish-tuh]

Pádraigín:
"Thank you."
Go raibh maith agat.
[guh ruh mah ah-gut]

"*You're* very clever, too!"
Tá tusa an-chliste, freisin!
[taw tuh-suh on khlish-tuh, fresh-in]

Lesson 70 – Talking About the Past

You've learned a lot of Irish! So far, we've been talking about what things are like now or what's happening now. You'll also want to talk about how something was or what someone was doing. Luckily, putting "**tá**" [taw] sentences into the past tense is easy.

The Past Tense of "Tá"

As we learned back in Lesson 2, a basic Irish sentence starts with a verb. Therefore, to turn a *present tense* sentence into a *past tense* sentence, all you have to do is change the first word. The past tense of "**tá**" [taw], "is," is "**bhí**" [vee], "was."

Examples

Let's take a look at a simple sentence in the *present tense*, and one in the *past tense* to compare:

"I <u>am</u> cold."
Tá mé fuar.
[taw may foo-uhr]

"I <u>was</u> cold."
Bhí mé fuar.
[vee may foo-uhr]

Here are sample sentences using all of the pronouns in the past tense:

"I was cold."
Bhí mé fuar.
[vee may foo-uhr]

"You were cold."
Bhí tú fuar.
[vee too foo-uhr]

"He was cold."
Bhí sé fuar.
[vee shay foo-uhr]

"She was cold."
Bhí sí fuar.
[vee shee foo-uhr]

"We were cold."
Bhí muid fuar.
[vee mwidj foo-uhr]

"Y'all were cold."
Bhí sibh fuar.
[vee shiv foo-uhr]

"They were cold."
Bhí siad fuar.
[vee shee-ud foo-uhr]

Vocabulary

To make your sentences more interesting, you can add words to the end of your sentence that describe when something happened.

"yesterday"
inné
[in-yay]

"last night"
aréir
[uh-rayr]

Examples

"The weather was hot yesterday."
Bhí an aimsir te inné.
[vee un am-sheer tcheh in-yay]

"Brian was sick last night."
Bhí Brian tinn aréir.
[vee bree-uhn tcheen uh-rayr]

"Patricia was reading yesterday."
Bhí Pádraigín ag léamh inné.
[vee paw-druh-geen ehg lay-uv in-yay]

"The floor was dirty last night."
Bhí an t-urlár salach aréir.
[vee un toor-lawr sahl-ahkh uh-rayr]

Lesson 71 – The Negative of "Bhí"

You've already learned that verbs in Irish don't change based on the person you're talking about, but they do change to make a sentence positive or negative. The *negative form* of "**bhí**" [vee], "was," is "**ní raibh**" [nee rev], "was not." So, to turn a positive statement into a negative statement in the past tense, you simply switch the word "**bhí**" [vee] with "**ní raibh**" [nee rev].

Examples

"The night wasn't cold last night."
Ní raibh an oíche fuar aréir.
[nee rev un ee-khuh foo-uhr uh-rayr]

"He didn't have a key."
Ní raibh eochair aige.
[nee rev ukh-er ehg-uh]

"Patricia wasn't running."
Ní raibh Pádraigín ag rith.
[nee rev paw-druh-geen ehg rih]

"There weren't three people there yesterday."
Ní raibh triúr ann inné.
[nee rev troo-ihr on in-yay]

"Brian wasn't sick."
Ní raibh Brian tinn.
[nee rev bree-uhn tcheen]

"They weren't outside."
Ní raibh siad amuigh.
[nee rev shee-ud uh-muh]

"It wasn't five o'clock."
Ní raibh sé a cúig a chlog.
[nee rev shay uh kooig uh khluhg]

Lesson 72 – The Question Forms of "Bhí"

Positive Questions

In the past tense, to turn a positive statement into a positive question, you simply switch the word "**bhí**" [vee], "was," with its question form, which is "**an raibh**" [un rev], "was?".

Examples

"Was it clean?"
An raibh sé glan?
[un rev shay glon]

"Did he have the ring?"
An raibh an fáinne aige?
[un rev un faw-nyuh ehg-uh]

"Were they working?"
An raibh siad ag obair?
[un rev shee-ud ehg uh-ber]

Negative Questions

To turn a positive statement in the past tense into a negative question, all you have to do is switch the word "**bhí**" [vee], "was," with its negative question form, which is "**nach raibh**" [nahkh rev], "wasn't?".

Examples

"Wasn't he laughing?"
Nach raibh sé ag gáire?
[nahkh rev shay ehg goy-ruh]

"Didn't you have a spoon?"
Nach raibh spúnóg agat?
[nahkh rev spoo-noeg ah-gut]

"Wasn't she well?"
Nach raibh sí go maith?
[nahkh rev shee guh mah]

Lesson 73 – Answering Past Questions

As we learned before, Irish has no simple words for "yes" and "no." Instead, you reply by repeating the positive form or the negative form of the verb. When you're asked questions in the past tense, you use the past tense forms of the verb when answering.

If you're asked a question using "**an raibh**" [un rev] or "**nach raibh**" [nahkh rev], this is how you answer:

"Yes."   "No."
Bhí.   **Ní raibh.**
[vee]   [nee rev]

As we saw before with the present tense, the "yes" and "no" answers literally mean "was" and "was not," or, loosely, "it was so" and "it was not so."

Examples

Let's take a look at some past tense questions with answers. Remember that you can answer simply, but it helps to answer with full sentences while you're learning, so you can get more practice.

"Was it hot yesterday?"
An raibh sé te inné?
[un rev shay tcheh in-yay]

"Yes, it was very hot yesterday!"
Bhí, bhí sé an-te inné!
[vee, vee shay on tcheh in-yay]

"Weren't there five people inside?"
Nach raibh cúigear istigh?
[nahkh rev kooih-gur iss-tchih]

"No, there weren't five people inside."
Ní raibh, ní raibh cúigear istigh.
[nee rev, nee rev kooih-gur iss-tchih]

"Were you running?"
An raibh tú ag rith?
[un rev too ehg rih]

"No. I was walking."
Ní raibh. Bhí mé ag siúl.
[nee rev. vee may ehg shool]

"Wasn't the chair small?"
Nach raibh an chathaoir beag?
[nahkh rev un khah-heer bayug]

"No. It was too big!"
Ní raibh. Bhí sí ró-mhór!"
[nee rev. vee shee roe wor]

"Did they have your box?"
An raibh do bhosca acu?
[un rev duh wuhss-kuh ah-kuh]

"Yes, they did have my box."
Bhí, bhí mo bhosca acu.
[vee, vee muh wuhss-kuh ah-kuh]

Conversation

Now we'll practice using the past tense with a conversation.

Pádraigín:
"The weather was cold yesterday."
Bhí an aimsir fuar inné.
[vee un am-sheer foo-uhr in-yay]

Brian:
"Yes. It was very wet last night."
Bhí. Bhí sé an-fhliuch aréir.
[vee. vee shay on lyukh uh-rayr]

"Were you working yesterday?"
An raibh tú ag obair inné?
[un rev too ehg uh-ber in-yay]

Pádraigín:
"No, I wasn't working."
Ní raibh. Ní raibh mé ag obair.
[nee rev. nee rev may ehg uh-ber]

"I was too sick."
Bhí mé ró-thinn.
[vee may roe heen]

Brian:

"Are you okay now?"

An bhfuil tú ceart go leor anois?

[un will too kyart guh leeyor uh-nish]

Pádraigín:

"Yes, I'm well now."

Tá. Tá mé go maith anois.

[taw. taw may guh mah uh-nish]

Lesson 74 – How Were You?

You can ask how someone was by changing any of the "How are you?" *Bonus Phrase* questions we learned in Lesson 1. Putting these common questions into the past tense is like putting a simple sentence into the past – you just change the verb. As these questions are *Bonus Phrases*, we won't go into the grammar of each one. For now, all you need to do is learn them "as-is."

Here are three common ways to ask "How are you?" in the present tense and the past tense to compare:

"How <u>are</u> you?"
Cén chaoi <u>a bhfuil</u> tú?
[keh hee will too]

"How <u>were</u> you?"
Cén chaoi <u>a raibh</u> tú?
[keh hee rev too]

"How <u>are</u> you?"
Conas <u>atá</u> tú?
[kun-us uh-taw too]

"How <u>were</u> you?"
Conas <u>a bhí</u> tú?
[kun-us uh vee too]

"How <u>are</u> you?"
Cad é mar <u>atá</u> tú?
[kuh-jay mar uh-taw too]

"How <u>were</u> you?"
Cad é mar <u>a bhí</u> tú?
[kuh-jay mar uh vee too]

Remember, you can replace the pronoun "**tú**" [too] with a different pronoun, name, or noun to ask about other people or things.

Examples

Let's take a look at some "How were you?" questions in the past tense with some answers.

"How was Patricia?"
Cén chaoi a raibh Pádraigín?
[keh hee rev paw-druh-geen]

"Patricia was well."
Bhí Pádraigín go maith.
[vee paw-druh-geen guh mah]

"How were they?"
Conas a bhí siad?
[kun-us uh vee shee-ud]

"They were sick."
Bhí siad tinn.
[vee shee-ud tcheen]

"How was he?"
Cad é mar a bhí sé?
[kuh-jay mar uh vee shay]

"He was fine."
Bhí sé go breá.
[vee shay guh braw]

"How was the weather?"
Cén chaoi a raibh an aimsir?
[keh hee rev un am-sheer]

"It was beautiful."
Bhí sí go h-álainn.
[vee shee guh haw-ling]

Conversation

Now we'll practice asking how things were in the past tense with a conversation.

Brian:
"How was the weather yesterday?"
Cén chaoi a raibh an aimsir inné?
[keh hee rev un am-sheer in-yay]

Pádraigín:
"It was cold, but it was dry."
Bhí sí fuar, ach bhí sí tirim.
[vee shee foo-uhr, akh vee shee tchih-ruhm]

Brian:
"And how were *you*?"
Agus cad é mar a bhí tusa?
[ah-gus kuh-jay mar uh vee tuh-suh]

Pádraigín:
"I was okay."
Bhí mé ceart go leor.
[vee may kyart guh leeyor]

"How were *you?*"
Conas a bhí tú féin?
[kun-us uh vee too fayn]

Brian:
"I was fine, thanks."
Bhí mé go breá, go raibh maith agat.
[vee may guh braw, guh ruh mah ah-gut]

Pádraigín:
"How was Noreen yesterday?"
Cén chaoi a raibh Noirín inné?
[keh hee rev nor-een in-yay]

Brian:
"She was sick."
Bhí sí tinn.
[vee shee tcheen]

Pádraigín:
"Was Liam sick, too?"
An raibh Liam tinn, freisin?
[un rev lee-um tcheen, fresh-in]

Brian:
"No. He was well."
Ní raibh. Bhí sé go maith.
[nee rev. vee shay guh mah]

Lesson 75 – How Many Did You Have?

You can use the "have" expression to ask how many things someone had in the past. To put the *Bonus Phrase* question, "How many do you have?" into the past tense, you switch the verb for its past tense form.

"How many boxes <u>do</u> you have?"
Cé mhéad bosca <u>atá</u> agat?
[kay vay-ud bus-kuh uh-taw ah-gut]

"How many boxes <u>did</u> you have?"
Cé mhéad bosca <u>a bhí</u> agat?
[kay vay-ud bus-kuh uh vee ah-gut]

To answer this question, you use a "have" statement in the past tense with a counting number.

"I had three boxes."
Bhí trí bhosca agam.
[vee tree wuhss-kuh ah-gum]

"I had three."
Bhí trí cinn agam.
[vee tree keen ah-gum]

You can also ask if someone has a specific number of things by using the "have" expression with one of the question forms of "**bhí**" [vee], a counted noun, and then a form of "**ag**" [ehg]. When answering these types of questions, don't forget to repeat the verb.

Examples

"Did you have eight keys?
An raibh ocht n-eochair agat?
[un rev awkht nukh-er ah-gut]

"Yes, I had eight."
Bhí. Bhí ocht gcinn agam.
[vee. vee awkht geen ah-gum]

"Didn't Patricia have four glasses?"
Nach raibh ceithre ghloine ag Pádraigín?
[nahkh rev keh-ruh ghlih-nyuh ehg paw-druh-geen]

"No. She only had two."
Ní raibh. Ní raibh ach dhá cheann aici.
[nee rev. nee rev akh ghaw khyawn ehk-ee]

Conversation

Let's practice talking about having things in the past with a conversation.

Pádraigín:
"Did you have your bag last night?"
An raibh do mhála agat aréir?
[un rev duh wah-luh ah-gut uh-rayr]

Brian:
"Yes, I had it."
Bhí. Bhí sé agam.
[vee. vee shay ah-gum]

Pádraigín:
"And did you have your book?"
Agus an raibh do leabhar agat?
[ah-gus un rev duh lyow-er ah-gut]

Brian:
"I had my book, but I didn't have a pen."
Bhí mo leabhar agam, ach ní raibh peann agam.
[vee muh lyow-er ah-gum, akh nee rev pyawn ah-gum]

Pádraigín:
"Didn't Liam have two pens?"
Nach raibh dhá pheann ag Liam?
[nahkh rev ghaw fyawn ehg lee-um]

Brian:
"No. He only had one."
Ní raibh. Ní raibh ach aon cheann amháin aige.
[nee rev. nee rev akh ayn khyawn uh-woyn ehg-uh]

Pádraigín:
"How many pens did Noreen have?"
Cé mhéad peann a bhí ag Noirín?
[kay vay-ud pyawn uh vee ehg nor-een]

Brian:
"She didn't have any pens."
Ní raibh peann ar bith aici.
[nee rev pyawn air bih ehk-ee]

Lesson 76 – What Were You Doing?

In the course of conversations, you'll often want to know what someone was doing. To put the *Bonus Phrase* question, "What are you doing?" into the past tense, you switch out the verb for its past tense form.

"What <u>are</u> you doing?"
Céard <u>atá</u> tú ag déanamh?
[kayrd uh-taw too ehg jay-nuv]

"What <u>were</u> you doing?"
Céard <u>a bhí</u> tú ag déanamh?
[kayrd uh vee too ehg jay-nuv]

Examples

Let's take a look at some "doing" questions in the past tense with answers.

"What were you doing?"
Céard a bhí tú ag déanamh?
[kayrd uh vee too ehg jay-nuv]

"I was talking."
Bhí mé ag caint.
[vee may ehg kyintch]

"What were y'all doing?"
Céard a bhí sibh ag déanamh?
[kayrd uh vee shiv ehg jay-nuv]

"We were eating."
Bhí muid ag ithe.
[vee mwidj ehg ih-huh]

"What was Brian doing?"
Céard a bhí Brian ag déanamh?
[kayrd uh vee bree-uhn ehg jay-nuv]

"Brian was laughing."
Bhí Brian ag gáire.
[vee bree-uhn ehg goy-ruh]

You can also ask if someone was doing something specific by using the progressive tense with one of the question forms of "**bhí**" [vee]. When answering these types of questions with full sentences, don't forget to repeat the verb.

Examples

"Was he walking?"
An raibh sé ag siúl?
[un rev shay ehg shool]

"Yes, he was walking."
Bhí. Bhí sé ag siúl.
[vee. vee shay ehg shool]

"Weren't they listening?"
Nach raibh siad ag éisteacht?
[nahkh rev shee-ud ehg aysh-tahkht]

"No, they weren't listening."
Ní raibh. Ní raibh siad ag éisteacht.
[nee rev. nee rev shee-ud ehg aysh-tahkht]

"Were you working?"
An raibh tú ag obair?
[un rev too ehg uh-ber]

"No. I was reading."
Ní raibh. Bhí mé ag léamh.
[nee rev. vee may ehg lay-uv]

"Wasn't Patricia running?"
Nach raibh Pádraigín ag rith?
[nahkh rev paw-druh-geen ehg rih]

"Yes, she was running."
Bhí. Bhí sí ag rith.
[vee. vee shee ehg rih]

Conversation

Let's practice talking about doing things in the past with a conversation.

Pádraigín:
"Were you working yesterday?"
An raibh tú ag obair inné?
[un rev too ehg uh-ber in-yay]

Brian:
"Yes, I was working."
Bhí. Bhí mé ag obair.
[vee. vee may ehg uh-ber]

Pádraigín:
"What were you doing last night?"
Céard a bhí tú ag déanamh aréir?
[kayrd uh vee too ehg jay-nuv uh-rayr]

Brian:
"Liam and I were eating and talking."
Bhí Liam agus mé féin ag ithe agus ag caint.
[vee lee-um ah-gus may fayn ehg ih-huh ah-gus ehg kyintch]

"What were *you* doing yesterday?"
Céard a bhí tusa ag déanamh inné?
[kayrd uh vee tuh-suh ehg jay-nuv in-yay]

Pádraigín:
"I was running in the afternoon."
Bhí mé ag rith sa tráthnóna.
[vee may ehg rih suh traw-no-nuh]

Brian:
"And what were you doing last night?"
Agus céard a bhí tú ag déanamh aréir?
[ah-gus kayrd uh vee too ehg jay-nuv uh-rayr]

Pádraigín:
"I was reading and learning."
Bhí mé ag léamh agus ag foghlaim.
[vee may ehg lay-uv ah-gus ehg foe-lum]

Lesson 77 – Where Was It?

Another handy *Bonus Phrase* question we learned was "Where is it?" Once again, to put this into the past tense, you switch out the present tense form of the verb with its past tense form.

"Where <u>is</u> it?"
Cá <u>bhfuil</u> sé?
[kaw will shay]

"Where <u>was</u> it?"
Cá <u>raibh</u> sé?
[kaw rev shay]

Examples

Let's take a look at a few "where" questions in the past tense with answers.

"Where was it?"
Cá raibh sé?
[kaw rev shay]

"It was here."
Bhí sé anseo.
[vee shay un-shuh]

"Where was Brian?"
Cá raibh Brian?
[kaw rev bree-uhn]

"Brian was inside."
Bhí Brian istigh.
[vee bree-uhn iss-tchih]

"Where was the box?"
Cá raibh an bosca?
[kaw rev un bus-kuh]

"It was outside."
Bhí sé amuigh.
[vee shay uh-muh]

Lesson 78 – Where Were You Going?

You can talk about where someone was going in the past by using the *Bonus Phrase* "Where are you going?" and switching its verb for its past tense form.

"Where <u>are</u> you going?"
Cá <u>bhfuil</u> tú ag dul?
[kaw will too ehg dull]

"Where <u>were</u> you going?"
Cá <u>raibh</u> tú ag dul?
[kaw rev too ehg dull]

Remember, when answering this question, the word you use for "to" depends upon the kind of place you're going.

Examples

"Where were you going?"
Cá raibh tú ag dul?
[kaw rev too ehg dull]

"I was going to a restaurant."
Bhí mé ag dul go bialann.
[vee may ehg dull guh bee-uh-luhn]

"Where was Brian going?"
Cá raibh Brian ag dul?
[kaw rev bree-uhn ehg dull]

"He was going to the store."
Bhí sé ag dul go dtí an siopa.
[vee shay ehg dull guh jee un shuhp-uh]

"Where were they going?"
Cá raibh siad ag dul?
[kaw rev shee-ud ehg dull]

"They were going to a party."
Bhí siad ag dul chuig cóisir.
[vee shee-ud ehg dull khig koe-sher]

Conversation

Let's practice talking about going different places in the past with a conversation.

Brian:
"Where were you going yesterday?"
Cá raibh tú ag dul inné?
[kaw rev too ehg dull in-yay]

Pádraigín:
"I was going to a movie."
Bhí mé ag dul chuig scannán.
[vee may ehg dull khig skuh-nawn]

Brian:
"Was Noreen going, too?"
An raibh Noirín ag dul ann, freisin?
[un rev nor-een ehg dull on, fresh-in]

Pádraigín:
"No. Noreen and Liam were going to the park."
Ní raibh. Bhí Noirín agus Liam ag dul go dtí an pháirc.
[nee rev. vee nor-een ah-gus lee-um ehg dull guh jee un fawrk]

"Weren't *you* also going to the park?"
Nach raibh tú féin ag dul go dtí an pháirc, freisin?
[nahkh rev too fayn ehg dull guh jee un fawrk, fresh-in]

Brian:
"No. I wasn't going there."
Ní raibh. Ní raibh mé ag dul ann.
[nee rev. nee rev may ehg dull on]

Pádraigín:
"Where were you going?"
Cá raibh tú ag dul?
[kaw rev too ehg dull]

Brian:
"I was going to a restaurant."
Bhí mé ag dul go bialann.
[vee may ehg dull guh bee-uh-luhn]

Lesson 79 – What Time Was It?

When you want to ask what time it was in Irish, there's a slight change to the *Bonus Phrase* question we learned in Lesson 52. In the sentence, "What time is it?" "**Cén t-am é?**" [kayn tom ay], the verb is only implied, so it's harder to put this into different tenses. Luckily, there's an alternate way of asking the time that uses a direct verb, which is easier to switch out for other forms.

To ask "What time is it?" in Irish, you can say:

"What time is it?"   "What time is it?
Cén t-am é?   or   **Cén t-am atá sé?**
[kayn tom ay]   [kayn tom uh-taw shay]

To put the second version into the past tense, you can switch out the verb "**atá**" [uh-taw] for its past tense form, "**a bhí**" [uh vee].

"What time <u>is</u> it?
Cén t-am <u>atá</u> sé?
[kayn tom uh-taw shay]

"What time <u>was</u> it?"
Cén t-am <u>a bhí</u> sé?
[kayn tom uh vee shay]

Examples

"What time was it?"
Cén t-am a bhí sé?
[kayn tom uh vee shay]

"It was four o'clock."
Bhí sé a ceathair a chlog.
[vee shay uh kya-her uh khluhg]

"What time was it?"
Cén t-am a bhí sé?
[kayn tom uh vee shay]

"It was half-past seven in the morning."
Bhí sé leathuair tar éis a seacht a chlog ar maidin.
[vee shay lah-hooir tar aysh uh shakht uh khluhg air ma-jin]

Lesson 80 – Talking About the Future

Being able to speak about the present as well as the past gives you lots of ways to say what you want in Irish. Now, we're going to expand that knowledge even further... into the future! Putting "**tá**" [taw] sentences into the future tense is as easy as it was putting them into the past.

The Future Tense of "Tá"

To turn a *present tense* sentence into a *future tense* sentence, you change the verb. The future tense of "**tá**" [taw], "is," is "**beidh**" [bay], "will be."

Examples

We'll look at a basic sentence in the *present tense*, and one in the *future tense* to compare:

"I <u>am</u> okay."
<u>Tá</u> mé ceart go leor.
[taw may kyart guh leeyor]

"I <u>will be</u> okay."
<u>Beidh</u> mé ceart go leor.
[bay may kyart guh leeyor]

Here are sample sentences using all of the pronouns in the future tense:

"I will be okay."
Beidh mé ceart go leor.
[bay may kyart guh leeyor]

"You will be okay."
Beidh tú ceart go leor.
[bay too kyart guh leeyor]

"He will be okay."
Beidh sé ceart go leor.
[bay shay kyart guh leeyor]

"She will be okay."
Beidh sí ceart go leor.
[bay shee kyart guh leeyor]

"We will be okay."
Beidh muid ceart go leor.
[bay mwidj kyart guh leeyor]

"Y'all will be okay."
Beidh sibh ceart go leor.
[bay shiv kyart guh leeyor]

"They will be okay."
Beidh siad ceart go leor.
[bay shee-ud kyart guh leeyor]

Vocabulary

To give your sentences more depth and variety, you can add words to the end of your sentence that describe when something will be happening.

"tomorrow"
amárach
[uh-maw-rahkh]

"tomorrow night"
oíche amárach
[ee-khuh uh-maw-rahkh]

Examples

"The weather will be hot tomorrow."
Beidh an aimsir te amárach.
[bay un am-sheer tcheh uh-maw-rahkh]

"Brian will be working tomorrow night."
Beidh Brian ag obair oíche amárach.
[bay bree-uhn ehg uh-ber ee-khuh uh-maw-rahkh]

"Patricia will be reading tomorrow."
Beidh Pádraigín ag léamh amárach.
[bay paw-druh-geen ehg lay-uv uh-maw-rahkh]

"The floor will be clean tomorrow night."
Beidh an t-urlár glan oíche amárach.
[bay un toor-lawr glon ee-khuh uh-maw-rahkh]

Lesson 81 – The Negative of "Beidh"

Verbs in Irish don't change to show the person you're talking about, but they do change to make a sentence positive or negative. The *negative form* of "**beidh**" [bay], "will be," is "**ní bheidh**" [nee vay], "will not be." So, to turn a positive statement into a negative statement in the future tense, you simply switch the word "**beidh**" [bay] with "**ní bheidh**" [nee vay].

Examples

"The day will not be hot tomorrow."
Ní bheidh an lá te amárach.
[nee vay un law tcheh uh-maw-rahkh]

"He will not have a key."
Ní bheidh eochair aige.
[nee vay ukh-er ehg-uh]

"Brian will not be running."
Ní bheidh Brian ag rith.
[nee vay bree-uhn ehg rih]

"There will not be two people there tomorrow night."
Ní bheidh beirt ann oíche amárach.
[nee vay baertch on ee-khuh uh-maw-rahkh]

"Patricia won't be sick."
Ní bheidh Pádraigín tinn.
[nee vay paw-druh-geen tcheen]

"They won't be inside."
Ní bheidh siad istigh.
[nee vay shee-ud iss-tchih]

"I won't be going home."
Ní bheidh mé ag dul abhaile.
[nee vay may ehg dull uh-wah-lyuh]

Lesson 82 – The Question Forms of "Beidh"

Positive Questions

To turn a positive statement into a positive question in the future tense, you simply switch the word "**beidh**" [bay], "will be," with its question form, "**an mbeidh**" [un may], "will be?".

Examples

"Will it be dry?"
An mbeidh sé tirim?
[un may shay tchih-ruhm]

"Will he have the ring?"
An mbeidh an fáinne aige?
[un may un faw-nyuh ehg-uh]

"Will they be working?"
An mbeidh siad ag obair?
[un may shee-ud ehg uh-ber]

Negative Questions

To make a future tense negative question, all you have to do is switch the word "**beidh**" [bay], "will be," with its negative question form, which is "**nach mbeidh**" [nahkh may], "won't be?".

Examples

"Won't she be eating?"
Nach mbeidh sí ag ithe?
[nahkh may shee ehg ih-huh]

"Won't you have a bag?"
Nach mbeidh mála agat?
[nahkh may maw-luh ah-gut]

"Won't they be well?"
Nach mbeidh siad go maith?
[nahkh may shee-ud guh mah]

Lesson 83 — Answering Future Questions

In Irish, you reply to a question by repeating the positive form or the negative form of the verb, instead of saying simple words for "yes" and "no." When you're asked questions in the future tense, you use the future tense forms of the verb when answering.

If you're asked a question using "**an mbeidh**" [un may], or "**nach mbeidh**" [nahkh may], you answer:

"Yes."   "No."
Beidh.   **Ní bheidh.**
[bay]   [nee vay]

As we saw before with the other tenses, the "yes" and "no" answers literally mean "will be" and "will not be," or, loosely "it will be so" and "it will not be so."

Examples

Let's look at some future tense questions with answers. Remember that you can answer simply, but it helps to answer with full questions while you're learning, so you can get more practice.

"Will it be wet tomorrow?"
An mbeidh sé fliuch amárach?
[un may shay flyukh uh-maw-rahkh]

"Yes, it will be very wet tomorrow!"
Beidh, beidh sé an-fhliuch amárach!"
[bay, bay shay on lyukh uh-maw-rahkh]

"Won't there be six people outside?"
Nach mbeidh seisear amuigh?
[nahkh may shesh-er uh-muh]

"No, there won't be six people outside."
Ní bheidh, ní bheidh seisear amuigh.
[nee vay, nee vay shesh-er uh-muh]

"Will you be running?"
An mbeidh tú ag rith?
[un may too ehg rih]

"No. I will be walking."
Ní bheidh. Beidh mé ag siúl.
[nee vay. bay may ehg shool]

"Won't the street be too small?"
Nach bheidh an tsráid ró-bheag?
[nahkh may un troyj roe vayug]

"No. It will be big!"
Ní bheidh. Beidh sí mór!"
[nee vay. bay shee mor]

"Will y'all have their boxes?"
An mbeidh a mboscaí agaibh?
[un may uh muss-kee ah-giv]

"Yes, we will have their boxes."
Beidh, beidh a mboscaí againn.
[bay, bay uh muss-kee ah-geen]

Conversation

Now we'll practice using the future tense with a conversation.

Pádraigín:
"Will the day be okay tomorrow?"
An mbeidh an lá ceart go leor amárach?
[un may un law kyart guh leeyor uh-maw-rahkh]

Brian:
"No. It will be cold and wet."
Ní bheidh. Beidh sé fuar agus fliuch.
[nee vay. bay shay foo-uhr ah-gus flyukh]

"Will you be running tomorrow?"
An mbeidh tú ag rith amárach?
[un may too ehg rih uh-maw-rahkh]

Pádraigín:
"No. I won't be running, now!"
Ní bheidh. Ní bheidh mé ag rith, anois!
[nee vay. nee vay may ehg rih, uh-nish]

"Won't it be dry tomorrow night?"
Nach mbeidh sé tirim oíche amárach?
[nahkh may shay tchih-ruhm ee-khuh uh-maw-rahkh]

Brian:
"Yes. It will be dry."
Beidh. Beidh sé tirim.
[bay. bay shay tchih-ruhm]

Pádraigín:
"I'll be reading tomorrow night."
Beidh mé ag léamh oíche amárach.
[bay may ehg lay-uv ee-khuh uh-maw-rahkh]

Brian:
"Me, too!"
Mise, freisin!
[mih-shuh, fresh-in]

Lesson 84 – Asking How the Weather Will Be

One thing about the future that you may be interested in is how the weather will be. To put any of the *Bonus Phrase* questions for "How is the weather?" into the future tense, you switch the verb for its future tense form.

"How <u>is</u> the weather?"
Cén chaoi <u>a bhfuil</u> an aimsir?
[keh hee will un am-sheer]

"How <u>will</u> the weather <u>be</u>?"
Cén chaoi <u>a mbeidh</u> an aimsir?
[keh hee may un am-sheer]

Examples

Let's take a look at some weather questions in the future tense with answers.

"How will the weather be?"
Cén chaoi a mbeidh an aimsir?
[keh hee may un am-sheer]

"The weather will be hot."
Beidh an aimsir te.
[bay un am-sheer tcheh]

"How will the weather be tomorrow?"
Conas a mbeidh an aimsir amárach?
[kun-us uh may un am-sheer uh-maw-rahkh]

"It won't be too cold."
Ní bheidh sí ró-fhuar.
[nee vay shee roe oo-uhr]

"How will the weather be tomorrow night?"
Cad é mar a mbeidh an aimsir oíche amárach?
[kuh-jay mar uh may un am-sheer ee-khuh uh-maw-rahkh]

"The night will be beautiful."
Beidh an oíche go h-álainn.
[bay un ee-khuh guh haw-ling]

Lesson 85 – How Many Will You Have?

The "have" expression can be used to say how many things someone will have. To put the *Bonus Phrase* question, "How many do you have?" into the future tense, you switch the verb for its future tense form.

"How many boxes <u>do</u> you have?"
Cé mhéad bosca <u>atá</u> agat?
[kay vay-ud bus-kuh uh-taw ah-gut]

"How many boxes <u>will</u> you have?"
Cé mhéad bosca <u>a mbeidh</u> agat?
[kay vay-ud bus-kuh uh may ah-gut]

To answer this question, you simply use a "have" statement in the future tense with a counting number.

"I will have nine boxes."
Beidh naoi mbosca agam.
[bay nee muss-kuh ah-gum]

"I will have nine."
Beidh naoi gcinn agam.
[bay nee geen ah-gum]

You can also ask if someone has a specific number of things by using the "have" expression with one of the question forms of "**beidh**" [bay], a counted noun, and then a form of "**ag**" [ehg]. Remember to repeat the verb when answering these types of questions.

"Will you have four bags?"
An mbeidh ceithre mhála agat?
[un may keh-ruh wah-luh ah-gut]

"Yes, I will have four."
Beidh, beidh ceithre cinn agam.
[bay, bay keh-ruh keen ah-gum]

"Won't Patricia have ten rings?"
Nach mbeidh deich bhfáinne ag Pádraigín?
[nahkh may jeh wah-nyuh ehg paw-druh-geen]

"No. She will only have six."
Ní bheidh. Ní bheidh ach sé cinn aici.
[nee vay. nee vay akh shay keen ehk-ee]

Conversation

Let's practice talking about having things in the future with a conversation.

Brian:
"How many boxes will you have tomorrow?"
Cé mhéad bosca a mbeidh agat amárach?
[kay vay-ud bus-kuh uh may ah-gut uh-maw-rahkh]

Pádraigín:
"I'll have two boxes."
Beidh dhá bhosca agam.
[bay ghaw wuhss-kuh ah-gum]

"How many apples will you have?"
Cé mhéad úll a mbeidh agat?
[kay vay-ud ool uh may ah-gut]

Brian:
"I'll have twenty apples."
Beidh fiche ceann agam.
[bay fih-huh kyawn ah-gum]

Pádraigín:
"I'll have my bicycle tomorrow."
Beidh mo rothar agam amárach.
[bay muh ruh-her ah-gum uh-maw-rahkh]

Brian:
"Won't you have your car?"
Nach mbeidh do charr agat?
[nahkh may duh khahr ah-gut]

Pádraigín:
"No. I don't have the key."
Ní bheidh. Níl an eochair agam.
[nee vay. neel un ukh-er ah-gum]

"But, I will have my key tomorrow night."
Ach, beidh m'eochair agam oíche amárach.
[akh, bay mukh-er ah-gum ee-khuh uh-maw-rahkh]

Brian:
"Good."
Go maith.
[guh mah]

Lesson 86 – What Will You Be Doing?

When you ask the *Bonus Phrase* "What are you doing?" in the future tense, you switch out its verb for its future tense form.

"What <u>are</u> you doing?"
Céard <u>atá</u> tú ag déanamh?
[kayrd uh-taw too ehg jay-nuv]

"What <u>will</u> you <u>be</u> doing?"
Céard <u>a mbeidh</u> tú ag déanamh?
[kayrd uh may too ehg jay-nuv]

Examples

Let's take a look at some "doing" questions in the future tense with answers.

"What will you be doing?"
Céard a mbeidh tú ag déanamh?
[kayrd uh may too ehg jay-nuv]

"I will be eating."
Beidh mé ag ithe.
[bay may ehg ih-huh]

"What will Brian be doing?"
Céard a mbeidh Brian ag déanamh?
[kayrd uh may bree-uhn ehg jay-nuv]

"Brian will be working."
Beidh Brian ag obair.
[bay bree-uhn ehg uh-ber]

"What will we be doing?"
Céard a mbeidh muid ag déanamh?
[kayrd uh may mwidj ehg jay-nuv]

"We will be learning!"
Beidh muid ag foghlaim!
[bay mwidj ehg foe-lum]

You can also ask if someone will be doing a specific thing by using the progressive tense with one of the question forms of "**beidh**" [bay]. When answering these with full sentences, don't forget to repeat the verb.

Examples

"Will they be waiting?"
An mbeidh siad ag fanacht?
[un may shee-ud ehg faw-nahkht]

"Yes, they will be waiting."
Beidh. Beidh siad ag fanacht.
[bay. bay shee-ud ehg faw-nahkht]

"Won't y'all be talking?"
Nach mbeidh sibh ag caint?
[nahkh may shiv ehg kyintch]

"No. We'll be listening."
Ní bheidh. Beidh muid ag éisteacht.
[nee vay. bay mwidj ehg aysh-tahkht]

Conversation

Let's practice talking about doing things in the future with a conversation.

Pádraigín:
"What will you be doing tomorrow night?"
Céard a mbeidh tú ag déanamh oíche amárach?
[kayrd uh may too ehg jay-nuv ee-khuh uh-maw-rahkh]

Brian:
"I'll be learning."
Beidh mé ag foghlaim.
[bay may ehg foe-lum]

Pádraigín:
"Will Liam and Noreen be learning too?"
An mbeidh Liam agus Noirín ag foghlaim, freisin?
[un may lee-um ah-gus nor-een ehg foe-lum, fresh-in]

Brian:
"Liam will be learning, but Noreen won't be learning."
Beidh Liam ag foghlaim, ach ní bheidh Noirín ag foghlaim.
[bay lee-um ehg foe-lum, akh nee vay nor-een ehg foe-lum]

Pádraigín:
"What will Noreen be doing?"
Céard a mbeidh Noirín ag déanamh?
[kayrd uh may nor-een ehg jay-nuv]

Brian:
"She'll be working."
Beidh sí ag obair.
[bay shee ehg uh-ber]

"What will *you* be doing tomorrow night?"
Céard a mbeidh tusa ag déanamh oíche amárach?
[kayrd uh may tuh-suh ehg jay-nuv ee-khuh uh-maw-rahkh]

Pádraigín:
"I'll be eating."
Beidh mé ag ithe.
[bay may ehg ih-huh]

Lesson 87 – Where Will It Be?

Something else that's useful to know about the future is where things will be. To ask the *Bonus Phrase* question, "Where is it?" in the future tense, you switch the present tense form of the verb for the future tense form.

"Where <u>is</u> it?"
Cá <u>bhfuil</u> sé?
[kaw will shay]

"Where <u>will</u> it <u>be</u>?"
Cá <u>mbeidh</u> sé?
[kaw may shay]

Examples

Let's take a look at a few "where" questions in the future tense with answers.

"Where will it be?"
Cá mbeidh sé?
[kaw may shay]

"It will be here."
Beidh sé anseo.
[bay shay un-shuh]

"Where will Patricia be?"
Cá mbeidh Pádraigín?
[kaw may paw-druh-geen]

"Patricia will be outside."
Beidh Pádraigín amuigh.
[bay paw-druh-geen uh-muh]

"Where will the table be?"
Cá mbeidh an bord?
[kaw may un bord]

"It will be there."
Beidh sé ansin.
[bay shay un-shin]

Lesson 88 – Where Will You Be Going?

When you want to talk about where someone will be going, you take the *Bonus Phrase* question "Where are you going?" and switch its verb for its future tense form.

"Where <u>are</u> you going?"
Cá <u>bhfuil</u> tú ag dul?
[kaw will too ehg dull]

"Where <u>will</u> you <u>be</u> going?"
Cá <u>mbeidh</u> tú ag dul?
[kaw may too ehg dull]

Remember, when answering this question, the word you use for "to" depends upon the kind of place you're going.

Examples

"Where will you be going?"
Cá mbeidh tú ag dul?
[kaw may too ehg dull]

"I will be going to a beach."
Beidh mé ag dul go trá.
[bay may ehg dull guh traw]

"Where will she be going?"
Cá mbeidh sí ag dul?
[kaw may shee ehg dull]

"She will be going to the hotel."
Beidh sí ag dul go dtí an t-óstán.
[bay shee ehg dull guh jee un toess-tawn]

"Where will Brian be going?"
Cá mbeidh Brian ag dul?
[kaw may bree-uhn ehg dull]

"Brian will be going to the meeting."
Beidh Brian ag dul chuig an gcruinniú.
[bay bree-uhn ehg dull khig un grin-nyew]

Conversation

Let's practice talking about going different places in the future with a conversation.

Brian:
"Where will you be going tomorrow?"
Cá mbeidh tú ag dul amárach?
[kaw may too ehg dull uh-maw-rahkh]

Pádraigín:
"I'll be going to a movie tomorrow night."
Beidh mé ag dul chuig scannán oíche amárach.
[bay may ehg dull khig skuh-nawn ee-khuh uh-maw-rahkh]

"Will *you* be going to a movie, too?"
An mbeidh tusa ag dul chuig scannán, freisin?
[un may tuh-suh ehg dull khig skuh-nawn, fresh-in]

Brian:
"No."
Ní bheidh.
[nee vay]

Pádraigín:
"Where will you be going?"
Cá mbeidh tú ag dul?
[kaw may too ehg dull]

Brian:
"I'll be going to a wedding tomorrow."
Beidh mé ag dul chuig bainis amárach.
[bay may ehg dull khig ban-ish uh-maw-rahkh]

Pádraigín:
"Lovely! Where will it be?"
Go h-álainn! Cá mbeidh sí?
[guh haw-ling! kaw may shee]

Brian:
"It will be outside."
Beidh sí amuigh.
[bay shee uh-muh]

"We'll be going to a park."
Beidh muid ag dul go páirc.
[bay mwidj ehg dull guh pawrk]

Lesson 89 – What Time Will It Be?

Another useful *Bonus Phrase* question you can use in the future tense is "What time will it be?" As we saw before, the basic phrase only implies the verb, but we can use an alternate phrase so that we can put it into different tenses. To put this *Bonus Phrase* into the future tense, you switch out the verb "**atá**" [uh-taw] for the future tense form, "**a mbeidh**" [uh may].

"What time <u>is</u> it?
Cén t-am <u>atá</u> sé?
[kayn tom uh-taw shay]

"What time <u>will</u> it <u>be</u>?"
Cén t-am <u>a mbeidh</u> sé?
[kayn tom uh may shay]

Examples

"What time will it be?"
Cén t-am a mbeidh sé?
[kayn tom uh may shay]

"It will be a quarter after seven o'clock."
Beidh sé ceathrú tar éis a seacht a chlog.
[bay shay kya-hroo tar aysh uh shakht uh khluhg]

"What time will it be?"
Cén t-am a mbeidh sé?
[kayn tom uh may shay]

"It will be three o'clock in the afternoon."
Beidh sé a trí a chlog sa tráthnóna.
[bay shay uh tree uh khluhg suh traw-no-nuh]

"What time will it be?"
Cén t-am a mbeidh sé?
[kayn tom uh may shay]

"It will be twenty minutes till one o'clock."
Beidh sé fiche nóiméad roimh a h-aon a chlog.
[bay shay fih-huh no-mayd riv uh hayn uh khluhg]

Lesson 90 – Talking About What Usually Happens

Things happened in the past. Things are happening now. Things will happen in the future. Things can also happen regularly, or *habitually*. These things may or may not be happening right now, but they *usually* happen.

To describe things that happen on a regular basis, whether often or only occasionally, Irish uses the *simple present tense*, also called the *habitual tense*. English also uses this same tense for regular occurrences, but Irish uses it more often.

Let's take a look at a few sentences in English to get a better idea of how this works. For example, if you say, "I eat breakfast," whether or not you're eating breakfast right now doesn't matter. Habitually, you do. You can be more specific about this habit by adding extra words. For example, you could say, "I eat breakfast <u>every day</u>," "I eat breakfast <u>from time to time</u>," "I <u>usually</u> eat breakfast," or even "I <u>rarely</u> eat breakfast."   All of these sentences express an action that takes place repeatedly over time.

The Habitual Tense of "Tá"

The habitual tense of "**tá**" [taw] is "**bíonn**" [bee-uhn]. When translating this into English, you often see helper words and phrases (like those in the above English examples) included as a reminder that this is a habitual action, even though no extra words are necessary in Irish to convey a strong habitual sense.

Habitual sentences are made the same way as a basic "**tá**" [taw] sentence. To turn a *present tense* sentence into a *habitual tense* sentence, you change the verb at the beginning.

Examples

We'll take a look at a simple sentence in the *present tense*, and one in the *habitual tense* to compare:

"I <u>am</u> cold."
Tá mé fuar.
[taw may foo-uhr]

"I <u>am (usually)</u> cold."
Bíonn mé fuar.
[bee-uhn may foo-uhr]

Once again, when "**bíonn**" [bee-uhn] sentences are translated into English, extra words are often added for clarity's sake. In Irish, however, "**bíonn**" [bee-uhn] speaks for itself, and you don't have to add anything for people to know that you're speaking about a regular occurrence. You may add extra words to be more specific, if you want to. Below are some words and phrases that are used frequently with "**bíonn**" [bee-uhn].

Vocabulary

"usually"
de ghnáth
[deh ghuh-naw]

"every day"
gach lá
[gahkh law]

"rarely"
go h-annamh
[guh hah-nuv]

"often"
go minic
[guh min-ik]

"from time to time"
ó am go h-am
[oe ahm guh hahm]

"sometimes"
uaireanta
[oor-en-tuh]

"always"
i gcónaí
[ih go-nee]

"now and again"
anois agus arís
[uh-nish ah-gus uh-reesh]

Examples

Now we'll take a look at some sample sentences using the habitual tense. To clarify that these are regular occurrences, we've included a note beside some of the English translations as a reminder.

"The weather is hot." (habitually)
Bíonn an aimsir te.
[bee-uhn un am-sheer tcheh]

"The weather is hot every day."
Bíonn an aimsir te gach lá.
[bee-uhn un am-sheer tcheh gahkh law]

"Brian is well." (habitually)
Bíonn Brian go maith.
[bee-uhn bree-uhn guh mah]

"Brian is usually well."
Bíonn Brian go maith de ghnáth.
[bee-uhn bree-uhn guh mah deh ghuh-naw]

"Patricia is reading." (habitually)
Bíonn Pádraigín ag léamh.
[bee-uhn paw-druh-geen ehg lay-uv]

"Patricia is always reading."
Bíonn Pádraigín ag léamh i gcónaí.
[bee-uhn paw-druh-geen ehg lay-uv ih go-nee]

"The floor is dirty." (habitually)
Bíonn an t-urlár salach.
[bee-uhn un toor-lawr sahl-ahkh]

"The floor is rarely dirty."
Bíonn an t-urlár salach go h-annamh.
[bee-uhn un toor-lawr sahl-ahkh guh hah-nuv]

Lesson 91 – The Negative of "Bíonn"

To make sentences about what doesn't usually happen, you switch out the positive form of "**bíonn**" [bee-uhn] for its negative form, which is "**ní bhíonn**" [nee vee-uhn].

Examples

Here are some sample sentences using the habitual tense in its negative form. To clarify that these are things that don't regularly occur, we've included a note beside some of the English translations as a reminder.

"It isn't cold." (habitually)
Ní bhíonn sé fuar.
[nee vee-uhn shay foo-uhr]

"It isn't often cold."
Ní bhíonn sé fuar go minic.
[nee vee-uhn shay foo-uhr guh min-ik]

"He doesn't have a key." (habitually)
Ní bhíonn eochair aige.
[nee vee-uhn ukh-er ehg-uh]

"He doesn't usually have a key."
Ní bhíonn eochair aige de ghnáth.
[nee vee-uhn ukh-er ehg-uh deh ghuh-naw]

"Patricia isn't running." (habitually)
Ní bhíonn Pádraigín ag rith.
[nee vee-uhn paw-druh-geen ehg rih]

"Patricia doesn't run every day."
Ní bhíonn Pádraigín ag rith gach lá.
[nee vee-uhn paw-druh-geen ehg rih gahkh law]

"There aren't three people there." (habitually)
Ní bhíonn triúr ann.
[nee vee-uhn troo-ihr on]

"There aren't three people there, sometimes."
Ní bhíonn triúr ann uaireanta.
[nee vee-uhn troo-ihr on oor-en-tuh]

Lesson 92 – The Question Forms of "Bíonn"

Positive Questions

When you want to turn a positive statement into a positive question in the habitual tense, you switch the word "**bíonn**" [bee-uhn] for its question form, "**an mbíonn**" [un me-uhn].

Examples

"Is it clean?" (habitually)
An mbíonn sé glan?
[un me-uhn shay glon]

"Is it clean now and again?"
An mbíonn sé glan anois agus arís?
[un me-uhn shay glon uh-nish ah-gus uh-reesh]

"Does he have a book?" (habitually)
An mbíonn leabhar aige?
[un me-uhn lyow-er ehg-uh]

"Does he always have a book?"
An mbíonn leabhar aige i gcónaí?
[un me-uhn lyow-er ehg-uh ih go-nee]

"Do they work?" (habitually)
An mbíonn siad ag obair?
[un me-uhn shee-ud ehg uh-ber]

"Do they often work?"
An mbíonn siad ag obair go minic?
[un me-uhn shee-ud ehg uh-ber guh min-ik]

Negative Questions

To turn a positive statement in the habitual tense into a negative question, you switch the word "**bíonn**" [bee-uhn] with its negative question form, "**nach mbíonn**" [nahkh me-uhn].

Examples

"Isn't he laughing?" (habitually)
Nach mbíonn sé ag gáire?
[nahkh me-uhn shay ehg goy-ruh]

"Isn't he laughing from time to time?"
Nach mbíonn sé ag gáire ó am go h-am?
[nahkh me-uhn shay ehg goy-ruh oe ahm guh hahm]

"Don't you have a bag?" (habitually)
Nach mbíonn mála agat?
[nahkh me-uhn maw-luh ah-gut]

"Don't you sometimes have a bag?"
Nach mbíonn mála agat uaireanta?
[nahkh me-uhn maw-luh ah-gut oor-en-tuh]

"Isn't she fine?" (habitually)
Nach mbíonn sí go breá?
[nahkh me-uhn shee guh braw]

"Isn't she fine now and again?"
Nach mbíonn sí go breá anois agus arís?
[nahkh me-uhn shee guh braw uh-nish ah-gus uh-reesh]

Lesson 93 – Answering Habitual Questions

In Irish, you answer a question by repeating the positive form or the negative form of the verb, rather than saying simple words for "yes" and "no." When you're asked a question using **"an mbíonn"** [un me-uhn] or **"nach mbíonn"** [nahkh me-uhn], you answer by saying:

"Yes."
Bíonn.
[bee-uhn]

"No."
Ní bhíonn.
[nee vee-uhn]

As we've seen with the other tenses, these "yes" and "no" answers loosely mean "it is usually so" and "it is not usually so."

Examples

Let's take a look at some habitual questions with answers. Once again, you can answer simply, but it helps to answer with full questions, so you can get more practice, especially when you're learning a concept like the habitual tense.

"Is it wet?" (habitually)
An mbíonn sé fliuch?
[un me-uhn shay flyukh]

"Yes, it is usually very wet."
Bíonn, bíonn sé an-fhliuch de ghnáth.
[bee-uhn, bee-uhn shay on lyukh deh ghuh-naw]

"Aren't there seven people outside?" (habitually)
Nach mbíonn seachtar amuigh?
[nahkh me-uhn shakh-tur uh-muh]

"No, there aren't seven people outside." (habitually)
Ní bhíonn, ní bhíonn seachtar amuigh.
[nee vee-uhn, nee vee-uhn shakh-tur uh-muh]

"Are you always running?"
An mbíonn tú ag rith í gcónaí?
[un me-uhn too ehg rih ih go-nee]

"No. I am often walking."
Ní bhíonn. Bíonn mé ag siúl go minic.
[nee vee-uhn. bee-uhn may ehg shool guh min-ik]

"Isn't the weather too cloudy?" (habitually)
Nach mbíonn an aimsir ró-scamallach?
[nahkh me-uhn un am-sheer roe skom-uh-lahkh]

"No. It's always sunny!"
Ní bhíonn. Bíonn sí grianmhar i gcónaí!
[nee vee-uhn. bee-uhn shee gree-un-wer ih go-nee]

"Is my chair usually here?"
An mbíonn mo chathaoir anseo de ghnáth?
[un mee-uhn muh khah-heer un-shuh deh ghuh-naw]

"Yes, your chair is here." (habitually)
Bíonn, bíonn do chathaoir anseo.
[bee-uhn, bee-uhn duh khah-heer un-shuh]

Conversation

Now we'll practice using the habitual tense with a conversation.

Pádraigín:
"Do you go to the beach?"
An mbíonn tú ag dul go dtí an trá?
[un me-uhn too ehg dull guh jee un traw]

Brian:
"No. I rarely go to the beach."
Ní bhíonn. Bíonn mé ag dul go dtí an trá go h-annamh.
[nee vee-uhn. bee-uhn may ehg dull guh jee un traw guh hah-nuv]

"I'm usually reading."
Bíonn mé ag léamh de ghnáth.
[bee-uhn may ehg lay-uv deh ghuh-naw]

Pádraigín:
"Do you always have a book?"
An mbíonn leabhar agat i gcónaí?
[un me-uhn lyow-er ah-gut ih go-nee]

Brian:
"Yes. I learn every day."
Bíonn. Bíonn mé ag foghlaim gach lá.
[bee-uhn. bee-uhn may ehg foe-lum gahkh law]

"Does Noreen go to the beach?"
An mbíonn Noirín ag dul go dtí an trá?
[un me-uhn nor-een ehg dull guh jee un traw]

Pádraigín:
"Yes. She's often there."
Bíonn. Bíonn sí ann go minic.
[bee-uhn. bee-uhn shee on guh min-ik]

Brian:
"Isn't Liam there from time to time, too?"
Nach mbíonn Liam ann ó am go h-am, freisin?
[nahkh me-uhn lee-um on oe ahm guh hahm, fresh-in]

Pádraigín:
"Yes. Liam goes now and again."
Bíonn. Bíonn sé ag dul ann anois agus arís.
[bee-uhn. bee-uhn shay ehg dull on uh-nish ah-gus uh-reesh]

Lesson 94 – Asking About the Weather in the Habitual

Sometimes, you may be curious to know how the weather usually is in a place. To ask questions about the weather in the habitual tense, you can use any of the *Bonus Phrase* questions for "How is the weather?" with the habitual tense form of "**tá**" [taw].

"How <u>is</u> the weather?"
Cén chaoi <u>a bhfuil</u> an aimsir?
[keh hee will un am-sheer]

"How <u>is</u> the weather?" (habitually)
Cén chaoi <u>a mbíonn</u> an aimsir?
[keh hee me-uhn un am-sheer]

Because you're talking in a habitual sense, you may find that these sentences work better with some words than others. For example, you're probably more likely to ask how "the days" usually are, rather than how "the day" usually is. For discussing how the weather habitually is, we'll also use the plural forms for "day" and "night."

Vocabulary

"the day"
an lá (m.)
[un law]

"the night"
an oíche (f.)
[un ee-khuh]

"the days"
na laethanta
[nuh lay-hen-tuh]

"the nights"
na h-oícheanta
[nuh hee-khen-tuh]

Examples

Let's take a look at some questions asking about how the weather, the days, and the nights usually are with some answers.

"How is the weather?" (habitually)
Cén chaoi a mbíonn an aimsir?
[keh hee me-uhn un am-sheer]

"It is dry." (habitually)
Bíonn sí tirim.
[bee-uhn shee tchih-ruhm]

"How are the days?" (habitually)
Conas a mbíonn na laethanta?
[kun-us uh me-uhn nuh lay-hen-tuh]

"They are cloudy from time to time."
Bíonn siad scamallach ó am go h-am.
[bee-uhn shee-ud skom-uh-lahkh oe ahm guh hahm]

"How are the nights usually?"
Cad é mar a mbíonn na h-oícheanta de ghnáth?
[kuh-jay mar uh me-uhn nuh hee-khen-tuh deh ghuh-naw]

"They are cold." (habitually)
Bíonn siad fuar.
[bee-uhn shee-ud foo-uhr]

Lesson 95 – How Many Do You Usually Have?

You can use the "have" expression to talk about how many things someone usually has. To change the *Bonus Phrase* question, "How many do you have?" into the habitual tense, you switch the verb for its habitual tense form. You can also add any of the words and phrases for the frequency of habits we learned before to make your questions and answers more specific.

Examples

"How many boxes <u>do</u> you have?"
Cé mhéad bosca <u>atá</u> agat?
[kay vay-ud bus-kuh uh-taw ah-gut]

"How many boxes <u>do</u> you have?" (<u>habitually</u>)
Cé mhéad bosca <u>a mbíonn</u> agat?
[kay vay-ud bus-kuh uh me-uhn ah-gut]

To answer this question, you use a "have" statement in the habitual tense with a counting number.

"I have three boxes." (habitually)
Bíonn trí bhosca agam.
[bee-uhn tree wuhss-kuh ah-gum]

"I have three." (habitually)
Bíonn trí cinn agam.
[bee-uhn tree keen ah-gum]

You can also ask if someone usually has a specific number of things by using the "have" expression with one of the question forms of "**bíonn**" [bee-uhn], a counted noun, and then a form of "**ag**" [ehg]. When answering these types of questions, don't forget to repeat the verb.

"Do you usually have eight chairs?"
An mbíonn ocht gcathaoir agat de ghnáth?
[un me-uhn awkht gah-heer ah-gut deh ghuh-naw]

"Yes, I have eight." (habitually)
Bíonn. Bíonn ocht gcinn agam.
[bee-uhn. bee-uhn awkht geen ah-gum]

"Doesn't Brian always have five books?"
Nach mbíonn cúig leabhar ag Brian i gcónaí?
[nahkh me-uhn kooig lyow-er ehg bree-uhn ih go-nee]

"No. He only has four sometimes."
Ní bhíonn. Ní bhíonn ach ceithre cinn aige uaireanta.
[nee vee-uhn. nee vee-uhn akh keh-ruh keen ehg-uh oor-en-tuh]

Conversation

Let's practice talking about what people usually have with a conversation.

Brian:
"Do you usually have the knives?"
An mbíonn na sceana agat de ghnáth?
[un me-uhn nuh shkyah-nuh ah-gut deh ghuh-naw]

Pádraigín:
"Yes."
Bíonn.
[bee-uhn]

Brian:
"How many do you have?"
Cé mhéad a mbíonn agat?
[kay vay-ud uh me-uhn ah-gut]

Pádraigín:
"I have eight."
Bíonn ocht gcinn agam.
[bee-uhn awkht geen ah-gum]

Brian:
"Don't Noreen and Liam usually have the spoons?"
Nach mbíonn na spúnóga ag Noirín agus Liam de ghnáth?
[nahkh me-uhn nuh spoo-noeg-uh ehg nor-een ah-gus lee-um deh ghuh-naw]

Pádraigín:
"Liam often has them, and sometimes Noreen has them."
Bíonn siad ag Liam go minic, agus bíonn siad ag Noirín uaireanta.
[bee-uhn shee-ud ehg lee-um guh min-ik, ah-gus bee-uhn shee-ud ehg nor-een oor-en-tuh]

Brian:
"How many spoons do they usually have?"
Cé mhéad spúnóg a mbíonn acu de ghnáth?
[kay vay-ud spoo-noeg uh me-uhn ah-kuh deh ghuh-naw]

Pádraigín:
"They have ten."
Bíonn deich gcinn acu.
[bee-uhn jeh geen ah-kuh]

Brian:
"Don't they always have twelve spoons?"
Nach mbíonn dhá spúnóg déag acu i gcónaí?
[nahkh me-uhn ghaw spoo-noeg jayug ah-kuh ih go-nee]

Pádraigín:
"No. They usually only have ten."
Ní bhíonn. Ní bhíonn ach deich gcinn acu de ghnáth.
[nee vee-uhn. nee vee-uhn akh jeh geen ah-kuh deh ghuh-naw]

Lesson 96 – What Are You Usually Doing?

When you use the *Bonus Phrase* question, "What are you doing?" in a habitual sense, you switch out its verb for its habitual tense form.

"What <u>are</u> you doing?"
Céard <u>atá</u> tú ag déanamh?
[kayrd uh-taw too ehg jay-nuv]

"What <u>do</u> you do?" (<u>habitually</u>)
Céard <u>a mbíonn</u> tú ag déanamh?
[kayrd uh me-uhn too ehg jay-nuv]

Examples

Here are a few sample questions with answers in the habitual tense.

"What do you do?" (habitually)
Céard a mbíonn tú ag déanamh?
[kayrd uh me-uhn too ehg jay-nuv]

"I read." (habitually)
Bíonn mé ag léamh.
[bee-uhn may ehg lay-uv]

"What does she do?" (habitually)
Céard a mbíonn sí ag déanamh?
[kayrd uh me-uhn shee ehg jay-nuv]

"She listens." (habitually)
Bíonn sí ag éisteacht.
[bee-uhn shee ehg aysh-tahkht]

"What does Brian usually do?"
Céard a mbíonn Brian ag déanamh de ghnáth?
[kayrd uh me-uhn bree-uhn ehg jay-nuv deh ghuh-naw]

"He is always learning."
Bíonn sé ag foghlaim i gcónaí.
[bee-uhn shay ehg foe-lum ih go-nee]

Lesson 97 – Where Is It Usually?

When you ask the *Bonus Phrase*, "Where is it?" in a habitual sense, you switch the present tense form of the verb for its habitual tense form.

"Where is it?"
Cá bhfuil sé?
[kaw will shay]

"Where is it?" (habitually)
Cá mbíonn sé?
[kaw me-uhn shay]

Examples

Let's take a look at a few "where" questions in the habitual tense with answers.

"Where is it?" (habitually)
Cá mbíonn sé?
[kaw me-uhn shay]

"It is here." (habitually)
Bíonn sé anseo.
[bee-uhn shay un-shuh]

"Where is the bicycle?" (habitually)
Cá mbíonn an rothar?
[kaw me-uhn un ruh-her]

"It is outside." (habitually)
Bíonn sé amuigh.
[bee-uhn shay uh-muh]

"Where are Brian and Patricia every day?"
Cá mbíonn Brian agus Pádraigín gach lá?
[kaw me-uhn bree-uhn ah-gus paw-druh-geen gahkh law]

"They are usually inside."
Bíonn siad istigh de ghnáth.
[bee-uhn shee-ud iss-tchih deh ghuh-naw]

Lesson 98 – Where Do You Usually Go?

You can ask about people's habits by asking them where they usually go. To ask where people often go, sometimes go, or rarely go, you can use the *Bonus Phrase* "Where are you going?" and switch its verb for its habitual tense form.

"Where <u>are</u> you going?"
Cá bhfuil tú ag dul?
[kaw will too ehg dull]

"Where <u>do</u> you go?" (<u>habitually</u>)
Cá mbíonn tú ag dul?
[kaw me-uhn too ehg dull]

Remember, when you answer this question, which word you use for "to" depends upon the kind of place you're going.

Examples

"Where do you go?" (habitually)
Cá mbíonn tú ag dul?
[kaw me-uhn too ehg dull]

"I go to a hotel." (habitually)
Bíonn mé ag dul go h-óstán.
[bee-uhn may ehg dull guh hoess-tawn]

"Where does Patricia go?" (habitually)
Cá mbíonn Pádraigín ag dul?
[kaw me-uhn paw-druh-geen ehg dull]

"She often goes to the beach."
Bíonn sí ag dul go dtí an trá go minic.
[bee-uhn shee ehg dull guh jee un traw guh min-ik]

"Where do y'all go?" (habitually)
Cá mbíonn sibh ag dul?
[kaw me-uhn shiv ehg dull]

"We are always going to a party!"
Bíonn muid ag dul chuig cóisir i gcónaí!
[bee-uhn mwidj ehg dull khig koe-sher ih go-nee]

Conversation

Let's practice talking about going different places in the habitual tense with a conversation.

Pádraigín:
"Where do you go?"
Cá mbíonn tú ag dul?
[kaw me-uhn too ehg dull]

Brian:
"I often go to the restaurant."
Bíonn mé ag dul go dtí an bhialann go minic.
[bee-uhn may ehg dull guh jee un vee-uh-luhn guh min-ik]

Pádraigín:
"Aren't the streets there dirty?"
Nach mbíonn na sráideanna ansin salach?
[nahkh me-uhn nuh sroy-jin-uh un-shin sahl-ahkh]

Brian:
"Sometimes they are, but they're not usually dirty."
Bíonn siad uaireanta, ach ní bhíonn siad salach de ghnáth.
[bee-uhn shee-ud oor-en-tuh, akh nee vee-uhn shee-ud sahl-ahkh deh ghuh-naw]

Pádraigín:
"Is the restaurant clean?"
An mbíonn an bhialann glan?
[un me-uhn un vee-uh-luhn glon]

Brian:
"Yes. It's always clean inside."
Bíonn. Bíonn sí glan istigh i gcónaí.
[bee-uhn. bee-uhn shee glon iss-tchih ih go-nee]

"Where do Liam and Noreen usually go?"
Cá mbíonn Liam agus Noirín ag dul de ghnáth?
[kaw me-uhn lee-um ah-gus nor-een ehg dull deh ghuh-naw]

Pádraigín:
"They go to a movie from time to time."
Bíonn siad ag dul chuig scannán ó am go h-am.
[bee-uhn shee-ud ehg dull khig skuh-nawn oe ahm guh hahm]

Lesson 99 – There Is Another "Is"

You've learned a lot of Irish! You can build lots of sentences using different subjects, tenses, and turns of phrase. So far, almost all of the sentences you've learned use some form of "**tá**" [taw]. which means "is." Now, we'll learn about the other verb which means "is" in Irish.

Like many languages, Irish uses two different verbs for "to be." This way, you can make a distinction between *how* things are, and *what* things are. The Irish verb "**tá**" [taw] is used to *describe* things. The Irish verb "**is**" [iss] is used to *classify* and *identify* things.

The Verb "Is"

There is a special kind of verb called a *copula*, or *linking verb*, which connects two nouns. For example, if you say, "It is a table," both the words "it" and "table" are referring to the same thing. The verb simply connects these words which *classify* or *identify* a thing.

In Irish, *the copula* is "**is**" [iss], which means "is."

The Difference Between "Tá" and "Is"

For native speakers of English and other languages which use one verb for "to be," it helps to explain the differences between "**tá**" [taw] and "**is**" [iss]. "**Tá**" [taw] is used to *describe* a thing, while "**is**" [iss] is used to *classify* or *identify* a thing. We could also say that "**tá**" [taw] is used to explain the *state* of a thing, and "**is**" [iss] is used to explain the *essence* of a thing.

As an example, let's take a chair. We can say, "The chair is cold." That *describes* the state of the thing. We can also say, "It is a chair." That *classifies* the essence of the thing. Now we'll pretend that someone has sat down in the chair. We can then say, "The chair is warm." Once again, that *describes* the state of the thing, which has changed since we last checked. Even so, we can still say, "It is a chair," because the essence of the thing has not changed.

Classify Versus Identify

The word "**is**" [iss] is used when you *classify* or *identify* someone or something. You build a sentence differently when you *classify* someone or something versus when you *identify* someone or something, so it's helpful to understand the difference between the two. When you *classify* someone or something, you're saying that it's a type of thing. When you *identify* someone or something, you're saying that it's a specific thing.

Let's use a box as an example. When you say, "It is *a* box," you're *classifying* the object. You're saying that it's some kind of box. When you say, "It is *the* box," you're *identifying* the object. You're saying that it's a specific box.

In the next lesson, we'll learn how to *classify* things. Later, we'll learn how to *identify* them.

Lesson 100 – A Basic Classifying Sentence Using "Is"

We learned in Lesson 2 that verbs come first in basic Irish sentences. So, being a verb, "**is**" [iss] comes at the beginning of the sentence. Here is a simple sentence to *classify* what something is:

"It is a box."
Is bosca é.
[iss bus-kuh ay]

This sentence is constructed like this:

is [iss] = "is"
bosca [bus-kuh] = "a box"
é [ay] = "it"

Notice how the "it" comes last in the Irish sentence. The noun, "box," goes in between.

The Pronouns for "Is" Sentences

We also learned in Lesson 2 about *pronouns*, short words that stand for nouns, such as "I," "you," and "they." In Irish, these change form a little when using the *copula*, "**is**" [iss]. That's because we will be using a different kind of pronoun.

The pronouns we were using before were *subject pronouns*. Those are used when the *pronoun* is *doing* the action of the sentence. These new pronouns are *object pronouns*. These are used when the *pronoun* is *receiving* the action of the sentence.

The biggest differences are in the third-person pronouns: "he," "she," and "they." The *subject pronouns* for them are "**sé**" [shay], "**sí**" [shee], and "**siad**" [shee-ud]. When using "**is**" [iss], you need to use *object pronouns*, which simply drop the "**s**" off the front of these forms.

"he"
sé *becomes* **é**
[shay] *becomes* [ay]

"she"
sí *becomes* **í**
[shee] *becomes* [ee]

"they"
siad *becomes* **iad**
[shee-ud] *becomes* [ee-ud]

Here is a list of the *object pronouns* that go with sentences that use "**is**" [iss]:

"I"
mé
[may]

"we"
muid
[mwidj]

"you"
tú
[too]

"y'all"
sibh
[shiv]

"he"
é
[ay]

"they"
iad
[ee-ud]

"she"
í
[ee]

Lesson 101 – Making Basic Classifying Sentences Using "Is"

When making a basic, *classifying* sentence using "**is**" [iss], "is," we start with the verb, followed by a noun, and then by an object pronoun. For example:

"It is a table."
Is bord é.
[iss bord ay]

Remember that nouns have a gender in Irish, so the object pronoun will change depending on what you're *classifying*. For example:

"It is a chair."
Is cathaoir í.
[iss kah-heer ee]

As plural pronouns don't specify gender, you simply use the object pronoun "**iad**" [ee-ud], "they," for any plural noun spoken about in the third-person.

"They are boxes."
Is boscaí iad.
[iss bus-kee ee-ud]

Examples

"It is a window."
Is fuinneog í.
[iss fwin-yoeg ee]

"It is a book."
Is leabhar é.
[iss lyow-er ay]

"They are people."
Is daoine iad.
[iss dee-nuh ee-ud]

Lesson 102 – Making More Classifying Sentences Using "Is"

Because "**is**" [iss] sentences are very useful, and they follow a slightly different pattern than "**tá**" [taw] sentences, we're going to practice them with some new vocabulary.

Vocabulary

"a computer"
ríomhaire (m.)
[ree-ver-uh]

"a plate"
pláta (m.)
[plaw-tuh]

"computers"
ríomhairí
[ree-ver-ee]

"plates"
plátaí
[plaw-tee]

"a brush" or "a broom"
scuab (f.)
[skoo-uhb]

"a map"
léarscáil (f.)
[layr-skoyl]

"brushes" or "brooms"
scuaba
[skoo-uh-buh]

"maps"
léarscáileanna
[layr-skoyl-uh-nuh]

Examples

"It is a computer."
Is ríomhaire é.
[iss ree-ver-uh ay]

"They are computers."
Is ríomhairí iad.
[iss ree-ver-ee ee-ud]

"It is a brush."
Is scuab í.
[iss skoo-uhb ee]

"They are brooms."
Is scuaba iad.
[iss skoo-uh-buh ee-ud]

"It is a plate."
Is pláta é.
[iss plaw-tuh ay]

"They are plates."
Is plátaí iad.
[iss plaw-tee ee-ud]

"It is a map."
Is léarscáil í.
[iss layr-skoyl ee]

"They are maps."
Is léarscáileanna iad.
[iss layr-skoyl-uh-nuh ee-ud]

Lesson 103 – Classifying People

We learned how to *describe* people in Lesson 9. Now, we're going to practice *classifying* them. Remember, "**is**" [iss] is used to *classify* the essence of someone or something. For example, to say, "I am cold," you use "**tá**" [taw], because that's a temporary state, but if you say, "I am a person," you use "**is**" [iss], because you're always a person.

Vocabulary

"a person"
duine (m.)
[din-uh]

"a child"
páiste (m.)
[paw-stchuh]

"people"
daoine
[dee-nuh]

"children"
páistí
[paw-stchee]

"a man"
fear (m.)
[far]

"a boy"
buachaill (m.)
[boo-uh-khil]

"men"
fir
[fihr]

"boys"
buachaillí
[boo-uh-khulee]

"a woman"
bean (f.)
[ban]

"a girl"
cailín (m.)
[kall-yeen]

"women"
mná
[mraw]

"girls"
cailíní
[kall-yeen-ee]

Even though the word for "girl," "**cailín**" [kall-yeen], is grammatically masculine, girls are always referred to by their natural gender. So, unless you're looking for trouble, use "**í**" [ee] when talking about a girl!

Examples

"She is a person."
Is duine í.
[iss din-uh ee]

"He is a man."
Is fear é.
[iss far ay]

"They are women."
Is mná iad.
[iss mraw ee-ud]

"They are children."
Is páistí iad.
[iss paw-stchee ee-ud]

"He is a boy."
Is buachaill é.
[iss boo-uh-khil ay]

"She is a girl."
Is cailín í.
[iss kall-yeen ee]

Lesson 104 – Occupations

Another way you can *classify* a person is by stating their occupation. This also uses the "**is**" [iɜs] construction, because you are saying they are a kind of person.

Examples

We'll look at a few examples that use the word "**dalta**" [dahl-tuh], "a student," which is masculine (m.), and the plural, "students," "**daltaí**" [dahl-tee].

"I am a student."
Is dalta mé.
[iss dahl-tuh may]

"She is a student."
Is dalta í.
[iss dahl-tuh ee]

"They are students."
Is daltaí iad.
[iss dahl-tee ee-ud]

Vocabulary

"a teacher" **múinteoir** (m.) [moon-chor]	"doctor" **dochtúir** (m.) [dokh-toor]	"a secretary" **rúnaí** (m.) [roo-nee]	"an engineer" **innealtóir** (m.) [in-yil-tor]
"teachers" **múinteoirí** [moon-chor-ee]	"doctors" **dochtúirí** [dokh-toor-ee]	"secretaries" **rúnaithe** [roo-nee-heh]	"engineers" **innealtóirí** [in-yil-tor-ee]
"a musician" **ceoltóir** (m.) [kyoel-tor]	"a dentist" **fiaclóir** (m.) [fee-uh-klor]	"a server" "(a waiter/a waitress)" **freastalaí** (m.) [fras-tuh-lee]	"a mechanic" **meicneoir** (m.) [mek-nyor]
"musicians" **ceoltóirí** [kyoel-tor-ee]	"dentists" **fiaclóirí** [fee-uh-klor-ee]	"servers" "(waiters/waitresses)" **freastalaithe** [fras-tuh-lee-huh]	"mechanics" **meicneoirí** [mek-nyor-ee]

Examples

"I am a teacher."
Is múinteoir mé.
[iss moon-chor may]

"You are a musician."
Is ceoltóir tú.
[iss kyoel-tor too]

"He is a doctor."
Is dochtúir é.
[iss dokh-toor ay]

"She is a dentist."
Is fiaclóir í.
[iss fee-uh-klor ee]

"We are secretaries."
Is rúnaithe muid.
[iss roo-nee-heh mwidj]

"Y'all are servers."
Is freastalaithe sibh.
[iss fras-tuh-lee-huh shiv]

"They are engineers."
Is innealtóirí iad.
[iss in-yil-tor-ee ee-ud]

"She is a mechanic."
Is meicneoir í.
[iss mek-nyor ee]

Lesson 105 – Classifying Named People

When you *classify* people, you may also want to be specific about who it is you're talking about. To name someone when you *classify* them using an "**is**" [iss] sentence, say their name, or names, after the appropriate pronoun. In English, we drop the pronoun and just say the name, but, in Irish, we say them both.

Examples

We'll compare some sentences that don't use a name to some that do:

"He is a teacher"
Is múinteoir é.
[iss moon-chor ay]

"Brian is a teacher."
Is múinteoir é Brian.
[iss moon-chor ay bree-uhn]

"She is a teacher."
Is múinteoir í.
[iss moon-chor ee]

"Patricia is a teacher."
Is múinteoir í Pádraigín.
[iss moon-chor ee paw-druh-geen]

"They are teachers."
Is múinteoirí iad.
[iss moon-chor-ee ee-ud]

"Brian and Patricia are teachers."
Is múinteoirí iad Brian agus Pádraigín.
[iss moon-chor-ee ee-ud bree-uhn ah-gus paw-druh-geen]

Notice that the pronouns are still included when you say the names.

Lesson 106 – Classifying a Specific Thing

You can also *classify* specific things using an "**is**" [iss] sentence. For example, you can say, "The woman is a doctor." You're saying that the specific woman is a type of person – a doctor. This sentence is built similarly to when you *classify* a named person, as we learned in Lesson 105.

"The woman is a doctor."
Is dochtúir í an bhean.
[iss dokh-toor ee un van]

Notice that we still keep the pronoun, "**í**" [ee]. This is like keeping the pronoun when using a person's name. Be careful that the pronoun matches the subject of your sentence. In this case, "**í**" [ee] matches "**an bhean**" [un van].

Vocabulary

"a fruit"
toradh (m.)
[tor-uh]

"a dish"
soitheach (m.)
[suh-hahkh]

"fruits"
torthaí
[tor-hee]

"dishes"
soithí
[suh-hee]

Examples

"The man is a dentist."
Is fiaclóir é an fear.
[iss fee-uh-klor ay un far]

"The girl is a student."
Is dalta í an cailín.
[iss dahl-tuh ee un kall-yeen]

"The women are people."
Is daoine iad na mná.
[iss dee-nuh ee-ud nuh mraw]

"The engineers are women."
Is mná iad na h-innealtóirí.
[iss mraw ee-ud nuh hin-yil-tor-ee]

"The children are boys."
Is buachaillí iad na páistí.
[iss boo-uh-khulee ee-ud nuh paw-stchee]

"The servers and the musicians are men."
Is fir iad na freastalaithe agus na ceoltóirí.
[iss fihr ee-ud nuh fras-tuh-lee-huh ah-gus nuh kyoel-tor-ee]

"The apple is a fruit."
Is toradh é an t-úll.
[iss tor-uh ay un tool]

"The plates are dishes."
Is soithí iad na plátaí.
[iss suh-hee ee-ud nuh plaw-tee]

Lesson 107 – Classifying with Possessives

Sometimes when you're *classifying* a person or thing, you want to say who or what they are in relation to someone or something else. You can use the possessive pronouns to express this. Possessive pronouns work just as they did before. It doesn't matter whether the possessive is in a "**tá**" [taw] sentence or an "**is**" [iss] sentence. To review possessive pronouns, see Lesson 25.

Examples

"My doctor is a woman."
Is bean í mo dhochtúir.
[iss ban ee muh ghokh-toor]

"Your teacher is a man."
Is fear é do mhúinteoir.
[iss far ay duh woon-chor]

"Our students are children."
Is páistí iad ár ndaltaí.
[iss paw-stchee ee-ud awr nahl-tee]

"Her apple is a fruit."
Is toradh é a h-úll.
[iss tor-uh ay uh hool]

"Their plates are dishes."
Is soithí iad a bplátaí.
[iss suh-hee ee-ud uh blaw-tee]

Lesson 108 – Classifying What It Is Not

Sometimes, you'll want to *classify* something by saying what it is not. You can make an "**is**" [iss] sentence negative by switching out the word "**is**" [iss] for its negative form. The negative form of "**is**" [iss] is "**ní**" [nee].

Let's take a look at an "**is**" [iss] sentence in the positive and in the negative to compare:

"He <u>is</u> a student."
Is dalta é.
[iss dahl-tuh ay]

"He <u>is not</u> a student."
Ní dalta é.
[nee dahl-tuh ay]

Examples

"I am not a mechanic."
Ní meicneoir mé.
[nee mek-nyor may]

"You are not an engineer."
Ní innealtóir tú.
[nee in-yil-tor too]

"He is not a server."
Ní freastalaí é.
[nee fras-tuh-lee ay]

"She is not a secretary."
Ní rúnaí í.
[nee roo-nee ee]

"We are not dentists."
Ní fiaclóirí muid.
[nee fee-uh-klor-ee mwidj]

"Y'all are not musicians."
Ní ceoltóirí sibh.
[nee kyoel-tor-ee shiv]

"They are not teachers."
Ní múinteoirí iad.
[nee moon-chor-ee ee-ud]

"Brian is not a girl."
Ní cailín é Brian.
[nee kall-yeen ay bree-uhn]

"Patricia is not a boy."
Ní buachaill í Pádraigín.
[nee boo-uh-khil ee paw-druh-geen]

"Brian and Patricia are not children."
Ní páistí iad Brian agus Pádraigín.
[nee paw-stchee ee-ud bree-uhn ah-gus paw-druh-geen]

"It is not a computer."
Ní ríomhaire é.
[nee ree-ver-uh ay]

"They are not boxes."
Ní boscaí iad.
[nee bus-kee ee-ud]

"The student is not a doctor."
Ní dochtúir é an dalta.
[nee dokh-toor ay un dahl-tuh]

Notice that in this case, the student is male. You can tell because of the pronoun "**é**" [ay].

"The musician is not a secretary."
Ní rúnaí í an ceoltóir.
[nee roo-nee ee un kyoel-tor]

Notice that in this case, the musician is a female. You can tell because of the pronoun "**í**" [ee].

"The knife is not a plate."
Ní pláta í an scian.
[nee plaw-tuh ee un shkee-un]

Notice that the pronoun "**í**" [ee] matches the grammatical gender of "**an scian**" [un shkee-un].

"The plate is not a knife."
Ní scian é an pláta.
[nee shkee-un ay un plaw-tuh]

Notice that the pronoun "**é**" [ay] matches the grammatical gender of "**an pláta**" [un plaw-tuh].

Lesson 109 – Asking Positive Classifying Questions

To ask a question with an "**is**" [iss] sentence, switch out the word "**is**" [iss] for its question form. The question form of "**is**" [iss] is "**an**" [un].

Let's take a look at an "**is**" [iss] statement and a question to compare:

"He is a student."
Is dalta é.
[iss dahl-tuh ay]

"Is he a student?"
An dalta é?
[un dahl-tuh ay]

Examples

"Am I musician?"
An ceoltóir mé?
[un kyoel-tor may]

"Are you a doctor?"
An dochtúir tú?
[un dokh-toor too]

"Is he a teacher?"
An múinteoir é?
[un moon-chor ay]

"Is she a mechanic?"
An meicneoir í?
[un mek-nyor ee]

"Are we men?"
An fir muid?
[un fihr mwidj]

"Are y'all servers?"
An freastalaithe sibh?
[un fras-tuh-lee-huh shiv]

"Are they brooms?"
An scuaba iad?
[un skoo-uh-buh ee-ud]

"Is it a pen?"
An peann é?
[un pyawn ay]

"Is it a map?"
An léarscáil í?
[un layr-skoyl ee]

"Is Brian an engineer?"
An innealtóir é Brian?
[un in-yil-tor ay bree-uhn]

"Is Patricia a dentist?"
An fiaclóir í Pádraigín?
[un fee-uh-klor ee paw-druh-geen]

"Are Brian and Patricia secretaries?"
An rúnaithe iad Brian agus Pádraigín?
[un roo-nee-heh ee-ud bree-uhn ah-gus paw-druh-geen]

"Is the book a map?"
An léarscáil é an leabhar?
[un layr-skoyl ay un lyow-er]

"Are the children girls?"
An cailíní iad na páistí?
[un kall-yeen-ee ee-ud nuh paw-stchee]

Lesson 110 – Asking Negative Classifying Questions

To ask a negative question with an "**is**" [iss] sentence, switch out the word "**is**" [iss] for its negative question form. The negative question form of "**is**" [iss] is "**nach**" [nahkh].

Let's take a look at an "**is**" [iss] statement and a negative question to compare:

"He is a student."
Is dalta é.
[iss dahl-tuh ay]

"Isn't he a student?"
Nach dalta é?
[nahkh dahl-tuh ay]

Examples

"Aren't I a secretary?"
Nach rúnaí mé?
[nahkh roo-nee may]

"Aren't you a mechanic?"
Nach meicneoir tú?
[nahkh mek-nyor too]

"Isn't he a musician?"
Nach ceoltóir é?
[nahkh kyoel-tor ay]

"Isn't she a dentist?"
Nach fiaclóir í?
[nahkh fee-uh-klor ee]

"Aren't we people?"
Nach daoine muid?
[nahkh dee-nuh mwidj]

"Aren't y'all engineers?"
Nach innealtóirí sibh?
[nahkh in-yil-tor-ee shiv]

"Aren't they doctors?"
Nach dochtúirí iad?
[nahkh dokh-toor-ee ee-ud]

"Isn't it an apple?"
Nach úll é?
[nahkh ool ay]

"Isn't it a chair?"
Nach cathaoir í?
[nahkh kah-heer ee]

' Isn't Patricia a woman?"
Nach bean í Pádraigín?
[nahkh ban ee paw-druh-geen]

"Isn't Brian a man?"
Nach fear é Brian?
[nahkh far ay bree-uhn]

"Aren't Brian and Patricia teachers?"
Nach múinteoirí iad Brian agus Pádraigín?
[nahkh moon-chor-ee ee-ud bree-uhn ah-gus paw-druh-geen]

"Isn't the student a girl?"
Nach cailín í an dalta?
[nahkh kall-yeen ee un dahl-tuh]

"Isn't the man a dentist?"
Nach fiaclóir é an fear?
[nahkh fee-uh-klor ay un far]

"Aren't the musicians boys?"
Nach buachaillí iad na ceoltóirí?
[nahkh boo-uh-khulee ee-ud nuh kyoel-tor-ee]

Lesson 111 – Answering Classifying Questions About Singulars

As we learned when working with all the tenses of "**tá**" [taw], there is no simple word for "yes" or "no" in Irish. You repeat the positive or negative form of the verb that was asked.

Because "**is**" [iss] is used when stating the nature of a thing, there's a slight difference when you answer with it. When answering "**is**" [iss] questions, you must include the "he," "she," or "it."

So far, we've been *classifying* things, like, "It is *a* computer," "I am *a* student," and so forth. We use a special pronoun for "he," "she," or "it" when answering a *classifying* question. This word is "**ea**" [a (like the word "at")], which has no gender, and it goes after the positive or negative forms of the verb, "**is**" [iss] or "**ní**" [nee].

"Yes" & "No" for *Classifying* "Is" Questions

To give a positive answer to a *classifying* "**is**" [iss] question, you say:

"Yes."
Is ea.
[sha]

You can pronounce this [iss a], but, as with anything that's said a lot, most people run these words together, so it's said [sha]. In fact, you'll often see it written as one word with an apostrophe in front of it: '**Sea** [sha].

For a negative answer to a *classifying* "**is**" [iss] question, you say:

"No."
Ní h-ea.
[nee ha]

Notice that there is an "**h-**" added to "**ea**" [a (like the word "at")] to make it easier to say.

Examples

"Is it a computer?"
An ríomhaire é?
[un ree-ver-uh ay]

"Yes."   "No."
Is ea.   **Ní h-ea.**
[sha]   [nee ha]

"Is it a brush?"
An scuab í?
[un skoo-uhb ee]

"Yes."   "No."
Is ea.   **Ní h-ea.**
[sha]   [nee ha]

"Is he a musician?"
An ceoltóir é?
[un kyoel-tor ay]

"Yes."   "No."
Is ea.   **Ní h-ea.**
[sha]   [nee ha]

"Is she an engineer?"
An innealtóir í?
[un in-yil-tor ee]

"Yes."   "No."
Is ea.   **Ní h-ea.**
[sha]   [nee ha]

"Are you a student?"
An dalta tú?
[un dahl-tuh too]

"Yes."   "No."
Is ea.   **Ní h-ea.**
[sha]   [nee ha]

"Is Brian a mechanic?"
An meicneoir é Brian?
[un mek-nyor ay bree-uhn]

"Yes."   "No."
Is ea.   **Ní h-ea.**
[sha]   [nee ha]

"Is the child a boy?"
An buachaill é an páiste?
[un boo-uh-khil ay un paw-stchuh]

"Yes."   "No."
Is ea.   **Ní h-ea.**
[sha]   [nee ha]

Lesson 112 – Answering Classifying Questions About Plurals

As we've seen, "**is**" [iss] is stating the nature of a thing, so you can't leave out the "it" when answering. This is also the case when answering for "they."

To answer *classifying* questions about plurals, you use the same word we used for singulars, "**ea**" [a (like the word "at")]. This special pronoun is used for both singular nouns, regardless of gender, as well as for plural nouns. It is only used along with the *copula* in certain phrases.

To give a positive or negative answer to a *classifying* "**is**" [iss] question, you say:

"Yes."
Is ea.
[sha]

"No."
Ní h-ea.
[nee ha]

Note that you will sometimes hear people using "**Is ea**" [sha] and "**Ní h-ea**" [nee ha] as general phrases for "yes" and "no." This is something to be aware of, but it's not a good habit to pick up. You should always use the positive or negative of whatever verb you were asked when answering questions with "yes" or "no."

Examples

"Are they plates?"
An plátaí iad?
[un plaw-tee ee-ud]

"Yes."   "No."
Is ea.   **Ní h-ea.**
[sha]   [nee ha]

"Are they maps?"
An léarscáileanna iad?
[un layr-skoyl-uh-nuh ee-ud]

"Yes."   "No."
Is ea.   **Ní h-ea.**
[sha]   [nee ha]

"Are they servers?"
An freastalaithe iad?
[un fras-tuh-lee-huh ee-ud]

"Yes."	"No."
Is ea.	**Ní h-ea.**
[sha]	[nee ha]

"Are Brian and Patricia dentists?"
An fiaclóirí iad Brian agus Pádraigín?
[un fee-uh-klor-ee ee-ud bree-uhn ah-gus paw-druh-geen]

"Yes."	"No."
Is ea.	**Ní h-ea.**
[sha]	[nee ha]

"Are the servers men?"
An fir iad na freastalaithe?
[un fihr ee-ud nuh fras-tuh-lee-huh]

"Yes."	"No."
Is ea.	**Ní h-ea.**
[sha]	[nee ha]

Lesson 113 – Expanding Your Answers

If you want to say more than just "yes," or "no," you can add a full sentence to your answer. Remember, in Irish, you have to repeat the verb before saying the complete sentence. This is true with all verbs, including "**is**" [iss].

Examples

"Is it a computer?"
An ríomhaire é?
[un ree-ver-uh ay]

"Yes, it's a computer."
Is ea. Is ríomhaire é.
[sha. iss ree-ver-uh ay]

"No, it isn't a computer."
Ní h-ea. Ní ríomhaire é.
[nee ha. nee ree-ver-uh ay]

"Is it a brush?"
An scuab í?
[un skoo-uhb ee]

"Yes, it's a brush."
Is ea. Is scuab í.
[sha. iss skoo-uhb ee]

"No, it isn't a brush."
Ní h-ea. Ní scuab í.
[nee ha. nee skoo-uhb ee]

"Is it a plate?"
An pláta é?
[un plaw-tuh ay]

"Yes, it's a plate."
Is ea. Is pláta é.
[sha. iss plaw-tuh ay]

"No, it's a map."
Ní h-ea. Is léarscáil í.
[nee ha. iss layr-skoyl ee]

"Are they plates?"
An plátaí iad?
[un plaw-tee ee-ud]

"Yes, they're plates."
Is ea. Is plátaí iad.
[sha. iss plaw-tee ee-ud]

"No, they aren't plates."
Ní h-ea. Ní plátaí iad.
[nee ha. nee plaw-tee ee-ud]

"Are they maps?"
An léarscáileanna iad?
[un layr-skoyl-uh-nuh ee-ud]

"Yes, they're maps."
Is ea. Is léarscáileanna iad.
[sha. iss layr-skoyl-uh-nuh ee-ud]

"No, they aren't maps."
Ní h-ea. Ní léarscáileanna iad.
[nee ha. nee layr-skoyl-uh-nuh ee-ud]

"Are they brushes?"
An scuaba iad?
[un skoo-uh-buh ee-ud]

"Yes, they're brushes."
Is ea. Is scuaba iad.
[sha. iss skoo-uh-buh ee-ud]

"No, they're computers."
Ní h-ea. Is ríomhairí iad.
[nee ha. iss ree-ver-ee ee-ud]

"Is she an engineer?"
An innealtóir í?
[un in-yil-tor ee]

"Yes, she is an engineer."
Is ea. Is innealtóir í.
[sha. iss in-yil-tor ee]

"No, she isn't an engineer."
Ní h-ea. Ní innealtóir í.
[nee ha. nee in-yil-tor ee]

"Are you a student?"
An dalta tú?
[un dahl-tuh too]

"Yes, I am a student."
Is ea. Is dalta mé.
[sha. iss dahl-tuh may]

"No, I am not a student."
Ní h-ea. Ní dalta mé.
[nee ha. nee dahl-tuh may]

"Is Brian a mechanic?"
An meicneoir é Brian?
[un mek-nyor ay bree-uhn]

"Yes, he is a mechanic."
Is ea. Is meicneoir é.
[sha. iss mek-nyor ay]

"No, he isn't a mechanic."
Ní h-ea. Ní meicneoir é.
[nee ha. nee mek-nyor ay]

"Is the child a boy?"
An buachaill é an páiste?
[un boo-uh-khil ay un paw-stchuh]

"Yes, he is a boy."
Is ea. Is buachaill é.
[sha. iss boo-uh-khil ay]

"No. The child is a girl."
Ní h-ea. Is cailín í an páiste.
[nee ha. iss kall-yeen ee un paw-stchuh]

Conversation

Now we'll practice what we've learned about *classifying* people with a conversation.

Brian:
"Is Liam a server?"
An freastalaí é Liam?
[un fras-tuh-lee ay lee-um]

Pádraigín:
"No. He's not a server."
Ní h-ea. Ní freastalaí é.
[nee ha. nee fras-tuh-lee ay]

"He's a musician."
Is ceoltóir é.
[iss kyoel-tor ay]

Brian:
"Isn't Noreen a musician, too?"
Nach ceoltóir í Noirín, freisin?
[nahkh kyoel-tor ee nor-een, fresh-in]

Pádraigín:
"Yes. She's a musician."
Is ea. Is ceoltóir í.
[sha. iss kyoel-tor ee]

Brian:
"Are Liam and Noreen teachers, also?"
An múinteoirí iad Liam agus Noirín, freisin?
[un moon-chor-ee ee-ud lee-um ah-gus nor-een, fresh-in]

Pádraigín:
"No. They're not teachers, but they are students."
Ní h-ea. Ní múinteoirí iad, ach is daltaí iad.
[nee ha. nee moon-chor-ee ee-ud, akh iss dahl-tee ee-ud]

Lesson 114 – Asking "What Is It?"

When asking about the nature of things, you may not know what the thing is at all. To ask what something is, you can say:

"What is it?"
Céard é?
[kayrd ay]

This sentence is constructed like this:

céard [kayrd] = "what"
é [ay] = "it"

You'll notice that there's no form of the verb "**is**" [iss] in this question, but that's okay. The question word "**céard**" [kayrd], "what," implies that you mean "what is."

You will also notice that the masculine "it," "**é**" [ay], is used. If you don't know what something is, it's okay to just say "**é**" [ay], because you can't guess if the word for it will be masculine or feminine until somebody answers you.

To ask what many things are, you simply switch the word for "it," "**é**" [ay], with the word for "they," "**iad**" [ee-ud].

"What are they?"
Céard iad?
[kayrd ee-ud]

Once again, there's no form of the verb "**is**" [iss], because the question word "**céard**" [kayrd], "what," implies "what are."

Answering "What Is It?"

To answer a "What is it?" question, all you have to do is say a simple "**is**" [iss] statement.

Examples

"What is it?"
Céard é?
[kayrd ay]

"It's a table."
Is bord é.
[iss bord ay]

"What is it?"
Céard é?
[kayrd ay]

"It's a chair."
Is cathaoir í.
[iss kah-heer ee]

"What are they?"
Céard iad?
[kayrd ee-ud]

"They're boxes."
Is boscaí iad.
[iss bus-kee ee-ud]

Lesson 115 – Identifying Things With "Is"

So far, we've been *classifying* nouns with "**is**" [iss]. A basic "**is**" [iss] sentence changes a little, however, when *identifying* things.

Let's review the difference between *classifying* and *identifying* something. We'll use a box as an example. When you say, "It is *a* box," you're *classifying* the object. You're saying that it's some kind of box. When you say, "It is *the* box," you're *identifying* the object. You're saying that it's a specific box.

In this and the next five lessons, we'll learn how to *identify* things while referring to them in the third-person. Remember that "he," "she," and "they" are "**é**" [ay], "**í**" [ee], and "**iad**" [ee-ud] in these kinds of "**is**" [iss] sentences. When you're *identifying* something in the third-person with an "**is**" [iss] sentence, you use the third-person pronoun twice in the sentence. It still comes after the noun at the end of the sentence, and it also shows up at the beginning, right after the word "**is**" [iss]. This "echoing" pronoun that comes right after the *copula* is referred to as a *proleptic pronoun* in more complicated grammar books.

Examples

Let's compare a *classifying* sentence and an *identifying* sentence:

"*It* is <u>a book</u>." (*classifying*)
Is <u>leabhar</u> *é*.
[iss lyow-er ay]

"*It* is <u>the book</u>." (*identifying*)
Is é <u>an leabhar</u> *é*.
[shay un lyow-er ay]

Notice how the first two words of the last sentence are run together when you say them. This is like what we saw in Lesson 111 with the answer "**is ea**" [sha]. It's okay to say these words separately, but, as with anything that's said a lot, most people run these words together.

The same repetition of "it" is true of sentences with feminine nouns:

"*It* is <u>a key</u>." (*classifying*)
Is <u>eochair</u> *í*.
[iss ukh-er ee]

"*It* is <u>the key</u>." (*identifying*)
Is í <u>an eochair</u> *í*.
[shee un ukh-er ee]

Finally, we see the same pattern of repeating the pronoun "they" with plural nouns:

"*They* are <u>boxes</u>." (*classifying*)
Is <u>boscaí</u> *iad*.
[iss bus-kee ee-ud]

"*They* are <u>the boxes</u>." (*identifying*)
Is iad <u>na boscaí</u> *iad*.
[shee-ud nuh bus-kee ee-ud]

In all three *identifying* examples, a pronoun follows the word "**is**" [iss]. Remembering this guideline will help you build correct *identifying* "**is**" [iss] sentences.

Examples

"It is the bicycle."
Is é an rothar é.
[shay un ruh-her ay]

"It is the window."
Is í an fhuinneog í.
[shee un in-yoeg ee]

"They are the tables."
Is iad na boird iad.
[shee-ud nuh bweerj ee-ud]

"It is the computer."
Is é an ríomhaire é.
[shay un ree-ver-uh ay]

"It is the map."
Is í an léarscáil í.
[shee un layr-skoyl ee]

"They are the brushes."
Is iad na scuaba iad.
[shee-ud nuh skoo-uh-buh ee-ud]

Lesson 116 – Identifying What It Is Not

To make a negative *identifying* statement, you replace the word "**is**" [iss] with its negative statement form, which is "**ní**" [nee]. When "**é**" [ay], "**í**" [ee], or "**iad**" [ee-ud] come immediately after the negative "**ní**" [nee], you add an "**h-**" to the front of them to make them easier to say.

Examples

Let's look at some negative *identifying* statements that use the pronouns "he," "she," or "they":

"It is not the book."
Ní h-é an leabhar é.
[nee hay un lyow-er ay]

"It is not the key."
Ní h-í an eochair í.
[nee hee un ukh-er ee]

"They are not the boxes."
Ní h-iad na boscaí iad.
[nee hee-ud nuh bus-kee ee-ud]

"It isn't the door."
Ní h-é an doras é.
[nee hay un dor-us ay]

"It isn't the chair."
Ní h-í an chathaoir í.
[nee hee un khah-heer ee]

"They aren't the spoons."
Ní h-iad na spúnóga iad.
[nee hee-ud nuh spoo-noeg-uh ee-ud]

Lesson 117 – Asking Identifying Questions

Positive *Identifying* Questions

Asking *identifying* questions is as easy as making *identifying* statements. To make a positive *identifying* question, you switch out "**is**" [iss] with its positive question form, "**an**" [un].

Examples

Let's look at some positive *identifying* questions that use the pronouns "he," "she," or "they,":

"Is it the book?"
An é an leabhar é?
[un ay un lyow-er ay]

"Is it the key?"
An í an eochair í?
[un ee un ukh-er ee]

"Are they the boxes?"
An iad na boscaí iad?
[un ee-ud nuh bus-kee ee-ud]

Negative *Identifying* Questions

When asking a negative *identifying* question, you switch out "**is**" [iss] with its negative question form, "**nach**" [nahkh].

EXAMPLES

Let's look at some negative *identifying* questions that use the pronouns "he," "she," or "they,":

"Isn't it the book?"
Nach é an leabhar é?
[nahkh ay un lyow-er ay]

"Isn't it the key?"
Nach í an eochair í?
[nahkh ee un ukh-er ee]

"Aren't they the boxes?"
Nach iad na boscaí iad?
[nahkh ee-ud nuh bus-kee ee-ud]

Lesson 118 – Answering Identifying Questions

When we answered *classifying* questions in Lesson 111, we used a special pronoun for "he," "she," or "it" when answering. Now that we're *identifying* things, we answer using the regular pronouns that go with "**is**" [iss] sentences: the masculine "**é**" [ay], the feminine "**í**" [ee], or the plural "**iad**" [ee-ud].

So, answering "yes" or "no" to an *identifying* question is just like starting an ordinary positive or negative *identifying* statement, except that you stop after the "he," "she," "it," or "they."

For a positive answer to an *identifying* question, you say:

"Yes."
Is é.
[shay]

"Yes."
Is í.
[shee]

"Yes."
Is iad.
[shee-ud]

For a negative answer to an *identifying* question, you say:

"No."
Ní h-é.
[nee hay]

"No."
Ní h-í.
[nee hee]

"No."
Ní h-iad.
[nee hee-ud]

Be sure that your answer matches the pronoun that you were asked about.

Examples

"Is it the book?"
An é an leabhar é?
[un ay un lyow-er ay]

"Yes."   "No."
Is é.   **Ní h-é.**
[shay]   [nee hay]

"Is it the key?"
An í an eochair í?
[un ee un ukh-er ee]

"Yes."   "No."
Is í.   **Ní h-í.**
[shee]   [nee hee]

"Are they the boxes?"
An iad na boscaí iad?
[un ee-ud nuh bus-kee ee-ud]

"Yes."   "No."
Is iad.   **Ní h-iad.**
[shee-ud]   [nee hee-ud]

"Isn't it the apple?"
Nach é an t-úll é?
[nahkh ay un tool ay]

"Yes."   "No."
Is é.   **Ní h-é.**
[shay]   [nee hay]

"Isn't it the street?"
Nach í an tsráid í?
[nahkh ee un troyj ee]

"Yes."   "No."
Is í.   **Ní h-í.**
[shee]   [nee hee]

"Aren't they the plates?"
Nach iad na plátaí iad?
[nahkh ee-ud nuh plaw-tee ee-ud]

"Yes."   "No."
Is iad.   **Ní h-iad.**
[shee-ud]   [nee hee-ud]

Lesson 119 – Expanding Your Answers

You can say more than just "yes" or "no" by adding a full sentence to your answer. Remember to repeat the verbal phrase before saying the complete sentence.

Examples

"Is it the book?"
An é an leabhar é?
[un ay un lyow-er ay]

"Yes, it is the book."
Is é. Is é an leabhar é.
[shay. shay un lyow-er ay]

"Is it the key?"
An í an eochair í?
[un ee un ukh-er ee]

"No, it is not the key."
Ní h-í. Ní h-í an eochair í.
[nee hee. nee hee un ukh-er ee]

"Are they the boxes?"
An iad na boscaí iad?
[un ee-ud nuh bus-kee ee-ud]

"Yes, they are the boxes."
Is iad. Is iad na boscaí iad.
[shee-ud. shee-ud nuh bus-kee ee-ud]

"Isn't it the apple?"
Nach é an t-úll é?
[nahkh ay un tool ay]

"No, it isn't the apple."
Ní h-é. Ní h-é an t-úll é.
[nee hay. nee hay un tool ay]

"Isn't it the street?"
Nach í an tsráid í?
[nahkh ee un troyj ee]

"Yes, it is the street."
Is í. Is í an tsráid í.
[shee. shee un troyj ee]

"Aren't they the plates?"
Nach iad na plátaí iad?
[nahkh ee-ud nuh plaw-tee ee-ud]

"No, they are the knives."
Ní h-iad. Is iad na sceana iad.
[nee hee-ud. shee-ud nuh shkyah-nuh ee-ud]

Conversation

Now we'll practice what we've learned about *identifying* things with a conversation.

Pádraigín:
"I have something."
Tá rud éigin agam.
[taw ruhd ay-gihn ah-gum]

Brian:
"What is it?"
Céard é?
[kayrd ay]

"Is it the book?"
An é an leabhar é?
[un ay un lyow-er ay]

Pádraigín:
"No. It's not the book."
Ní h-é. Ní h-é an leabhar é.
[nee hay. nee hay un lyow-er ay]

Brian:
"Is it the map?"
An í an léarscáil í?
[un ee un layr-skoyl ee]

Pádraigín:
"Yes. It's the map."
Is í. Is í an léarscáil í.
[shee. shee un layr-skoyl ee]

Brian:
"I have something, too."
Tá rud éigin agam, freisin.
[taw ruhd ay-gihn ah-gum, fresh-in]

Pádraigín:
"Isn't it the key?"
Nach í an eochair í?
[nahkh ee un ukh-er ee]

Brian:
"Yes. It's the key."
Is í. Is í an eochair í.
[shee. shee un ukh-er ee]

Lesson 120 – Identifying People with "He," "She," and "They"

We learned how to *classify* people using "**is**" [iss] in Lesson 103. You can also use "**is**" [iss] to *identify* "the" person or "the" people. When we use the third-person pronouns "he," "she," or "they," *identifying* people is done in the same way as we saw when *identifying* things in Lesson 115.

Examples

Let's compare some *classifying* sentences and some *identifying* sentences:

"*He* is <u>a musician</u>." (*classifying*)
Is <u>ceoltóir</u> *é.*
[iss kyoel-tor ay]

"*He* is <u>the musician</u>." (*identifying*)
Is é <u>an ceoltóir</u> *é.*
[shay un kyoel-tor ay]

"*She* is <u>a musician</u>." (*classifying*)
Is <u>ceoltóir</u> *í.*
[iss kyoel-tor ee]

"*She* is <u>the musician</u>." (*identifying*)
Is í <u>an ceoltóir</u> *í.*
[shee un kyoel-tor ee]

"*They* are <u>musicians</u>." (*classifying*)
Is <u>ceoltóirí</u> *iad.*
[iss kyoel-tor-ee ee-ud]

"*They* are <u>the musicians</u>." (*identifying*)
Is iad <u>na ceoltóirí</u> *iad.*
[shee-ud nuh kyoel-tor-ee ee-ud]

Notice that the "**é**" [ay], "**í**" [ee], and "**iad**" [ee-ud] are repeated, just like they were when *identifying* things.

Identifying People with All Forms of "Is" [iss]

Just like with things, you can make *identifying* sentences about people using all the forms of "**is**" [iss], as well.

Examples

"He is not the mechanic."
Ní h-é an meicneoir é.
[nee hay un mek-nyor ay]

"She is not the student."
Ní h-í an dalta í.
[nee hee un dahl-tuh ee]

"They are not the servers."
Ní h-iad na freastalaithe iad.
[nee hee-ud nuh fras-tuh-lee-huh ee-ud]

"Is he the teacher?"
An é an múinteoir é?
[un ay un moon-chor ay]

"Is she the dentist?"
An í an fiaclóir í?
[un ee un fee-uh-klor ee]

"Are they the secretaries?"
An iad na rúnaithe iad?
[un ee-ud nuh roo-nee-heh ee-ud]

"Isn't he the engineer?"
Nach é an t-innealtóir é?
[nahkh ay un tin-yil-tor ay]

"Isn't she the musician?"
Nach í an ceoltóir í?
[nahkh ee un kyoel-tor ee]

"Aren't they the doctors?"
Nach iad na dochtúirí iad?
[nahkh ee-ud nuh dokh-toor-ee ee-ud]

Lesson 121 – Identifying People with "I," "You," "We," and "Y'all"

When talking about other people, you use the same sentence structure as when talking about things. However, when talking directly to people or about yourself, the pattern changes a little. When using "I," "you," "we," or "y'all," you don't use the pronoun at the end of the sentence. You only say the pronoun after "**is**" [iss].

Examples

Let's compare some *classifying* sentences in the first- or second-person to some *identifying* sentences in the first- or second-person:

"*I* am <u>an engineer</u>." (*classifying*)
Is <u>innealtóir</u> *mé*.
[iss in-yil-tor may]

"*I* am <u>the engineer</u>." (*identifying*)
Is *mé* **<u>an t-innealtóir</u>**.
[iss may un tin-yil-tor]

"*You* are <u>an engineer</u>." (*classifying*)
Is <u>innealtóir</u> *tú*.
[iss in-yil-tor too]

"*You* are <u>the engineer</u>." (*identifying*)
Is *tú* **<u>an t-innealtóir</u>**.
[iss too un tin-yil-tor]

"*We* are <u>engineers</u>." (*classifying*)
Is <u>innealtóirí</u> *muid*.
[iss in-yil-tor-ee mwidj]

"*We* are <u>the engineers</u>." (*identifying*)
Is *muid* **<u>na h-innealtóirí</u>**.
[iss mwidj nuh hin-yil-tor-ee]

"*Y'all* are <u>engineers</u>." (*classifying*)
Is <u>innealtóirí</u> *sibh*.
[iss in-yil-tor-ee shiv]

"*Y'all* are <u>the engineers</u>." (*identifying*)
Is *sibh* **na h-innealtóirí.**
[iss shiv nuh hin-yil-tor-ee]

Notice that the first- and second-person pronouns appear after "**is**" [iss] in the *identifying* sentences, but not at the end.

Identifying People with All Forms of "Is" [iss]

You can *identify* people with all the forms of "**is**" [iss] that you've used before.

Examples

"I'm not the server."
Ní mé an freastalaí.
[nee may un fras-tuh-lee]

"You aren't the secretary."
Ní tú an rúnaí.
[nee too un roo-nee]

"We aren't the musicians."
Ní muid na ceoltóirí.
[nee mwidj nuh kyoel-tor-ee]

"Y'all aren't the mechanics."
Ní sibh na meicneoirí.
[nee shiv nuh mek-nyor-ee]

"Am I the student?"
An mé an dalta?
[un may un dahl-tuh]

"Are you the doctor?"
An tú an dochtúir?
[un too un dokh-toor]

"Are we the dentists?"
An muid na fiaclóirí?
[un mwidj nuh fee-uh-klor-ee]

"Are y'all the servers?"
An sibh na freastalaithe?
[un shiv nuh fras-tuh-lee-huh]

"Aren't I the engineer?"
Nach mé an t-innealtóir?
[nahkh may un tin-yil-tor]

"Aren't you the musician?"
Nach tú an ceoltóir?
[nahkh too un kyoel-tor]

"Aren't we the teachers?"
Nach muid na múinteoirí?
[nahkh mwidj nuh moon-chor-ee]

"Aren't y'all the secretaries?"
Nach sibh na rúnaithe?
[nahkh shiv nuh roo-nee-heh]

Lesson 122 – Identifying People by Name

You can *identify* people by name, too. All you have to do is say the name after the pronoun at the beginning of the sentence. You don't use the pronoun at the end of the sentence, even though it's for a third-person ("he," "she," "they"), when only using names.

Examples

"Brian is the secretary."
Is é Brian an rúnaí.
[shay bree-uhn un roo-nee]

"Patricia is the secretary."
Is í Pádraigín an rúnaí.
[shee paw-druh-geen un roo-nee]

"Brian and Patricia are the secretaries."
Is iad Brian agus Pádraigín na rúnaithe.
[shee-ud bree-uhn ah-gus paw-druh-geen nuh roo-nee-heh]

"Liam isn't the dentist."
Ní h-é Liam an fiaclóir.
[nee hay lee-um un fee-uh-klor]

"Noreen isn't the dentist."
Ní h-í Noirín an fiaclóir.
[nee hee nor-een un fee-uh-klor]

"Liam and Noreen aren't the dentists."
Ní h-iad Liam agus Noirín na fiaclóirí.
[nee hee-ud lee-um ah-gus nor-een nuh fee-uh-klor-ee]

"Is Brian the musician?"
An é Brian an ceoltóir?
[un ay bree-uhn un kyoel-tor]

"Is Patricia the musician?"
An í Pádraigín an ceoltóir?
[un ee paw-druh-geen un kyoel-tor]

"Are Brian and Patricia the musicians?"
An iad Brian agus Pádraigín na ceoltóirí?
[un ee-ud bree-uhn ah-gus paw-druh-geen nuh kyoel-tor-ee]

"Isn't <u>Liam</u> the engineer?"
Nach <u>é</u> <u>Liam</u> an t-innealtóir?
[nahkh ay lee-um un tin-yil-tor]

"Isn't <u>Noreen</u> the engineer?"
Nach <u>í</u> <u>Noirín</u> an t-innealtóir?
[nahkh ee nor-een un tin-yil-tor]

"Aren't <u>Liam and Noreen</u> the engineers?"
Nach <u>iad Liam agus Noirín</u> na h-innealtóirí?
[nahkh ee-ud lee-um ah-gus nor-een nuh hin-yil-tor-ee]

Lesson 123 – Identifying Specific Subjects

Identifying a specific someone or something is similar to making an *identifying* sentence using a third-person pronoun. In this case, the third-person pronoun is only used once, right after "**is**" [iss]. Let's look at two sentences to compare:

"She is the teacher."
Is í an múinteoir í.
[shee un moon-chor ee]

"The woman is the teacher."
Is í an múinteoir an bhean.
[shee un moon-chor un van]

Notice that when "the woman" was the specific subject, the pronoun "**í**" [ee] was only used once, right after "**is**" [iss].

Examples

"The man is the musician."
Is é an ceoltóir an fear.
[shay un kyoel-tor un far]

"The children are the students."
Is iad na daltaí na páistí.
[shee-ud nuh dahl-tee nuh paw-stchee]

"The man isn't the doctor."
Ní h-é an dochtúir an fear.
[nee hay un dokh-toor un far]

"The woman isn't the secretary."
Ní h-í an rúnaí an bhean.
[nee hee un roo-nee un van]

"The children aren't the teachers."
Ní h-iad na múinteoirí na páistí.
[nee hee-ud nuh moon-chor-ee nuh paw-stchee]

"Is the man the engineer?"
An é an t-innealtóir an fear?
[un ay un tin-yil-tor un far]

"Is the woman the mechanic?"
An í an meicneoir an bhean?
[un ee un mek-nyor un van]

"Are the children the servers?"
An iad na freastalaithe na páistí?
[un ee-ud nuh fras-tuh-lee-huh nuh paw-stchee]

"Isn't the man the dentist?"
Nach é an fiaclóir an fear?
[nahkh ay un fee-uh-klor un far]

"Isn't the woman the musician?"
Nach í an ceoltóir an bhean?
[nahkh ee un kyoel-tor un van]

"Aren't the children the students?"
Nach iad na daltaí na páistí?
[nahkh ee-ud nuh dahl-tee nuh paw-stchee]

Conversation

Now we'll practice what we've learned about *identifying* people with a conversation.

Brian:
"Is Noreen the teacher?"
An í Noirín an múinteoir?
[un ee nor-een un moon-chor]

Pádraigín:
"No. She's not the teacher."
Ní h-í. Ní h-í an múinteoir í.
[nee hee. nee hee un moon-chor ee]

"She's the secretary."
Is í an rúnaí í.
[shee un roo-nee ee]

Brian:
"Is Liam the teacher?"
An é Liam an múinteoir?
[un ay lee-um un moon-chor]

Pádraigín:
"Yes. He's the teacher."
Is é. Is é an múinteoir é.
[shay. shay un moon-chor ay]

Brian:
"Are the children the students?"
An iad na daltaí na páistí?
[un ee-ud nuh dahl-tee nuh paw-stchee]

Pádraigín:
"No. They're not the students."
Ní h-iad. Ní h-iad na daltaí iad.
[nee hee-ud. nee hee-ud nuh dahl-tee ee-ud]

"The men and women are the students."
Is iad na daltaí na fir agus na mná.
[shee-ud nuh dahl-tee nuh fihr ah-gus nuh mraw]

Lesson 124 – Emphatic Pronouns with "Is"

As we learned in Lesson 10, instead of just using tone of voice to show emphasis, Irish changes the words themselves into their *emphatic forms*. Like the regular pronouns, these are mostly the same between "**tá**" [taw] sentences and "**is**" [iss] sentences, except the third-person pronouns drop the "**s**" off the front.

When you use third-person emphatic pronouns, you don't need to use the pronoun at the end of the sentence as you normally would. All you have to do is use the third-person emphatic pronoun after "**is**" [iss].

Vocabulary

Here is a list of emphatic pronouns that go with sentences that use "**is**" [iss]:

"I!"
mise
[mih-shuh]

"we!"
muide
[mwidj-uh]

"you!"
tusa
[tuh-suh]

"y'all!"
sibhse
[shiv-shuh]

"he!"
eisean
[esh-in]

"they!"
iadsan
[ee-ud-sun]

"she!"
ise
[ih-shuh]

Examples

Let's compare some *identifying* sentences with regular pronouns to some with emphatic pronouns:

"I am the doctor."
Is me an dochtúir.
[iss may un dokh-toor]

"I am the doctor."
Is mise an dochtúir.
[iss mih-shuh un dokh-toor]

"You are the server."
Is tú an freastalaí.
[iss too un fras-tuh-lee]

"*You* are the server."
Is tusa an freastalaí.
[iss tuh-suh un fras-tuh-lee]

"He is the man."
Is é an fear é.
[shay un far ay]

"*He* is the man."
Is eisean an fear.
[shesh-in un far]

"She is the woman."
Is í an bhean í.
[shee un van ee]

"*She* is the woman."
Is ise an bhean.
[shih-shuh un van]

"We are the students."
Is muid na daltaí.
[iss mwidj nuh dahl-tee]

"*We* are the students."
Is muide na daltaí.
[iss mwidj-uh nuh dahl-tee]

"Y'all are the children."
Is sibh na páistí.
[iss shiv nuh paw-stchee]

"*Y'all* are the children."
Is sibhse na páistí.
[iss shiv-shuh nuh paw-stchee]

"They are the teachers."
Is iad na múinteoirí iad.
[shee-ud nuh moon-chor-ee ee-ud]

"*They* are the teachers."
Is iadsan na múinteoirí.
[shee-ud-sun nuh moon-chor-ee]

Lesson 125 – Mixing Names and Pronouns

You can also mix names and pronouns in the same *identifying* sentence. This works for both regular pronouns, as well as emphatic pronouns. Though you'd probably be more likely to use these sentences with emphatic pronouns, we'll look at sentences with both to practice.

"Brian and I are the students."
Is <u>mé agus Brian</u> na daltaí.
[iss may ah-gus bree-uhn nuh dahl-tee]

"Brian and *I* are the students."
Is <u>mise agus Brian</u> na daltaí.
[iss mih-shuh ah-gus bree-uhn nuh dahl-tee]

"You and Patricia are the teachers."
Is <u>tú agus Pádraigín</u> na múinteoirí.
[iss too ah-gus paw-druh-geen nuh moon-chor-ee]

"*You* and Patricia are the teachers."
Is <u>*túsa* agus Pádraigín</u> na múinteoirí.
[iss tuh-suh ah-gus paw-druh-geen nuh moon-chor-ee]

Notice how in the sentences using "I," the "**mé**" [may] or "**mise**" [mih-shuh] comes before "**Brian**" [bree-uhn]. While, in English, it is considered polite to put yourself, "I," after all others in a list of people, in Irish, the final spot is reserved for the person who is given the most respect.

Examples

"Are Patricia and *I* the teachers?"
An mise agus Pádraigín na múinteoirí?
[un mih-shuh ah-gus paw-druh-geen nuh moon-chor-ee]

"Yes, *you* and Patricia are the teachers."
Is sibh. Is tusa agus Pádraigín na múinteoirí.
[iss shiv. iss tuh-suh ah-gus paw-druh-geen nuh moon-chor-ee]

"Aren't *you* and Brian the musicians?"
Nach tusa agus Brian na ceoltóirí?
[nahkh tuh-suh ah-gus bree-uhn nuh kyoel-tor-ee]

"Yes, Brian and *I* are the musicians."
Is muid. Is mise agus Brian na ceoltóirí.
[iss mwidj. iss mih-shuh ah-gus bree-uhn nuh kyoel-tor-ee]

"Are *he* and Patricia the doctors?"
An eisean agus Pádraigín na dochtúirí?
[un esh-in ah-gus paw-druh-geen nuh dokh-toor-ee]

"Yes, *he* and Patricia are the doctors."
Is iad. Is eisean agus Pádraigín na dochtúirí.
[shee-ud. shesh-in ah-gus paw-druh-geen nuh dokh-toor-ee]

"Aren't *she* and Brian the dentists?"
Nach ise agus Brian na fiaclóirí?
[nahkh ih-shuh ah-gus bree-uhn nuh fee-uh-klor-ee]

"No, *she* and Brian are the doctors."
Ní h-iad. Is ise agus Brian na dochtúirí.
[nee hee-ud. shih-shuh ah-gus bree-uhn nuh dokh-toor-ee]

"Are *we* and Liam the mechanics?"
An muide agus Liam na meicneoirí?
[un mwidj-uh ah-gus lee-um nuh mek-nyor-ee]

"No, *we* and Liam aren't the mechanics."
Ní muide. Ní muide agus Liam na meicneoirí.
[nee mwidj-uh. nee mwidj-uh ah-gus lee-um nuh mek-nyor-ee]

"Aren't *y'all* and Noreen the engineers?"
Nach sibhse agus Noirín na h-innealtóirí?
[nahkh shiv-shuh ah-gus nor-een nuh hin-yil-tor-ee]

"Yes, *we* and Noreen are the engineers."
Is muide. Is muide agus Noirín na h-innealtóirí.
[iss mwidj-uh. iss mwidj-uh ah-gus nor-een nuh hin-yil-tor-ee]

"Are *they* and Patricia the servers?"
An iadsan agus Pádraigín na freastalaithe?
[un ee-ud-sun ah-gus paw-druh-geen nuh fras-tuh-lee-huh]

"No, *they* and Patricia are the secretaries."
Ní h-iadsan. Is iadan agus Pádraigín na rúnaithe.
[nee hee-ud-sun. shee-ud-sun ah-gus paw-druh-geen nuh roo-nee-heh]

Lesson 126 – Identifying with Possessives

Sometimes when you're *identifying* a person or thing, you want to say who or what they are in relation to someone or something else. You can use the possessive pronouns to express this, and they work just as they did before. It doesn't matter whether the possessive is in a "**tá**" [taw] sentence or an "**is**" [iss] sentence. To review possessive pronouns, see Lessons 25 and 26.

Vocabulary

"a friend"
cara (m.)
[kahr-uh]

"friends"
cairde
[kahr-juh]

"the friend"
an cara
[un kahr-uh]

"the friends"
na cairde
[nuh kahr-juh]

Examples

"He is my friend."
Is é mo chara é.
[shay muh khahr-uh ay]

"He is your friend."
Is é do chara é.
[shay duh khahr-uh ay]

"He is his friend."
Is é a chara é.
[shay uh khahr-uh ay]

"He is her friend."
Is é a cara é.
[shay uh kahr-uh ay]

"He is our friend."
Is é ár gcara é.
[shay awr gahr-uh ay]

"He is y'all's friend."
Is é bhur gcara é.
[shay woor gahr-uh ay]

"He is their friend."
Is é a gcara é.
[shay uh gahr-uh ay]

Vocabulary

Let's learn some more words for people that you'd be likely to use with a possessive.

"a father"
athair (m.)
[ah-her]

"a son"
mac (m.)
[mahk]

"a mother"
máthair (f.)
[maw-her]

"sons"
mic
[mik]

"a brother"
deartháir (m.)
[dreh-har]

"a daughter"
iníon (f.)
[in-yeen]

"brothers"
deartháireacha
[dreh-har-uh-khuh]

"daughters"
iníonacha
[in-yeen-ih-khuh]

"a sister"
deirfiúr (f.)
[drih-foor]

"a husband"
fear céile (m.)
[far kay-leh]

"sisters"
deirfiúracha
[drih-foor-uh-khuh]

"a wife"
bean chéile (f.)
[ban khay-leh]

Examples

"He is my father."
Is é m'athair é.
[shay mah-her ay]

"I am your friend."
Is mé do chara.
[iss may duh khahr-uh]

"They aren't y'all's sons."
Ní h-iad bhur mic iad.
[nee hee-ud woor mik ee-ud]

"Is she is our doctor?"
An í ár ndochtúir í?
[un ee awr nokh-toor ee]

"Isn't she their mother?"
Nach í a máthair í?
[nahkh ee uh maw-her ee]

"My wife is the teacher."
Is í an múinteoir mo bhean chéile.
[shee un moon-chor muh van khay-leh]

"The musician is my husband."
Is é m'fhear céile an ceoltóir.
[shay mar kay-leh un kyoel-tor]

"Noreen is his daughter."
Is í Noirín a iníon.
[shee nor-een uh in-yeen]

"Liam is her brother."
Is é Liam a deartháir.
[shay lee-um uh dreh-har]

"Are our plates the dishes?"
An iad na soithí ár bplátaí?
[un ee-ud nuh suh-hee awr blaw-tee]

Lesson 127 – "This," "That," "These," and "Those"

Sometimes you'll want to be more specific about what you're talking about. This is where the words "this," "that," "these," and "those" come in handy. Irish uses different words to indicate whether something is near or far ("this" versus "that"). Whether it's plural or singular ("this" versus "these," or "that" versus "those") is handled by the noun or pronoun.

Vocabulary

"this" or "these"
seo
[shuh]

"that" or "those"
sin
[shin]

Notice how the word for "this," "**seo**" [shuh], looks a lot like the word we learned in Lesson 39 for "here," "**anseo**" [un-shuh]. And notice how the word for "that," "**sin**" [shin], looks a lot like the word we learned for "there," "**ansin**" [un-shin]. This is here, and that is there!

Just like in English, you can use these terms pretty loosely, but "**seo**" [shuh] tends to be used for things close to you, and "**sin**" [shin] tends to be used for things far from you. Use whichever seems appropriate to you at the time.

Using "This" and "That" When *Classifying* Nouns

To use these location words in a *classifying* "**is**" [iss] sentence, you simply say "**seo**" [shuh] or "**sin**" [shin] after the pronoun.

Examples

Let's look at some *classifying* sentences by themselves, and then using "**seo**" [shuh] and "**sin**" [shin] to compare.

"It is a box."
Is bosca é.
[iss bus-kuh ay]

"This is a box."
Is bosca é seo.
[iss bus-kuh ay shuh]

"That is a box."
Is bosca é sin.
[iss bus-kuh ay shin]

"It is a brush."
Is scuab í.
[iss skoo-uhb ee]

"This is a brush."
Is scuab í seo.
[iss skoo-uhb ee shuh]

"That is a brush."
Is scuab í sin.
[iss skoo-uhb ee shin]

"They are plates."
Is plátaí iad.
[iss plaw-tee ee-ud]

"These are plates."
Is plátaí iad seo.
[iss plaw-tee ee-ud shuh]

"Those are plates."
Is plátaí iad sin.
[iss plaw-tee ee-ud shin]

Lesson 128 – More About Classifying "This" and "That"

To say "**seo**" [shuh] and "**sin**" [shin] in negative *classifying* statements and *classifying* questions, you simply use the other forms of "**is**" [iss].

Examples

"This isn't a computer."
Ní ríomhaire é seo.
[nee ree-ver-uh ay shuh]

"That isn't a key."
Ní eochar í sin.
[nee ukh-er ee shin]

"These aren't tables."
Ní boird iad seo.
[nee bweerj ee-ud shuh]

"Is that a chair?"
An cathaoir í sin?
[un kah-heer ee shin]

"Aren't these boxes?"
Nach boscaí iad seo?
[nahkh bus-kee ee-ud shuh]

Answering *Classifying* Questions with "This" and "That"

To answer a *classifying* question using "**seo**" [shuh] or "**sin**" [shin], you use the "yes" or "no" that goes with *classifying* "**is**" [iss] questions. You can also expand your answer by saying a full sentence after the "yes" or "no." Remember to repeat the verb.

Examples

"Is this a fork?"
An gabhlóg í seo?
[un gow-loeg ee shuh]

"Yes. This is a fork."
Is ea. Is gabhlóg í seo.
[sha. iss gow-loeg ee shuh]

"No. This is not a fork."
Ní h-ea. Ní gabhlóg í seo.
[nee ha. nee gow-loeg ee shuh]

"No. This is a spoon."
Ní h-ea. Is spúnóg í seo.
[nee ha. iss spoo-noeg ee shuh]

"Are those doors?"
An doirse iad sin?
[un deer-shuh ee-ud shin]

"Yes. Those are doors."
Is ea. Is doirse iad sin.
[sha. iss deer-shuh ee-ud shin]

"No. Those are not doors."
Ní h-ea. Ní doirse iad sin.
[nee ha. nee deer-shuh ee-ud shin]

"No. Those are windows."
Ní h-ea. Is fuinneoga iad sin.
[nee ha. iss fwin-yoeg-uh ee-ud shin]

Lesson 129 – Identifying "This," "That," "These," and "Those"

To use "**seo**" [shuh] or "**sin**" [shin] in an *identifying* "**is**" [iss] sentence, you say "**seo**" [shuh] or "**sin**" [shin] after the pronoun. In these types of *identifying* sentences, you don't need to use the pronoun at the end.

Examples

Let's look some *identifying* "**is**" [iss] sentences, and then add "**seo**" [shuh] and "**sin**" [shin] to compare.

"It is the book."
Is é an leabhar é.
[shay un lyow-er ay]

"This is the book."
Is é seo an leabhar.
[shay shuh un lyow-er]

"That is the book."
Is é sin an leabhar.
[shay shin un lyow-er]

"It is the key."
Is í an eochair í.
[shee un ukh-er ee]

"This is the key."
Is í seo an eochair.
[shee shuh un ukh-er]

"That is the key."
Is í sin an eochair.
[shee shin un ukh-er]

"They are the boxes."
Is iad na boscaí iad.
[shee-ud nuh bus-kee ee-ud]

"These are the boxes."
Is iad seo na boscaí.
[shee-ud shuh nuh bus-kee]

"Those are the boxes."
Is iad sin na boscaí.
[shee-ud shin nuh bus-kee]

Lesson 130 – More About Identifying "This" and "That"

To say "**seo**" [shuh] and "**sin**" [shin] in negative *identifying* statements and *identifying* questions, you simply use the other forms of "**is**" [iss].

Examples

"This isn't the book."
Ní h-é seo an leabhar.
[nee hay shuh un lyow-er]

"That isn't the key."
Ní h-í sin an eochair.
[nee hee shin un ukh-er]

"These aren't the boxes."
Ní h-iad seo na boscaí.
[nee hee-ud shuh nuh bus-kee]

"Those aren't the knives."
Ní h-iad sin na sceana.
[nee hee-ud shin nuh shkyah-nuh]

"Is that the bicycle?"
An é sin an rothar?
[un ay shin un ruh-her]

"Aren't these the drinks?"
Nach iad seo na deochanna?
[nahkh ee-ud shuh nuh jawkh-uh-nuh]

Answering *Identifying* Questions with "This" and "That"

To answer an *identifying* question using "**seo**" [shuh] or "**sin**" [shin], you use the "yes" or "no" that goes with *identifying* "**is**" [iss] questions. You can also expand your answer by saying a full sentence after the "yes" or "no." Remember to repeat the verb.

Examples

"Is this the cup?"
An é seo an cupán?
[un ay shuh un kuh-pawn]

"Yes. This is the cup."
Is é. Is é seo an cupán.
[shay. shay shuh un kuh-pawn]

"No. This is not the cup."
Ní h-é. Ní h-é seo an cupán.
[nee hay. nee hay shuh un kuh-pawn]

"No. This is the glass."
Ní h-é. Is í seo an ghloine.
[nee hay. shee shuh un ghlih-nyuh]

"Are those the boys?"
An iad sin na buachaillí?
[un ee-ud shin nuh boo-uh-khulee]

"Yes. Those are the boys."
Is iad. Is iad sin na buachaillí.
[shee-ud. shee-ud shin nuh boo-uh-khulee]

"No. Those are not the boys."
Ní h-iad. Ní h-iad sin na buachaillí.
[nee hee-ud. nee hee-ud shin nuh boo-uh-khulee]

"No. Those are the girls."
Ní h-iad. Is iad sin na cailíní.
[nee hee-ud. shee-ud shin nuh kall-yeen-ee]

Lesson 131 – Saying "This" and "That" the Short Way

As with many things that are said a lot, there is a shorter way of making "**is**" [iss] sentences with "**seo**" [shuh] and "**sin**" [shin].

Short Versions of *Classifying* "This" and "That"

To use "**seo**" [shuh] and "**sin**" [shin] in *classifying* sentences, you replace the "**is**" [iss] at the beginning of the sentence with "**seo**" [shuh] or "**sin**" [shin]. You do not need any pronoun at the end of the sentence.

Examples

Let's compare some regular *classifying* sentences that use "**seo**" [shuh] or "**sin**" [shin] to their shorter versions.

"This is a book."
Is leabhar é seo.
[iss lyow-er ay shuh]

"This is a book."
Seo leabhar.
[shuh lyow-er]

"These are plates."
Is plataí iad seo.
[iss plaw-tee ee-ud shuh]

"These are plates."
Seo plataí.
[shuh plaw-tee]

"That is a pen."
Is peann é sin.
[iss pyawn ay shin]

"That is a pen."
Sin peann.
[shin pyawn]

"Those are boxes."
Is boscaí iad sin.
[iss bus-kee ee-ud shin]

"Those are boxes."
Sin boscaí.
[shin bus-kee]

Short Versions of *Identifying* "This" and "That"

To use "**seo**" [shuh] or "**sin**" [shin] in *identifying* "**is**" [iss] statements, you replace "**is**" [iss] at the beginning of the sentence with "**seo**" [shuh] or "**sin**" [shin].

Examples

Let's compare some regular *identifying* sentences that use "**seo**" [shuh] or "**sin**" [shin] to their shorter versions.

"This is the computer."
Is é seo an ríomhaire.
[shay shuh un ree-ver-uh]

"This is the computer."
Seo é an ríomhaire.
[shuh ay un ree-ver-uh]

"These are the maps."
Is iad seo na léarscáileanna.
[shee-ud shuh nuh layr-skoyl-uh-nuh]

"These are the maps."
Seo iad na léarscáileanna.
[shuh ee-ud nuh layr-skoyl-uh-nuh]

"That is the chair."
Is í sin an chathaoir.
[shee shin un khah-heer]

"That is the chair."
Sin í an chathaoir.
[shin ee un khah-heer]

"Those are the brushes."
Is iad sin na scuaba.
[shee-ud shin nuh skoo-uh-buh]

"Those are the brushes."
Sin iad na scuaba.
[shin ee-ud nuh skoo-uh-buh]

Lesson 132 – What Is This?

You can ask about what "this" or "that" is by taking the sentence, "What is it?" and adding "**seo**" [shuh] or "**sin**" [shin] to the end of it. Once again, you use the masculine "it," "**é**" [ay], since you don't know if the noun in question is masculine or feminine. The plural "**iad**" [ee-ud] is used for both "these" and "those."

Examples

"What is this?"
Céard é seo?
[kayrd ay shuh]

"What is that?"
Céard é sin?
[kayrd ay shin]

"What are these?"
Céard iad seo?
[kayrd ee-ud shuh]

"What are those?"
Céard iad sin?
[kayrd ee-ud shin]

Answering "What Is This?"

When answering these questions, you can use any appropriate "**is**" [iss] statement you've learned.

Examples

"What is this?"
Céard é seo?
[kayrd ay shuh]

"This is a chair."
Is cathaoir í seo.
[iss kah-heer ee shuh]

"What is that"
Céard é sin?
[kayrd ay shin]

"That is a table."
Is bord é sin.
[iss bord ay shin]

"What are these?"
Céard iad seo?
[kayrd ee-ud shuh]

"These are the boxes."
Is iad seo na boscaí.
[shee-ud shuh nuh bus-kee]

"What are those?"
Céard iad sin?
[kayrd ee-ud shin]

"Those are my keys."
Is iad sin m'eochracha.
[shee-ud shin mukh-rukh-uh]

Conversation

Now we'll practice what we've learned about using "this" and "that" with people and things through a conversation.

Pádraigín:
"What are those?"
Céard iad sin?
[kayrd ee-ud shin]

Brian:
"These are the maps."
Is iad seo na léarscáileanna.
[shee-ud shuh nuh layr-skoyl-uh-nuh]

Pádraigín:
"And what is this?"
Agus céard é seo?
[ah-gus kayrd ay shuh]

Brian:
"That is the book."
Sin é an leabhar.
[shin ay un lyow-er]

Pádraigín:
"Is that person your teacher?"
An é do mhúinteoir an duine sin?
[un ay duh woon-chor un din-uh shin]

Brian:
"No. He's not my teacher."
Ní h-é. Ní h-é mo mhúinteoir é.
[nee hay. nee hay muh woon-chor ay]

"He's a student."
Sin dalta.
[shin dahl-tuh]

Lesson 133 – Who Is This?

When talking about people, you'll sometimes want to ask who someone is. To do this, you start with the question word "who," "cé" [kay], followed by "he," "she," or "they." This is often followed by the word for "this" or "that," because you'll usually ask "Who is this?" or "Who is that?" rather than simply asking "Who is?"

Examples

"Who is this?" (for a man)
Cé h-é seo?
[kay hay shuh]

"Who is that?" (for a man)
Cé h-é sin?
[kay hay shin]

"Who is this?" (for a woman)
Cé h-í seo?
[kay hee shuh]

"Who is that?" (for a woman)
Cé h-í sin?
[kay hee shin]

"Who are these (people)?"
Cé h-iad seo?
[kay hee-ud shuh]

"Who are those (people)?"
Cé h-iad sin?
[kay hee-ud shin]

You'll notice that there's no form of the verb "is" in these questions, but that's okay. The question word "**cé**" [kay] "who," implies that you mean "who is." Also, notice that there's an "**h-**" added to the pronouns that start with vowels to make them easier to say.

Answering a "Who Is" Question

To answer a "who is" question, all you have to do is use an "**is**" [iss] sentence. When you're using a name, you're talking about a specific person, so you use the pattern for *identifying* people.

Examples

"Who is that?"
Cé h-é sin?
[kay hay shin]

"That's Brian."
Is é sin Brian.
[shay shin bree-uhn]

"That's Brian."
Sin é Brian.
[shin ay bree-uhn]

"Who is that?"
Cé h-í sin?
[kay hee shin]

"That's Patricia."
Is í sin Pádraigín.
[shee shin paw-druh-geen]

"That's Patricia."
Sin í Pádraigín.
[shin ee paw-druh-geen]

"Who are they?"
Cé h-iad sin?
[kay hee-ud shin]

"They are Brian and Patricia."
Is iad sin Brian agus Pádraigín.
[shee-ud shin bree-uhn ah-gus paw-druh-geen]

"They are Brian and Patricia."
Sin iad Brian agus Pádraigín.
[shin ee-ud bree-uhn ah-gus paw-druh-geen]

"Who is this?"
Cé h-é seo?
[kay hay shuh]

"This is a musician."
Is ceoltóir é seo.
[iss kyoel-tor ay shuh]

"This is a musician."
Seo ceoltóir.
[shuh kyoel-tor]

"Who is this?"
Cé h-í seo?
[kay hee shuh]

"This is the engineer."
Is í seo an t-innealtóir.
[shee shuh un tin-yil-tor]

"This is the engineer."
Seo í an t-innealtóir.
[shuh ee un tin-yil-tor]

"Who are they?"
Cé h-iad seo?
[kay hee-ud shuh]

"They are my teachers."
Is iad sin mo mhúinteoirí.
[shee-ud shin muh woon-chor]

"They are my teachers."
Sin iad mo mhúinteoirí.
[shin ee-ud muh woon-chor-ee]

Lesson 134 – Being More Specific with "Who Is?"

You can be more specific by asking and answering with nouns, too. You simply start by saying "who is," then a pronoun, and then a definite noun.

Examples

"Who is the doctor?"
Cé h-é an dochtúir?
[kay hay un dokh-toor]

"Who is the woman?"
Cé h-í an bhean?
[kay hee un van]

"Who are the students?"
Cé h-iad na daltaí?
[kay hee-ud nuh dahl-tee]

"Who is Brian?"
Cé h-é Brian?
[kay hay bree-uhn]

"Who is your friend?"
Cé h-í do chara?
[kay hee duh khahr-uh]

Answering "Who Is" with the Noun

You can answer these "who is" questions with any kind of "**is**" [iss] statement.

Examples

"Who is the doctor?"
Cé h-é an dochtúir?
[kay hay un dokh-toor]

"Liam is the doctor."
Is é Liam an dochtúir.
[shay lee-um un dokh-toor]

"Who is the woman?"
Cé h-í an bhean?
[kay hee un van]

"The woman is the dentist."
Is í an fiaclóir an bhean.
[shee un fee-uh-klor un van]

"Who are the students?"
Cé h-iad na daltaí?
[kay hee-ud nuh dahl-tee]

"The students are the children."
Is iad na páistí na daltaí.
[shee-ud nuh paw-stchee nuh dahl-tee]

"Who is Brian?"
Cé h-é Brian?
[kay hay bree-uhn]

"He is our teacher."
Is é ár múinteoir é.
[shay awr moon-chor ay]

"Who is your friend?"
Cé h-í do chara?
[kay hee duh khahr-uh]

"This is Patricia!"
Seo í Pádraigín!
[shuh ee paw-druh-geen]

Conversation

Now we'll practice asking and answering about who people are with a conversation.

Brian:
"Who are they?"
Cé h-iad sin?
[kay hee-ud shin]

Pádraigín:
"They are the teachers."
Is iad sin na múinteoirí.
[shee-ud shin nuh moon-chor-ee]

Brian:
"And who is that man?"
Agus cé h-é an fear sin?
[ah-gus kay hay un far shin]

Pádraigín:
"That's Liam."
Is é sin Liam.
[shay shin lee-um]

Brian:
"Isn't Liam the dentist?"
Nach é Liam an fiaclóir?
[nahkh ay lee-um un fee-uh-klor]

Pádraigín:
"No. He's the engineer."
Ní h-é. Is é an t-innealtóir é.
[nee hay. shay un tin-yil-tor ay]

Brian:
"Who is the dentist?"
Cé h-é an fiaclóir?
[kay hay un fee-uh-klor]

Pádraigín:
"That's Noreen."
Sin í Noirín.
[shin ee nor-een]

Lesson 135 – Having More

You've learned a lot of Irish! You can express yourself in many ways, including some turns of phrase that use *prepositions*.

As we learned in Lesson 28, the word "**ag**" [ehg], "at," can be used to create broader meanings than when something is just physically at a place. One of those meanings is how to express "having" something in Irish. All you have to do is say a form of the verb "**tá**" [taw], then a noun, and then a form of "**ag**" [ehg].

Examples

"Brian has a box."
Tá bosca ag Brian.
[taw bus-kuh ehg bree-uhn]

"I have a bag."
Tá mála agam.
[taw maw-luh ah-gum]

Having Different Kinds of Things

You can have things other than physical objects, too. For example, you can "have" a question, or a job, even though you can't hold such a thing in your hands. In Irish, when you say that you speak a language (whether fluently or just a few words), you say that you "have" that language.

To express that you know something in Irish, you say that you "have" knowledge of it. Because you're talking about having "its knowledge," you use the masculine possessive "**a**" [uh], for "it," before the word for knowledge.

Vocabulary

Here are some nouns for intangible things you can have, including languages:

"a question"	"knowledge"	"Irish" (language)
ceist (f.)	**fios** (m.)	**Gaeilge** (f.)
[kesht]	[fiss]	[gay-lih-guh]
"a story, news"	"its knowledge"	"English" (language)
scéal (m.)	**a fhios**	**Béarla** (m.)
[shkayl]	[uh iss]	[baer-luh]
"a job"		"Spanish" (language)
post (m.)		**Spáinnis** (f.)
[pust]		[spawn-ish]
		"French" (language)
		Fraincis (f.)
		[fran-keesh]

Examples

"I have a question."
Tá ceist agam.
[taw kesht ah-gum]

"Do you have any news?"
An bhfuil aon scéal agat?
[un will ayn shkayl ah-gut]

"He has a job."
Tá post aige.
[taw pust ehg-uh]

"Doesn't she know?"
Nach bhfuil a fhios aici?
[nahkh will iss ehk-ee]

"We speak Irish."
Tá Gaeilge againn.
[taw gay-lih-guh ah-geen]

"Y'all don't speak English."
Níl Béarla agaibh.
[neel baer-luh ah-giv]

"Do they speak Spanish?"
An bhfuil Spáinnis acu?
[un will spawn-ish ah-kuh]

"She spoke French."
Bhí Fraincis aici.
[vee fran-keesh ehk-ee]

"Patricia will have a question."
Beidh ceist ag Pádraigín.
[bay kesht ehg paw-druh-geen]

"Brian always has a story."
Bíonn scéal ag Brian i gcónaí.
[bee-uhn shkayl ehg bree-uhn ih go-nee]

"My friend speaks Irish."
Tá Gaeilge ag mo chara.
[taw gay-lih-guh ehg muh khahr-uh]

Conversation

Let's practice talking about having different kinds of things with a conversation.

Brian:
"Excuse me."
Gabh mo leithscéal.
[guhv muh leh-shkayl]

"Do you speak Irish?"
An bhfuil Gaeilge agat?
[un will gay-lih-guh ah-gut]

Pádraigín:
"Yes, I do speak Irish."
Tá. Tá Gaeilge agam.
[taw. taw gay-lih-guh ah-gum]

Brian:
"Wonderful!"
Go h-iontach!
[guh hee-un-tahkh]

Pádraigín:
"I also speak English."
Tá Béarla agam, freisin.
[taw baer-luh ah-gum, fresh-in]

Brian:
"I don't speak English, but I do speak Spanish."
Níl Béarla agam, ach tá Spáinnis agam.
[reel baer-luh ah-gum, akh taw spawn-ish ah-gum]

Pádraigín:
"I speak Spanish, too."
Tá Spáinnis agam, freisin.
[taw spawn-ish ah-gum, fresh-in]

Brian:
"I have a question."
Tá ceist agam.
[taw kesht ah-gum]

"Where is the hotel?"
Cá bhfuil an t-óstán?
[kaw will un toess-tawn]

Pádraigín:
"I know."
Tá a fhios agam.
[taw iss ah-gum]

"It's there."
Tá sé ansin.
[taw shay un-shin]

Brian:
"Thanks!"
Go raibh maith agat!
[guh ruh mah ah-gut]

Pádraigín:
"You're welcome."
Tá fáilte romhat.
[taw fawl-tchuh roet]

Brian:
"Bye!"
Slán agat!
[slawn ah-gut]

Pádraigín:
"Bye!"
Slán leat!
[slawn lyat]

Lesson 136 – Using "At" with "The"

Sometimes, when *prepositions* work together with the *definite article*, "the," they change the word that comes after them. By itself, "**ag**" [ehg] doesn't change the word that follows it. However, when "**ag**" [ehg] is used with "**an**" [un], together they will *eclipse* the next word. Also, certain feminine words starting with "**s**" will take a "**t**" in front of them. These words start with "**sl**," "**sn**," "**sr**," or "**s**" followed by a vowel.

Words that start with "**d**" or "**t**" are exceptions in this case. If the word after "**ag an**" [ehg un] begins with the letter "**d**" or "**t**," the "**d**" or the "**t**" *does not get eclipsed*.

When "**ag**" [ehg] and "**na**" [nuh] come together, they cause no change to the following word. If the next word after "**ag na**" [ehg nuh] begins with a vowel, you add an "**h-**" in front of it to make it easier to say.

Examples

Let's take a look at some sentences that talk about what people have using "the."

"The woman has the boxes."
Tá na boscaí ag an mbean.
[taw nuh bus-kee ehg un man]

"The child doesn't have a spoon."
Níl spúnóg ag an bpáiste.
[neel spoo-noeg ehg un baw-stchuh]

"The student often has a question."
Bíonn ceist ag an dalta go minic.
[bee-uhn kesht ehg un dahl-tuh guh min-ik]

"Did the man have brooms?"
An raibh scuaba ag an bhfear?
[un rev skoo-uh-buh ehg un var]

"Will the musicians have chairs?"
An mbeidh cathaoireacha ag na ceoltóirí?
[un may kah-heer-ih-khuh ehg nuh kyoel-tor-ee]

"Don't the engineers have computers?"
Nach bhfuil ríomhairí ag na h-innealtóirí?
[nahkh will ree-ver-ee ehg nuh hin-yil-tor-ee]

"Does the father have the key?"
An bhfuil an eochair ag an athair?
[un will un ukh-er ehg un ah-her]

"The daughter speaks Spanish."
Tá Spáinnis ag an iníon.
[taw spawn-ish ehg un in-yeen]

"That server has the knives."
Tá na sceana ag an bhfreastalaí sin.
[taw nuh shkyah-nuh ehg un vras-tuh-lee shin]

Conversation

Let's practice talking about definite people having things with a conversation.

Pádraigín:
"Does the man have the plates?"
An bhfuil na plátaí ag an bhfear?
[un will nuh plaw-tee ehg un var]

Brian:
"No. The servers have them."
Níl. Tá siad ag na freastalaithe.
[neel. taw shee-ud ehg nuh fras-tuh-lee-huh]

Pádraigín:
"Do the servers have the knife, too?"
An bhfuil an scian ag na freastalaithe, freisin?
[un will un shkee-un ehg nuh fras-tuh-lee-huh, fresh-in]

Brian:
"No. The woman has it."
Níl. Tá sí ag an mbean.
[neel. taw shee ehg un man]

Pádraigín:
"Doesn't the musician have spoons?"
Nach bhfuil spúnóga ag an gceoltóir?
[nahkh will spoo-noeg-uh ehg un gyoel-tor]

Brian:
"Yes. The musician has spoons."
Tá. Tá spúnóga ag an gceoltóir.
[taw. taw spoo-noeg-uh ehg un gyoel-tor]

Lesson 137 – The Word "On"

As we learned before, a *preposition* is a word like "in," "for," "with," etc., that shows a noun's relationship to some other thing in the sentence. We've learned how to say a lot with the preposition "**ag**" [ehg]. Now, we'll look at another very useful preposition in Irish: "**ar**" [air], which means "on."

The Forms of "Ar"

By itself, "**ar**" [air] will *soften* a noun that comes after it. When "**ar**" [air] comes together with "**an**" [un], they will *eclipse* the next word. Also, certain feminine words starting with "**s**" will take a "**t**" in front of them. These words start with "**sl**," "**sn**," "**sr**," or "**s**" followed by a vowel.

Words that start with "**d**" or "**t**" are exceptions in this case. If the word after "**ar an**" [air un] begins with the letter "**d**" or "**t**," the "**d**" or the "**t**" *does not get eclipsed*.

When "**ar**" [air] and "**na**" [nuh] come together, they cause no change to the following word. If the next word after "**ar na**" [air nuh] begins with a vowel, you add an "**h-**" in front of it.

Vocabulary

When a *preposition* (like "on") and a *pronoun* (like "I") come together, they merge into one word called a *prepositional pronoun*. Here are the forms for "**ar**" [air]:

"on"	"on me"	"on us"
ar	**orm**	**orainn**
[air]	[or-um]	[or-een]
	"on you"	"on y'all"
	ort	**oraibh**
	[ort]	[or-iv]
	"on him" ("on it")	"on them"
	air	**orthu**
	[air]	[or-huh]
	"on her" ("on it")	
	uirthi	
	[ur-hee]	

Lesson 138 – Wearing Clothes

There are a lot of things that can be on you in Irish, but the most basic things are those that are physically on you. Therefore, we'll start by talking about clothes.

To express that you're wearing a piece of clothing, you say that it is on you. All you have to do is say a form of "**tá**" [taw], then a piece of clothing, and then a form of "**ar**" [air], "on."

Vocabulary

Here are some nouns for clothing:

"a coat"	"a shirt"	"a sock"
cóta (m.)	**léine** (f.)	**stoca** (m.)
[ko-tuh]	[lay-nuh]	[stuhk-uh]
"a dress"	"a shoe"	"socks"
gúna (m.)	**bróg** (f.)	**stocaí**
[goo-nuh]	[broeg]	[stuh-kee]
"a hat"	"shoes"	
hata (m.)	**bróga**	
[hot-uh]	[bro-guh]	
"pants"	"a skirt"	
bríste (m.)	**sciorta** (m.)	
[breesh-tuh]	[skir-tuh]	

Examples

"I'm wearing a coat."
Tá cóta orm.
[taw ko-tuh or-um]

"You're not wearing a dress."
Níl gúna ort.
[neel goo-nuh ort]

"Is he wearing a hat?"
An bhfuil hata air?
[un will hot-uh air]

"She's wearing pants."
Tá bríste uirthi.
[taw breesh-tuh ur-hee]

"We're not wearing shoes."
Níl bróga orainn.
[neel bro-guh or-een]

"Are y'all wearing socks?"
An bhfuil stocaí oraibh?
[un will stuh-kee or-iv]

"Aren't they wearing shoes?"
Nach bhfuil bróga orthu?
[nahkh will bro-guh or-huh]

"Brian is wearing a shirt."
Tá léine ar Bhrian.
[taw lay-nuh air vree-uhn]

"Is Patricia wearing a skirt?"
An bhfuil sciorta ar Phádraigín?
[un will skir-tuh air faw-druh-geen]

"Are you wearing one sock?"
An bhfuil stoca amháin ort?
[un will stuhk-uh uh-woyn ort]

"The man was wearing one shoe."
Bhí bróg amháin ar an bhfear.
[vee broeg uh-woyn air un var]

"Are the girls wearing shoes?"
An bhfuil bróga ar na cailíní?
[un will bro-guh air nuh kall-yeen-ee]

Conversation

Let's practice talking about what people are wearing with a conversation.

Brian:
"I was cold yesterday."
Bhí mé fuar inné.
[vee may foo-uhr in-yay]

Pádraigín:
"Were you wearing a coat?"
An raibh cóta ort?
[un rev ko-tuh ort]

Brian:
"Yes. I was wearing a coat, but I wasn't wearing a hat."
Bhí. Bhí cóta orm, ach ní raibh hata orm.
[vee. vee ko-tuh or-um, akh nee rev hot-uh or-um]

Pádraigín:
"Was Liam wearing a coat?"
An raibh cóta ar Liam?
[un rev ko-tuh air lee-um]

Brian:
"No. He was only wearing socks."
Ní raibh. Ní raibh ach stocaí air.
[nee rev. nee rev akh stuh-kee air]

Pádraigín:
"Wasn't the man wearing shoes?"
Nach raibh bróga ar an bhfear?
[nahkh rev bro-guh air un var]

Brian:
"No. He was inside."
Ní raibh. Bhí sé istigh.
[nee rev. vee shay iss-tchih]

Lesson 139 – Physical Conditions

Another thing that is considered to be "on" you in Irish are physical conditions, like hunger or sleepiness. Once again, to make a sentence to express this, all you have to do is say a form of "**tá**" [taw], the condition, and a form of "**ar**" [air], "on."

Vocabulary

Here are some nouns for physical conditions:

"hunger" **ocras** (m.) [uhk-russ]	"tiredness" **tuirse** (f.) [teer-shuh]	"a cold" **slaghdán** (m.) [sly-dawn]	"improvement" **biseach** (m.) [bih-shahkh]
"thirst" **tart** (m.) [tart]	"sleep" **codladh** (m.) [kull-uh]	"sickness, an ache" **tinneas** (m.) [tchih-nuss]	

Examples

"I'm hungry."
Tá ocras orm.
[taw uhk-russ or-um]

"Are you thirsty?"
An bhfuil tart ort?
[un will tart ort]

"He's not tired."
Níl tuirse air.
[neel teer-shuh air]

"Isn't she sleepy?"
Nach bhfuil codladh uirthi?
[nahkh will kull-uh ur-hee]

"I have a cold."
Tá slaghdán orm.
[taw sly-dawn or-um]

"We're not sick."
Níl tinneas orainn.
[neel tchih-nuss or-een]

"Are y'all better?"
An bhfuil biseach oraibh?
[un will bih-shahkh or-iv]

"Aren't they always hungry?"
Nach mbíonn ocras orthu i gcónaí?
[nahkh me-uhn uhk-russ or-huh ih go-nee]

"Patricia will be thirsty."
Beidh tart ar Phádraigín.
[bay tart air faw-druh-geen]

"Does the doctor have a cold?"
An bhfuil slaghdán ar an dochtúir?
[un will sly-dawn air un dokh-toor]

"Are the servers better?"
An bhfuil biseach ar na freastalaithe?
[un will bih-shahkh air nuh fras-tuh-lee-huh]

"The engineers were tired."
Bhí tuirse ar na h-innealtóirí.
[vee teer-shuh air nuh hin-yil-tor-ee]

Conversation

Let's practice talking about some physical conditions that people can have with a conversation.

Pádraigín:
"I'm going to the restaurant."
Tá mé ag dul go dtí an bhialann.
[taw may ehg dull guh jee un vee-uh-luhn]

Brian:
"Are you hungry?"
An bhfuil ocras ort?
[un will uhk-russ ort]

Pádraigín:
"Yes, and I'm thirsty, too."
Tá. Agus tá tart orm, freisin.
[taw. ah-gus taw tart or-um, fresh-in]

"Will *you* be going to the restaurant, too?"
An mbeidh tusa ag dul go dtí an bhialann, freisin?
[un may tuh-suh ehg dull guh jee un vee-uh-luhn, fresh-in]

Brian:
"No. I'm tired."
Ní bheidh. Tá tuirse orm.
[nee vay. taw teer-shuh or-um]

Pádraigín:
"Are you sick?"
An bhfuil tinneas ort?
[un will tchih-nuss ort]

Brian:
"Yes. I have a cold, but I will be better tomorrow."
Tá. Tá slaghdán orm, ach beidh biseach orm amárach.
[taw. taw sly-dawn or-um, akh bay bih-shahkh or-um uh-maw-rahkh]

Lesson 140 – Emotions

Like physical conditions, emotional states are also considered to be "on" you in Irish. As with the other turns of phrase using "**ar**" [air], to make a sentence expressing emotion, all you have to do is say a form of "**tá**" [taw], the emotional state, and a form of "**ar**" [air], "on."

Vocabulary

Here are some nouns for emotions:

"gladness"	"fear"	"worry"	"doubt"
áthas (m.)	**eagla** (f.)	**imní** (f.)	**amhras** (m.)
[aw-huss]	[og-luh]	[im-ree]	[ow-russ]

"sorrow"	"anger"	"surprise"	"hurry"
brón (m.)	**fearg** (f.)	**ionadh** (m.)	**deifir** (f.)
[broen]	[far-ihg]	[ee-nuh]	[jef-fer]

Examples

"I'm glad."
Tá áthas orm.
[taw aw-huss or-um]

"Are you sorry?"
An bhfuil brón ort?
[un will broen ort]

"He's not afraid."
Níl eagla air.
[neel og-luh air]

"Wasn't she angry?"
Nach raibh fearg uirthi?
[nahkh rev far-ihg ur-hee]

"We're worried."
Tá imní orainn.
[taw im-ree or-een]

"Y'all will be surprised."
Beidh ionadh oraibh.
[bay ee-nuh or-iv]

"Are they doubtful?"
An bhfuil amhras orthu?
[un will ow-russ or-huh]

"Brian is in a hurry."
Tá deifir ar Bhrian.
[taw jef-fer air vree-uhn]

"Was the friend afraid?"
An raibh eagla ar an gcara?
[un rev og-luh air un gahr-uh]

"The musicians won't be angry."
Ní bheidh fearg ar na ceoltóirí.
[nee vay far-ihg air nuh kyoel-tor-ee]

Conversation

Let's practice talking about how people are feeling with a conversation.

Brian:
"Noreen's not going to the park."
Níl Noirín ag dul go dtí an pháirc.
[neel nor-een ehg dull guh jee un fawrk]

Pádraigín:
"I'm surprised."
Tá ionadh orm.
[taw ee-nuh or-um]

"Where is she going now?"
Cá bhfuil sí ag dul anois?
[kaw will shee ehg dull uh-nish]

Brian:
"She's going to a meeting, and she's in a hurry."
Tá sí ag dul chuig cruinniú, agus tá deifir uirthi.
[taw shee ehg dull khig krin-nyew, ah-gus taw jef-fer ur-hee]

Pádraigín:
"Good."
Go maith.
[guh mah]

"I was worried."
Bhí imní orm.
[vee im-ree or-um]

"Will she be going to the party tomorrow night?"
An mbiedh sí ag dul chuig an gcóisir oíche amárach.
[un may shee ehg dull khig un goe-sher ee-khuh uh-maw-rahkh]

Brian:
"Yes, she'll be there."
Beidh. Beidh sí ann.
[bay. bay shee on]

Pádraigín:
"I'm glad!"
Tá áthas orm!
[taw aw-huss or-um]

Lesson 141 – Colors

Irish uses the word "on" to describe the colors of things. To say that something is a particular color, you say that a color is "on" it. This is similar to other "**ar**" [air] sentences, only you also say the word "color" before the actual color.

Vocabulary

"color"	"brown"	"orange"	"red"
dath (m.)	**donn**	**oráiste**	**dearg**
[dah]	[duhn]	[or-awsh-tuh]	[jer-uhg]
"black"	"green"	"pink"	"white"
dubh	**glas**	**bándearg**	**bán**
[duhv]	[gloss]	[bawn-jer-uhg]	[bawn]
"blue"	"grey"	"purple"	"yellow"
gorm	**liath**	**corcra**	**buí**
[gor-um]	[lee-uh]	[kor-kuh-ruh]	[bwee]

Examples

Now we'll practice saying what colors things are using prepositional pronouns as well as nouns.

"It is black." (on a masculine noun)
Tá dath dubh air.
[taw dah duhv air]

"It is blue." (on a feminine noun)
Tá dath gorm uirthi.
[taw dah gor-um ur-hee]

"They are brown."
Tá dath donn orthu.
[taw dah duhn or-huh]

"The land is green."
Tá dath glas ar an tír.
[taw dah gloss air un tcheer]

"The streets are grey."
Tá dath liath ar na sráideanna.
[taw dah lee-uh air nuh sroy-jin-uh]

"The drinks are orange."
Tá dath oráiste ar na deochanna.
[taw dah or-awsh-tuh air nuh jawkh-uh-nuh]

"The pen is pink."
Tá dath bándearg ar an bpeann.
[taw dah bawn-jer-uhg air un byawn]

"The bag is purple."
Tá dath corcra ar an mála.
[taw dah kor-kuh-ruh air un maw-luh]

"The apple is red."
Tá dath dearg ar an úll.
[taw dah jer-uhg air un ool]

"The floors are white."
Tá dath bán ar na h-urláir.
[taw dah bawn air nuh hoor-lawyer]

"The door is yellow."
Tá dath buí ar an doras.
[taw dah bwee air un dor-us]

Lesson 142 – Spatially On the Thing

We've learned a lot of turns of phrase that use "**ar**" [air] to express different ideas, but you can also use "**ar**" [air] to express when something is literally on another thing.

Vocabulary

Here are some nouns we've seen before, shown with the phrase "on the" preceding them:

"on the table"
ar an mbord
[air un mord]

"on the box"
ar an mbosca
[air un muss-kuh]

"on the tables"
ar na boird
[air nuh bweerj]

"on the boxes"
ar na boscaí
[air nuh bus-kee]

"on the chair"
ar an gcathaoir
[air un gah-heer]

"on the floor"
ar an urlár
[air un oor-lawr]

"on the chairs"
ar na cathaoireacha
[air nuh kah-heer-ih-khuh]

"on the floors"
ar na h-urláir
[air nuh hoor-lawyer]

Examples

"A bag is on the table."
Tá mála ar an mbord.
[taw maw-luh air un mord]

"The spoons are on the tables."
Tá na spúnóga ar na boird.
[taw nuh spoo-noeg-uh air nuh bweerj]

"Is my coat on the chair?"
An bhfuil mo chóta ar an gcathaoir?
[un will muh kho-tuh air un gah-heer]

"Boxes are on the chairs."
Tá boscaí ar na cathaoireacha.
[taw bus-kee air nuh kah-heer-ih-khuh]

"A knife is on the box."
Tá scian ar an mbosca.
[taw shkee-un air un muss-kuh]

"Isn't the book on the boxes?"
Nach bhfuil an leabhar ar na boscaí.
[nahkh will un lyow-er air nuh bus-kee]

"The boy is on the floor."
Tá an buachaill ar an urlár.
[taw un boo-uh-khil air un oor-lawr]

"There is nothing on the floors."
Níl rud ar bith ar na h-urláir
[neel ruhd air bih air nuh hoor-lawyer]

Conversation

Let's practice talking about things that are physically on other things with a conversation.

Pádraigín:
"Where is my pen?"
Cá bhfuil mo pheann?
[kaw will muh fyawn]

Brian:
"Your pen is on the box."
Tá do pheann ar an mbosca.
[taw duh fyawn air un muss-kuh]

Pádraigín:
"But where is the box?"
Ach cá bhfuil an bosca?
[akh kaw will un bus-kuh]

Brian:
"It's on the table."
Tá sé ar an mbord.
[taw shay air un mord]

Pádraigín:
"Is my bag on it, too?"
An bhfuil mo mhála air, freisin?
[un will muh wah-luh air, fresh-in]

Brian:
"No. It's on the floor."
Níl. Tá sé ar an urlár.
[neel. taw shay air un oor-lawr]

Lesson 143 – Under

We can use many prepositions to describe where something is in relation to other things. The word for "under" in Irish is "**faoi**" [fwee]. Like all the prepositions, it combines with pronouns to form prepositional pronouns. By itself, "**faoi**" [fwee] will *soften* the following word.

Vocabulary

Here are all of the prepositional pronouns for "**faoi**" [fwee]:

"under"
faoi
[fwee]
softens

"under me"
fúm
[foom]

"under you"
fút
[foot (rhymes with "boot")]

"under him" ("under it")
faoi
[fwee]

"under her" ("under it")
fúithi
[foo-hee]

"under us"
fúinn
[foo-een]

"under y'all"
fúibh
[foo-iv]

"under them"
fúthu
[foo-huh]

Examples

"The floor is under Brian."
Tá an t-urlár faoi Bhrian.
[taw un toor-lawr fwee vree-uhn]

"The shoes are under a chair."
Tá na bróga faoi chathaoir.
[taw nuh bro-guh fwee khah-heer]

"My coat is under me."
Tá mo chóta fúm.
[taw muh kho-tuh foom]

"Your hat is under you."
Tá do hata fút.
[taw duh hot-uh foot (rhymes with "boot")]

"The key is under it." (a masculine noun)
Tá an eochair faoi.
[taw un ukh-er fwee]

"The bag is under it." (a feminine noun)
Tá an mála fúithi.
[taw un maw-luh foo-hee]

"The streets are under us."
Tá na sráideanna fúinn.
[taw nuh sroy-jin-uh foo-een]

"Something is under y'all."
Tá rud éigin fúibh.
[taw ruhd ay-gihn foo-iv]

"The box is under them."
Tá an bosca fúthu.
[taw un bus-kuh foo-huh]

Lesson 144 – Under The

The word "**faoi**" [fwee] will combine with "**an**" [un] to form the contraction "**faoin**" [fween], "under the." You could say "**faoi an**" [fwee un] and still be understood, but most people contract these words. The word "**faoi**" [fwee] doesn't contract with the plural "the," "**na**" [nuh].

As we learned in Lesson 136, when prepositions work together with the definite article, "the," sometimes they change the word that comes after them. "**Faoin**" [fween] will *eclipse* the next word. Also, certain feminine words starting with "**s**" will take a "**t**" in front of them. These words start with "**sl**," "**sn**," "**sr**," or "**s**" followed by a vowel.

Words that start with "**d**" or "**t**" are exceptions in this case. If the word after "**faoin**" [fween] begins with the letter "**d**" or "**t**," the "**d**" or the "**t**" *does not get eclipsed*.

When "**faoi**" [fwee] and "**na**" [nuh] come together, they cause no change to the following word. If the next word after "**faoi na**" [fwee nuh] begins with a vowel, you add an "**h-**" in front of it to make it easier to say.

Vocabulary

Here are some nouns with the phrase "under the" preceding them:

"under the table"	"under the chair"	"under the box"
faoin mbord	**faoin gcathaoir**	**faoin mbosca**
[fween mord]	[fween gah-heer]	[fween muss-kuh]

"under the tables"	"under the chairs"	"under the boxes"
faoi na boird	**faoi na cathaoirecha**	**faoi na boscaí**
[fwee nuh bweerj]	[fwee nuh kah-heer-ih-khuh]	[fwee nuh bus-kee]

Examples

"The plates are under the table."
Tá na plátaí faoin mbord.
[taw nuh plaw-tee fween mord]

"The computers are under the tables."
Tá na ríomhairí faoi na boird.
[taw nuh ree-ver-ee fwee nuh bweerj]

"The socks under the chair."
Tá na stocaí faoin gcathaoir.
[taw nuh stuh-kee fween gah-heer]

"Their shoes are under the chairs."
Tá a mbróga faoi na cathaoirecha.
[taw uh mro-guh fwee nuh kah-heer-ih-khuh]

"The child is under the box."
Tá an páiste faoin mbosca.
[taw un paw-stchuh fween muss-kuh]

"The map is under the boxes."
Tá an léarscáil faoi na boscaí.
[taw un layr-skoyl fwee nuh bus-kee]

Conversation

Now we'll practice talking about things that are under other things with a conversation.

Brian:
"Where are my shoes?"
Cá bhfuil mo bhróga?
[kaw will muh vro-guh]

Pádraigín:
"Your shoes are under the table."
Tá do bhróga faoin mbord.
[taw duh vro-guh fween mord]

Brian:
"Aren't my socks under the table, too?"
Nach bhfuil mo stocaí faoin mbord, freisin?
[nahkh will muh stuh-kee fween mord, fresh-in]

Pádraigín:
"No. They're under the chair."
Níl. Tá siad faoin gcathaoir.
[neel. taw shee-ud fween gah-heer]

Brian:
"And where are our keys?"
Agus cá bhfuil ár n-eochracha?
[ah-gus kaw will awr nukh-rukh-uh]

Pádraigín:
"They're under this box."
Tá siad faoin mbosca seo.
[taw shee-ud fween muss-kuh shuh]

Lesson 145 – In

We've been learning how to describe where something is in relation to other things. The word for "in" in Irish is "**i**" [ih]. Like the other prepositions, it combines with pronouns to form prepositional pronouns. By itself, "**i**" [ih] will *eclipse* the following word. If the next word begins with a vowel, you put an "**n**" at the end of the word "**i**" [ih], making it "**in**" [ihn]. This is done to make it easier to say before a vowel, and will cause no change to the next word.

Vocabulary

Here are all of the prepositional pronouns for "**i**" [ih]:

"in"	"in me"	"in us"
i	**ionam**	**ionainn**
[ih]	[un-um]	[un-een]
eclipses		
	"in you"	"in y'all"
	ionat	**ionaibh**
	[un-ut]	[un-iv]
	"in him" ("in it")	"in them"
	ann	**iontu**
	[on]	[un-tuh]
	"in her" ("in it")	
	inti	
	[in-tchee]	

Examples

Now we'll take a look at some examples using "in a," "in it" and "in them" to say where things are. Though you can use the other prepositional pronouns to state that something is literally "in me," " in you," "in him," etc., those forms tend to be used only in expressions.

"Is the map in a car?"
An bhfuil an léarscáil i gcarr?
[un will un layr-skoyl ih gahr]

"Yes, the map is in it."
Tá, tá an léarscáil ann.
[taw, taw un layr-skoyl on]

"Is the spoon in a glass?"
An bhfuil an spúnóg i ngloine?
[un will un spoo-noeg ih nglih-nyuh]

"Yes, the spoon is in it."
Tá, tá an spúnóg inti.
[taw, taw un spoo-noeg in-tchee]

"Are the keys in boxes?"
An bhfuil na h-eochracha i mboscaí?
[un will nuh hukh-rukh-uh ih muss-kee]

"Yes, the keys are in them."
Tá, tá na h-eochracha iontu.
[taw, taw nuh hukh-rukh-uh un-tuh]

Lesson 146 – In The

When "**i**" [ih] comes together with the singular "the," "**an**" [un], it contracts into the word "**sa**" [suh], which will *soften* the next word. However, certain feminine words starting with "**s**" will take a "**t**" in front of them instead of *softening*. These words start with "**sl**," "**sn**," "**sr**," or "**s**" followed by a vowel.

Words that start with "**d**" or "**t**" are exceptions in this case. If the word after "**sa**" [suh] begins with the letter "**d**" or "**t**," the "**d**" or the "**t**" *does not get softened*.

If the next word starts with a vowel, "**sa**" [suh] becomes "**san**" [sun] to make it easier to say. Remember that a softened "**f**" becomes silent. So, words that start with a softened "**f**" immediately followed by a vowel are treated as if they started with a vowel.

Example

"a ring"
fáinne (m.)
[faw-nyuh]

"the ring"
an fáinne
[un faw-nyuh]

"in the ring"
san fháinne
[sun aw-nyuh]

When "**i**" [ih] comes together with the plural "the," "**na**" [nuh], it contracts into the word "**sna**" [snuh], which does not change the next word. If the word after "**sna**" [snuh] starts with a vowel, you add an "**h-**" to the front of it to make it easier to say.

Vocabulary

Here are a few nouns with the phrase "in the" preceding them:

"in the box"	"cars"	"in the car"
sa bhosca	**carranna**	**sa charr**
[suh wuhss-kuh]	[kahr-uh-nuh]	[suh khahr]
"in the boxes"		"in the cars"
sna boscaí		**sna carranna**
[snuh bus-kee]		[snuh kahr-uh-nuh]

Examples

"The spoon is in the box."
Tá an spúnóg sa bhosca.
[taw un spoo-noeg suh wuhss-kuh]

"The spoons are in the boxes."
Tá na spúnóga sna boscaí.
[taw nuh spoo-noeg-uh snuh bus-kee]

"The children are in the car."
Tá na páistí sa charr.
[taw nuh paw-stchee suh khahr]

"The children are in the cars."
Tá na páistí sna carranna.
[taw nuh paw-stchee snuh kahr-uh-nuh]

Conversation

Let's practice talking about things that are inside of other things with a conversation.

Pádraigín:
"Where are the drinks?"
Cá bhfuil na deochanna?
[kaw will nuh jawkh-uh-nuh]

Brian:
"They're in the boxes."
Tá siad sna boscaí.
[taw shee-ud snuh bus-kee]

Pádraigín:
"And where are the boxes?"
Agus cá bhfuil na boscaí?
[ah-gus kaw will nuh bus-kee]

Brian:
"They're in the car."
Tá siad sa charr.
[taw shee-ud suh khahr]

Pádraigín:
"Is my bag in the car, too?"
An bhfuil mo mhála sa charr, freisin?
[un will muh wah-luh suh khahr, fresh-in]

Brian:

"No, your bag's not in it."

Níl. Níl do mhála ann.

[neel. neel duh wah-luh on]

"It's here."

Tá sé anseo.

[taw shay un-shuh]

Pádraigín:

"Is a pen in the bag?"

An bhfuil peann sa mhála?

[un will pyawn suh wah-luh]

Brian:

"No. There's no pen in it."

Níl. Níl peann ar bith ann.

[neel. neel pyawn air bih on]

Lesson 147 – Using "In" with Places

The word "**i**" [ih], "in," is also used when talking about being in geographical places, like cities or countries.

As we learned in Lesson 145, by itself, "**i**" [ih] will *eclipse* the following word. Also, if the next word begins with a vowel, "**i**" [ih] turns into "**in**" [ihn], which causes no change to the next word.

Vocabulary

Here are some names of countries shown by themselves and with the word "in":

"America"
Meiriceá (m.)
[mair-ih-kaw]

"in America"
i Meiriceá
[ih mair-ih-kaw]

"Canada"
Ceanada (m.)
[kya-nuh-duh]

"in Canada"
i gCeanada
[ih gya-nuh-duh]

"Mexico"
Meicsiceo (m.)
[mek-shih-ko]

"in Mexico"
i Meicsiceo
[ih mek-shih-ko]

"Scotland"
Albain (f.)
[all-uh-bin]

"in Scotland"
in Albain
[ihn all-uh-bin]

"England"
Sasana (m.)
[soss-uh-nuh]

"in England"
i Sasana
[ih soss-uh-nuh]

"Ireland"
Éire (f.)
[air-uh]

"in Ireland"
in Éirinn
[ihn air-ihn]

Placenames That Use "The"

There are relatively very few country placenames in English that use the word "the" in the name, such as "The Netherlands," or "The U.S." However, Irish has many more. When you talk about these places with "**i**" [ih], what we learned before about when "in" and "the" come together still applies.

Vocabulary

Here are some names of countries that use the definite article shown by themselves and with the word "in":

"(The) Australia"
an Astráil (f.)
[un aws-trawyil]

"(The) France"
an Fhrainc (f.)
[un rank]

"The United States"
na Stáit Aontaithe (m.)
[nuh stoych ayn-tih-huh]

"in (The) Australia"
san Astráil
[sun aws-trawyil]

"in (The) France"
sa Fhrainc
[suh rank]

"in The United States"
sna Stáit Aontaithe
[snuh stoych ayn-tih-huh]

"(The) China"
an tSín (f.)
[un tcheen]

"(The) Germany"
an Ghearmáin (f.)
[un yah-ruh-moyn]

"in (The) China"
sa tSín
[suh tcheen]

"in (The) Germany"
sa Ghearmáin
[suh yah-ruh-moyn]

Conversation

Let's practice talking about being in places with a conversation.

Brian:
"Where is Liam?"
Cá bhfuil Liam?
[kaw will lee-um]

Pádraigín:
"He's in Scotland."
Tá sé in Albain.
[taw shay ihn all-uh-bin]

Brian:
"Was he in Scotland yesterday?"
An raibh sé in Albain inné?
[un rev shay ihn all-uh-bin in-yay]

Pádraigín:
"No. He was in France last night, and he will be in Ireland tomorrow."
Ní raibh. Bhí sé sa Fhrainc aréir, agus beidh sé in Éirinn amárach.
[nee rev. vee shay suh rank uh-rayr, ah-gus bay shay ihn air-ihn uh-maw-rahkh]

Brian:
"Isn't Noreen in Ireland right now?"
Nach bhfuil Noirín in Éirinn anois díreach?
[nahkh will nor-een ihn air-ihn uh-nish jee-rahkh]

Pádraigín:
"No. She's in Australia."
Níl. Tá sí san Astráil.
[neel. taw shee sun aws-trawyil]

Lesson 148 – Saying Where You Live

The word "**i**" [ih], "in," is very useful for saying where you live. It's so useful in fact, that it's actually used twice in the sentence. To say you live somewhere, you say:

"I live in X."
Tá mé i mo chónaí i X.
[taw may ih muh khoe-nee ih ...]

This sentence literally translates as, "I am in my residence in X," and is made like this:

Tá [taw] = "am"
mé [may] = "I"
i [ih] = "in"
mo [muh] = "my"
cónaí [khoe-nee] = "residence"
i [ih] = "in"

The word for "residence" in Irish is "**cónaí**" [koe-nee], which is masculine (m.). Notice that, because it's after the possessive "my," "**mo**" [muh], it is *softened*. What we learned in Lesson 25 about possessives applies here. Therefore, if you are talking about where other people are in "their residences," you'll use the appropriate possessive, along with the matching pronoun.

Also, notice that the first "**i**" [ih] doesn't eclipse the possessive word which follows it. If the possessive pronoun begins with a vowel, "**i**" [ih] becomes "**in**" [ihn], and will contract with the possessive pronoun. Therefore, "**i**" [ih] contracts with "**a**" [uh] to become "**ina**" [ihn-uh], and "**i**" [ih] contracts with "**ár**" [awr] to become "**inár**" [ihn-awr].

Examples

Let's look at some sentences about where people live.

"I live in America."
Tá mé i mo chonaí i Meiriceá.
[taw may ih muh khoe-nee ih mair-ih-kaw]

"Do you live in Canada?"
An bhfuil tú i do chonaí i gCeanada?
[un will too ih duh khoe-nee ih gya-nuh-duh]

"He doesn't live in Ireland."
Níl sé ina chonaí in Éirinn.
[neel shay ihn-uh khoe-nee ihn air-ihn]

"Doesn't she live in Australia?"
Nach bhfuil sí ina conaí san Astráil?
[nahkh will shee ihn-uh koe-nee sun aws-trawyil]

"We lived in Germany."
Bhí muid inár gconaí sa Ghearmáin.
[vee mwidj ihn-awr goe-nee suh yah-ruh-moyn]

"Y'all will live in Scotland."
Beidh sibh i bhur gconaí in Albain.
[bay shiv ih woor goe-nee ihn all-uh-bin]

"They live in China."
Tá siad ina gconaí sa tSín.
[taw shee-ud ihn-uh goe-nee suh tcheen]

"Liam lives in France."
Tá Liam ina chónaí sa Fhrainc.
[taw lee-um ihn-uh khoe-nee suh rank]

"Noreen lives in Mexico."
Tá Noirín ina cónaí i Meicsiceo.
[taw nor-een ihn-uh koe-nee ih mek-shih-ko]

"Brian and Patricia live in The United States."
Tá Brian agus Pádraigín ina gcónaí sna Stáit Aontaithe.
[taw bree-uhn ah-gus paw-druh-geen ihn-uh goe-nee snuh stoych ayn-tih-huh]

Lesson 149 – Asking Where Somebody Lives

Asking where somebody lives is like saying where they live, with one small change. All you have to do is replace the form of "**tá**" [taw] with the words "**cá bhfuil**" [kaw will], "where is." This is just like when we learned to ask "Where is it?" in Lesson 38.

To ask, "Where do you live?" in Irish, you say:

"Where do you live?"
Cá bhfuil tú i do chónaí?
[kaw will too ih duh khoe-nee]

You can use this question to ask where other people live by using a name or another pronoun in place of "**tú**" [too]. Make sure to use the appropriate possessive that matches the name or pronoun. To answer, all you have to do is say a statement about where someone lives using the phrases we learned in the previous lesson.

Examples

"Where do you live?"
Cá bhfuil tú i do chónaí?
[kaw will too ih duh khoe-nee]

"I live in America."
Tá mé i mo chonaí i Meiriceá.
[taw may ih muh khoe-nee ih mair-ih-kaw]

"Where does he live?"
Cá bhfuil sé ina chónaí?
[kaw will shay ihn-uh khoe-nee]

"He lives in England."
Tá sé ina chonaí i Sasana.
[taw shay ihn-uh khoe-nee ih soss-uh-nuh]

"Where do she and Brian live?"
Cá bhfuil sí agus Brian ina gcónaí?
[kaw will shee ah-gus bree-uhn ihn-uh goe-nee]

"They live in the United States."
Tá siad ina gconaí sna Stáit Aontaithe.
[taw shee-ud ihn-uh goe-nee snuh stoych ayn-tih-huh]

Conversation

Let's practice talking about where people live with a conversation.

Pádraigín:
"Hello."
Dia duit.
[jee-uh ghitch]

Brian:
"Hello."
Dia 's Muire duit.
[jee-uh smwir-uh ghitch]

"I'm Brian."
Is mise Brian.
[iss mih-shuh bree-uhn]

"What's *your* name?"
Cén t-ainm atá ortsa?
[kayn tan-um uh-taw ort-suh]

Pádraigín:
"I'm Patricia."
Is mise Pádraigín.
[iss mih-shuh paw-druh-geen]

"Where do you live, Brian."
Cá bhfuil tú i do chónaí, a Bhriain?
[kaw will too ih duh khoe-nee, uh vree-in]

Brian:
"I live in the United States."
Tá mé i mo chonaí sna Stáit Aontaithe.
[taw may ih muh khoe-nee snuh stoych ayn-tih-huh]

"And where do *you* live, Patricia?"
Agus cá bhfuil tusa i do chónaí, a Phádraigín?
[ah-gus kaw will tuh-suh ih duh khoe-nee, uh faw-druh-geen]

Pádraigín:
"I live in Canada."
Tá mé i mo chonaí i gCeanada.
[taw may ih muh khoe-nee ih gya-nuh-duh]

Brian:
"*He* lives in Canada, too."
Tá seisean ina chonaí i gCeanada, freisin.
[taw shesh-in ihn-uh khoe-nee ih gya-nuh-duh, fresh-in]

Pádraigín:
"That's Liam."
Sin é Liam.
[shin ay lee-um]

"His daughter lives in Mexico."
Tá a iníon ina conaí i Meicsiceo.
[taw uh in-yeen ihn-uh koe-nee ih mek-shih-ko]

Brian:
"My friends live in Mexico, too!"
Tá mo chairde ina gconaí i Meicsiceo, freisin!
[taw muh khahr-juh ihn-uh goe-nee ih mek-shih-ko, fresh-in]

Lesson 150 – Saying Where You Are From

To ask where someone is from, you use the preposition "**as**" [oss], which means "out of." By itself, "**as**" [oss] causes no change to the word that follows it. When "**as**" [oss] comes together with the singular "the," "**an**" [un], together they will *eclipse* the next word. Also, certain feminine words starting with "**s**" will take a "**t**" in front of them. These words start with "**sl**," "**sn**," "**sr**," or "**s**" followed by a vowel.

Words that start with "**d**" or "**t**" are exceptions in this case. If the word after "**as an**" [oss un] begins with the letter "**d**" or "**t**," the "**d**" or the "**t**" *does not get eclipsed*.

When you use "**as**" [oss] with the plural "the," "**na**" [nuh], they cause no change to the following word. If the next word after "**as na**" [oss nuh] begins with a vowel, you add an "**h-**" in front of it to make it easier to say.

Though we won't be learning expressions that use the prepositional pronoun forms of "**as**" [oss] here, we'll show them below just for practice, as well as reference for your future learning of Irish.

Vocabulary

"out of"	"out of me"	"out of us"
as	**asam**	**asainn**
[oss]	[oss-um]	[oss-een]
	"out of you"	"out of y'all"
	asat	**asaibh**
	[oss-it]	[oss-iv]
	"out of him"	"out of them"
	as	**astu**
	[oss]	[oss-tuh]
	"out of her"	
	aisti	
	[ash-tchee]	

Saying Where Someone is From

Since where you're from is a more permanent concept, we use the verb "**is**" [iss] in this expression, rather than "**tá**" [taw]. To say where someone is from, you start with "**is**" [iss], then say "**as**" [oss], then the place, and then a pronoun or a pronoun followed by a noun.

Examples

"I am from Canada."
Is as Ceanada mé.
[iss oss kya-nuh-duh may]

"She is from Ireland."
Is as Éirinn í.
[iss oss air-in ee]

"Y'all are from the United States."
Is as na Stáit Aontaithe sibh.
[iss oss nuh stoych ayn-tih-huh shiv]

"Noreen is from China."
Is as an tSín í Noirín.
[iss oss un tcheen ee nor-een]

"The man is from France."
Is as an bhFrainc é an fear.
[iss oss un vrank ay un far]

Lesson 151 – Asking Where You Are From

When you want to ask where someone is from, you can say:

"Where are you from?"
Cé as tú?
[kay oss too]

You can ask where other people are from by using another pronoun or a pronoun followed by a name in place of "**tú**" [too]. Because this question is related to an "**is**" [iss] answer, remember to use the pronouns that go with "**is**" [iss] in the question. To answer, all you have to do is say a statement about where someone is from.

Examples

"Where are you from?"
Cé as tú?
[kay oss too]

"I am from Scotland."
Is as Albain mé.
[iss oss all-uh-bin may]

"Where is she from?"
Cé as í?
[kay oss ee]

"She is from the United States."
Is as na Stáit Aontaithe í.
[iss oss nuh stoych ayn-tih-huh ee]

"Where are they from?"
Cé as iad?
[kay oss ee-ud]

"They are from Germany."
Is as an nGearmáin iad.
[iss oss un yah-ruh-moyn ee-ud]

"Where is Liam from?"
Cé as é Liam?
[kay oss ay lee-um]

"Liam is from Mexico."
Is as Meicsiceo é Liam.
[iss oss mek-shih-ko ay lee-um]

Conversation

We'll practice talking about where people are from with a conversation.

Brian:
"Where is Noreen from?"
Cé as í Noirín?
[kay oss ee nor-een]

Pádraigín:
"She's from Canada."
Is as Ceanada í.
[iss oss kya-nuh-duh ee]

Brian:
"Is Liam from Canada, too?"
An as Ceanada é Liam, freisin?
[un oss kya-nuh-duh ay lee-um, fresh-in]

Pádraigín:
"No. He's not from Canada."
Ní h-ea. Ní as Ceanada é.
[nee ha. nee oss kya-nuh-duh ay]

"He's from Ireland."
Is as Éirinn é.
[iss oss air-in ay]

Brian:
"Aren't *you* from Ireland, too?"
Nach as Éirinn tú féin, freisin?
[nahkh oss air-in too fayn, fresh-in]

Pádraigín:
"No. I'm from France."
Ní h-ea. Is as an bhFrainc mé.
[nee ha. iss oss un vrank may]

"Where are *you* from?"
Cé as tusa?
[kay oss tuh-suh]

Brian:
"I'm from Australia."
Is as an Astráil mé.
[iss oss un aws-trawyil may]

Lesson 152 – "For" or "To"

Another useful preposition in Irish is "**do**" [duh], which means "for" or "to." This is used a lot when giving things, or when saying who a thing is for. We've actually seen this one before, because it's used in the greetings "**Dia duit**" [jee-uh ghitch], and "**Dia daoibh**" [jee-uh yeev].

By itself, "**do**" [duh] will *soften* the following word. If the next word starts with a vowel or an "**f**," which becomes silent when *softened*, you run the words together, and use a "**d'**" (d+apostrophe) when writing them.

When "**do**" [duh] comes together with the singular "the," "**an**" [un], it contracts into the word "**don**" [duhn], which will still *soften* the next word. However, certain feminine words starting with "**s**" will take a "**t**" in front of them instead of *softening*. These words start with "**sl**," "**sn**," "**sr**," or "**s**" followed by a vowel.

Words that start with "**d**" or "**t**" are exceptions in this case. If the word after "**don**" [duhn] begins with the letter "**d**" or "**t**," the "**d**" or the "**t**" *does not get softened*.

"**Do**" [duh] doesn't contract with the plural "the," "**na**" [nuh], and this combination doesn't change the next word. If the next word after "**do na**" [duh nuh] begins with a vowel, you add an "**h-**" in front of it to make it easier to say.

Vocabulary

Here are all of the prepositional pronouns for "**do**" [duh]:

"for/to" **do** [duh] *softens*	"for me/to me" **dom** [dum]	"for us/to us" **dúinn** [doo-een]	"for Brian/to Brian" **do Bhrian** [duh vree-uhn]
	"for you/to you" **duit** [ditch]	"for y'all/to y'all" **daoibh** [deev]	"for the boy/to the boy" **don bhuachaill** [duhn woo-uh-khil]
	"for him/to him" **dó** [doe]	"for them/to them" **dóibh** [doe-iv]	"for the girls/to the girls" **do na cailíní** [duh nuh kall-yeen-ee]
	"for her/to her" **di** [jih]		

You may notice that "**duit**" [ditch] and "**daoibh**" [deev] are pronounced differently that what we saw in the greeting *Bonus Phrases*. Because greetings are said so often, the pronunciations of the words will sometimes vary. The standard pronunciations for "**duit**" [ditch] and "**daoibh**" [deev] are as above, but sometimes you'll hear people using the alternate versions in more than just the greeting phrases.

The Emphatic Forms of "Do"

Because "**do**" [duh], "for/to," is often used with giving, you may want to be emphatic about who you're giving something to. Therefore, you'll commonly see the emphatic forms of "**do**" [duh] used.

Vocabulary

Here are the emphatic forms for the preposition pronouns for "**do**" [duh]:

"for *me*/to *me*"
domsa
[dum-suh]

"for *us*/to *us*"
dúinne
[doo-een-uh]

"for *you*/to *you*"
duitse
[dih-tchuh]

"for *y'all*/to *y'all*"
daoibhse
[deev-shuh]

"for *him*/to *him*"
dósan
[doe-sun]

"for *them*/to *them*"
dóibhsean
[doe-iv-shun]

"for *her*/to *her*"
dise
[jih-shuh]

Lesson 153 – This Is For You!

When you're in the act of giving someone something, you often say something to them while doing so. In English, we say things like, "Here you go," or "There you are," which, ironically, mean the same thing. In Irish, you very often say, "**Seo duit**" [shuh ghitch], which translates as, "This for you." The plural is "**Seo daoibh**" [shuh yeev].

Because these phrases are said often, you'll hear people using the alternate forms of "**duit**" [ditch] and "**daoibh**" [deev] when saying them. This is just like what we saw with the greeting phrases, "**Dia duit**" [jee-uh ghitch] and "**Dia daoibh**" [jee-uh yeev]. When giving things, you can use either pronunciation and still be understood.

Vocabulary

"a gift"
bronntanas (m.)
[brun-tun-us]

"gifts"
bronntanais
[brun-tun-ish]

Examples

Let's take a look at a few sentences to see how these giving phrases are used:

"It's a gift."
Is bronntanas é.
[iss brun-tun-us ay]

"Here you go!"
Seo duit!
[shuh ghitch]

"They're gifts."
Is bronntanais iad.
[iss brun-tun-ish ee-ud]

"Here y'all go!"
Seo daoibh!
[shuh yeev]

Lesson 154 – I Have Something For You

One of the nice things about prepositions is that you can use two of them together to create a more complex sentence. You can combine "**ag**" [ehg], in its sense of having, with "**do**" [duh], to express that you "have" something "for" someone else. All you have to do is say the form of "**do**" [duh] after the form of "**ag**" [ehg] in any "have" sentence.

Examples

"*I have* a gift <u>for you</u>."
***Tá* bronntanas *agam* <u>duit</u>.**
[taw brun-tun-us ah-gum ditch]

"*He has* a story <u>for us</u>."
***Tá* scéal *aige* <u>duinn</u>.**
[taw shkayl ehg-uh doo-een]

"*Brian has* the key <u>for Patricia</u>."
***Tá* an eochair *ag Brian* <u>do Phádraigín</u>.**
[taw un ukh-er ehg bree-uhn duh faw-druh-geen]

Conversation

Let's practice talking about having things for people with a conversation.

Brian:
"I have something for Noreen."
Tá rud éigin agam do Noirín.
[taw ruhd ay-gihn ah-gum duh nor-een]

Pádraigín:
"What is it?"
Céard é?
[kayrd ay]

Brian:
"It's a book."
Is leabhar é.
[iss lyow-er ay]

Pádraigín:
"Do you have a book for Liam, too?"
An bhfuil leabhar agat do Liam, freisin?
[un will lyow-er ah-gut duh lee-um, fresh-in]

Brian:
"Yes, I have one for him, also."
Tá. Tá ceann agam dó, freisin.
[taw. taw kyawn ah-gum doe, fresh-in]

"Do you have any boxes for them?"
An bhfuil aon bhoscaí agat dóibh?
[un will ayn wuhss-kee ah-gut doe-iv]

Pádraigín:
"I have a box *for him,* but I don't have a box *for her.*"
Tá bosca agam dósan, ach níl bosca agam dise.
[taw bus-kuh ah-gum doe-sun, akh neel bus-kuh ah-gum jih-shuh]

Brian:
"That's okay."
Tá sé sin ceart go leor.
[taw shay shin kyart guh leeyor]

"I have boxes for them."
Tá boscaí agam dóibh.
[taw bus-kee ah-gum doe-iv]

Lesson 155 – I Love You

As we've seen before, there are many kinds of things, both tangible and intangible, that you can "have" in Irish. One of these things is "love," **grá** [graw], which is grammatically masculine (m.). To tell someone you love them, you say that you "have" love "for" them.

This expression is only used for affectionate love. We'll learn how to talk about a having strong liking for something, as in "I love ice cream," in a later lesson.

Vocabulary

Here are a few things you can use this affectionate love expression with, aside from people:

"a cat"	"a dog"
cat (m.)	**madra** (m.)
[kot]	[mah-druh]

Examples

"I love you."
Tá grá agam duit.
[taw graw ah-gum ditch]

"Do you love me?"
An bhfuil grá agat dom?
[un will graw ah-gut dum]

"The man loves the woman."
Tá grá ag an bhfear don bhean.
[taw graw ehg un var duhn van]

"Patricia loves Brian."
Tá grá ag Pádraigin do Bhrian.
[taw graw ehg paw-druh-geen duh vree-uhn]

"The woman loves the cat."
Tá grá ag an mbean don chat.
[taw graw ehg un man duhn khot]

"The boy loves the dog."
Tá grá ag an mbuachaill don mhadra.
[taw graw ehg un moo-uh-khil duhn wah-druh]

Lesson 156 – I Have a Question For You

In Irish, when you have a question for someone, you express it as having a question "on" someone. You use the same pattern that we learned in Lesson 154 about having something for someone. All you have to do is say the form of "**ar**" [air], "on," after the form of "**ag**" [ehg] in any "have" sentence.

Examples

"*I have* a question <u>for you</u>."
Tá ceist *agam* <u>ort</u>.
[taw kesht ah-gum ort]

"*He doesn't have* a question <u>for her</u>."
Níl ceist *aige* <u>uirthi</u>.
[neel kesht ehg-uh ur-hee]

"*Do y'all have* a question <u>for me</u>?"
An bhfuil ceist *agaibh* <u>orm</u>?
[un will kesht ah-giv or-um]

"*Doesn't Patricia have* a question <u>for Brian</u>?"
Nach bhfuil ceist *ag Pádraigín* <u>ar Bhrian</u>?
[nahkh will kesht ehg paw-druh-geen air vree-uhn]

"*Does the child have* a question <u>for the dentist</u>?"
An bhfuil ceist *ag an bpáiste* <u>ar an bhfiaclóir</u>?
[un will kesht ehg un baw-stchuh air un vee-uh-klor]

Conversation

Let's practice talking about having questions with a conversation.

Pádraigín:
"I have a question for you."
Tá ceist agam ort.
[taw kesht ah-gum ort]

Brian:
"What is it?"
Céard é?
[kayrd ay]

Pádraigín:
"Do you have the movie for Liam and Noreen?"
An bhfuil an scannán agat do Liam agus Noirín?
[un will un skuh-nawn ah-gut duh lee-um ah-gus nor-een]

Brian:
"Yes. I have it for them."
Tá. Tá sé agam dóibh.
[taw. taw shay ah-gum doe-iv]

"Now, I have a question for *you*."
Anois, tá ceist agam ortsa.
[un-nish, taw kesht ah-gum ort-suh]

Pádraigín:
"What is it?"
Céard é?
[kayrd ay]

Brian:
"Do you have my key?"
An bhfuil m'eochair agat?
[un will mukh-er ah-gut]

Pádraigín:
"Yes. I have it for you."
Tá. Tá sí agam duit.
[taw. taw shee ah-gum ditch]

"Here you are."
Seo duit.
[shuh ghitch]

Brian:
"Thanks."
Go raibh maith agat.
[guh ruh mah ah-gut]

Pádraigín:
"You're welcome."
Tá fáilte romhat.
[taw fawl-tchuh roet]

Lesson 157 – Need

When you want to express a need in Irish, you say that something is "from" you. The word for "from" is "**ó**" [oe]. By itself, "**ó**" [oe] will *soften* the following word. When "**ó**" [oe] comes together with the singular "the," "**an**" [un], it contracts into the word "**ón**" [oen], which will *eclipse* the next word. Also, certain feminine words starting with "**s**" will take a "**t**" in front of them. These words start with "**sl**," "**sn**," "**sr**," or "**s**" followed by a vowel.

Words that start with "**d**" or "**t**" are exceptions in this case. If the word after "**ón**" [oen] begins with the letter "**d**" or "**t**," the "**d**" or the "**t**" *does not get eclipsed*.

"**Ó**" [oe] doesn't contract with the plural "the," "**na**" [nuh], and this combination doesn't change the next word. If the next word after "**ó na**" [oe nuh] begins with a vowel, you add an "**h-**" in front of it to make it easier to say.

Vocabulary

Here are all of the prepositional pronouns for "**ó**" [oe]:

"from" **ó** [oe] *softens*	"from me" **uaim** [wem]	"from us" **uainn** [weng]	"from Brian" **ó Bhrian** [oe vree-uhn]
	"from you" **uait** [wet]	"from y'all" **uaibh** [wev]	"from the boy" **ón mbuachaill** [oen moo-uh-khil]
	"from him" **uaidh** [wy]	"from them" **uathu** [wuh-huh]	"from the girls" **ó na cailíní** [oe nuh kall-yeen-ee]
	"from her" **uaithi** [wuh-hee]		

Examples

To say that you need something in Irish, all you have to do is say a form of "**tá**" [taw], a noun, and then a form of "**ó**" [oe].

"I need a pen."
Tá peann uaim.
[taw pyawn wem]

"Do you need a drink?"
An bhfuil deoch uait?
[un will jawkh wet]

"Doesn't he need a broom?"
Nach bhfuil scuab uaidh?
[nahkh will skoo-uhb wy]

"She doesn't need anything."
Níl rud ar bith uaithi.
[neel ruhd air bih wuh-hee]

"We didn't need a car."
Ní raibh carr uainn.
[nee rev kahr weng]

"Did y'all need something?"
An raibh rud éigin uaibh?
[un rev ruhd ay-gihn wev]

"They will need a book."
Beidh leabhar uathu.
[bay lyow-er wuh-huh]

"Patricia needs her computer."
Tá a ríomhaire ó Phádraigín.
[taw uh ree-ver-uh oe faw-druh-geen]

"Didn't the musician need a chair?"
Nach raibh cathaoir ón gceoltóir?
[nahkh rev kah-heer oen gyoel-tor]

"Will the mechanics need boxes?"
An mbeidh boscaí ó na meicneoirí?
[un may bus-kee oe nuh mek-nyor-ee]

Conversation

Let's practice talking about needing things with a conversation.

Brian:
"Patricia, I need socks."
A Phádraigín, tá stocaí uaim.
[uh faw-druh-geen, taw stuh-kee wem]

Pádraigín:
"Here you are."
Seo duit.
[shuh ghitch]

"Do you need shoes, too?"
An bhfuil bróga uait, freisin?
[un will bro-guh wet, fresh-in]

Brian:
"No. I have my shoes."
Níl. Tá mo bhróga agam.
[neel. taw muh vro-guh ah-gum]

Pádraigín:
"Do the children need socks, too?"
An bhfuil stocaí ó na páistí, freisin?
[un will stuh-kee oe nuh paw-stchee, fresh-in]

Brian:
"The girl doesn't need socks, but the boy needs socks and shoes."
Níl stocaí ón gcailín, ach tá stocaí agus bróga ón mbuachaill.
[neel stuh-kee oen gall-yeen, akh taw stuh-kee ah-gus bro-guh oen moo-uh-khil]

Lesson 158 – I Would Like It

You can express a need by using "**ó**" [oe], "from," but asking for something by stating bluntly that you need it isn't terribly polite. To say that you "would like" something, you use a form of "**is**" [iss] with the word "with," "**le**" [leh].

To say that you would like something in Irish, you use this *Bonus Phrase*:

"I would like X."
Ba mhaith liom X.
[buh wah lyum ...]

This loosely translates as, "X would be good with me." Although this is a *Bonus Phrase*, we'll take a brief look at how it's made. In this sentence, the verb "**is**" [iss] is in the *conditional mood*. (Yes, verbs have moods, too. The *conditional mood* is used when a verb describes an action that is uncertain or hypothetical.) The next word is "good," "**maith**" [mah], and it's softened. So, the first two words, "**ba mhaith**" [buh wah], mean, "would be good."

"With"

The word "with" is "**le**" [leh] in Irish. By itself, "**le**" [leh] does nothing to the following word. When "**le**" [leh] comes together with the singular "the," "**an**" [un], it works a little differently than other prepositions. In this case, you use the prepositional pronoun form for "with him," "**leis**" [lesh] (instead of just "**le**" [leh] by itself), followed by "**an**" [un]. So, to say "with the" you say, "**leis an**" [lesh un]. This combination will *eclipse* the next word. Also, certain feminine words starting with "**s**" will take a "**t**" in front of them. These words start with "**sl**," "**sn**," "**sr**," or "**s**" followed by a vowel.

Words that start with "**d**" or "**t**" are exceptions in this case. If the word after "**leis an**" [lesh un] begins with the letter "**d**" or "**t**," the "**d**" or the "**t**" *does not get eclipsed*.

When "**le**" [leh] comes together with the plural "the," "**na**" [nuh], you also use the form for "with him," "**leis**" [lesh], and say "**leis na**" [lesh nuh]. This combination doesn't change the next word. If the next word after "**leis na**" [lesh nuh] begins with a vowel, you add an "**h-**" in front of it to make it easier to say.

Vocabulary

Here are all of the prepositional pronouns for "**le**" [leh]:

"with"	"with me"	"with us"	"with Brian"
le	**liom**	**linn**	**le Brian**
[leh]	[lyum]	[leeng]	[leh bree-uhn]

	"with you"	"with y'all"	"with the boy"
	leat	**libh**	**leis an mbuachaill**
	[lyat]	[liv]	[lesh un moo-uh-khil]

	"with him"	"with them"	"with the girls"
	leis	**leo**	**leis na cailíní**
	[lesh]	[lyo]	[lesh nuh kall-yeen-ee]

	"with her"
	léi
	[lay-ih]

Examples

"I would like a bag."
Ba mhaith liom mála.
[buh wah lyum maw-luh]

"You would like it."
Ba mhaith leat é.
[buh wah lyat ay]

"He would like an apple."
Ba mhaith leis úll.
[buh wah lesh ool]

"She would like a pen."
Ba mhaith léi peann.
[buh wah lay-ih pyawn]

"We would like the map."
Ba mhaith linn an léarscáil.
[buh wah leeng un layr-skoyl]

"Y'all would like the story."
Ba mhaith libh an scéal.
[buh wah liv un shkayl]

"They would like boxes."
Ba mhaith leo boscaí.
[buh wah lyo bus-kee]

"Patricia would like this dress."
Ba mhaith le Pádraigín an gúna seo.
[buh wah leh paw-druh-geen un goo-nuh shuh]

"The child would like a bicycle."
Ba mhaith leis an bpáiste rothar.
[buh wah lesh un baw-stchuh ruh-her]

"The people would like chairs."
Ba mhaith leis na daoine cathaoireacha.
[buh wah lesh nuh dee-nuh kah-heer-ih-khuh]

Lesson 159 – More Things To Like

There are plenty of things to like. One kind of thing everybody would like from time to time is something to eat or drink. We'll practice talking about what people would like by learning some nouns for foods and drinks.

Vocabulary

"coffee"
caife (m.)
[kaf-ay]

"milk"
bainne (m.)
[bon-yuh]

"a salad"
sailéad (m.)
[sal-ayd]

"an apple"
úll (m.)
[ool]

"tea"
tae (m.)
[tay]

"sugar"
siúcra (m.)
[shoo-kruh]

"a cookie"
briosca (m.)
[bris-kuh]

"apples"
úlla
[ool-uh]

"water"
uisce (m.)
[ish-kuh]

"a sandwich"
ceapaire (m.)
[kya-puh-ruh]

"cookies"
brioscaí
[bris-kee]

Examples

"I would like coffee."
Ba mhaith liom caife.
[buh wah lyum kaf-ay]

"He would like tea."
Ba mhaith leis tae.
[buh wah lesh tay]

"They would like water."
Ba mhaith leo uisce.
[buh wah lyo ish-kuh]

"The cat would like milk."
Ba mhaith leis an gcat bainne.
[buh wah lesh un got bon-yuh]

"The woman would like sugar."
Ba mhaith leis an mbean siúcra.
[buh wah lesh un man shoo-kruh]

"Brian would like a sandwich."
Ba mhaith le Brian ceapaire.
[buh wah leh bree-uhn kya-puh-ruh]

"She would like a salad."
Ba mhaith léi sailéad.
[buh wah lay-ih sal-ayd]

"Patricia would like a cookie."
Ba mhaith le Pádraigín briosca.
[buh wah leh paw-druh-geen bris-kuh]

"The children would like cookies."
Ba mhaith leis na páistí brioscaí.
[buh wah lesh nuh paw-stchee bris-kee]

"The doctor would like an apple."
Ba mhaith leis an dochtúir úll.
[buh wah lesh un dokh-toor ool]

"The friends would like apples."
Ba mhaith leis na cairde úlla.
[buh wah lesh nuh kahr-juh ool-uh]

Lesson 160 – I Wouldn't Like It

Sometimes, you'll want to say what you wouldn't like. To make this *Bonus Phrase* negative, all you have to do is switch out the word "**ba**" [buh] for its negative form, which is "**níor**" [neer]. For example:

"I <u>would</u> like tea."
Ba mhaith liom tae.
[buh wah lyum tay]

"I <u>wouldn't</u> like tea."
Níor mhaith liom tae.
[neer wah lyum tay]

Examples

"I wouldn't like milk."
Níor mhaith liom bainne.
[neer wah lyum bon-yuh]

"She wouldn't like sugar."
Níor mhaith léi siúcra.
[neer wah lay-ih shoo-kruh]

"They wouldn't like water."
Níor mhaith leo uisce.
[neer wah lyo ish-kuh]

"Brian wouldn't like coffee."
Níor mhaith le Brian caife.
[neer wah leh bree-uhn kaf-ay]

"The mechanic wouldn't like a salad."
Níor mhaith leis an meicneoir sailéad.
[neer wah lesh un mek-nyor sal-ayd]

"The secretaries wouldn't like apples."
Níor mhaith leis na rúnaithe úlla.
[neer wah lesh nuh roo-nee-heh ool-uh]

Lesson 161 – Asking About What You Would Like

To ask about what people would like, all you have to do is switch out the word "**ba**" [buh] with its question form, which is "**ar**" [ur]. For example:

"You <u>would</u> like water."
Ba mhaith leat uisce.
[buh wah lyat ish-kuh]

"<u>Would</u> you like water?"
Ar mhaith leat uisce?
[ur wah lyat ish-kuh]

TIP!   Be careful! The question word "**ar**" [ur] may look like the preposition for "on," "**ar**" [air], but it's a very different word, and is pronounced differently. A clue to tell them apart is that verbs appear at the beginnings of sentences, so if you see this word at the start of a sentence, it will most likely be the question indicator "**ar**" [ur].

Examples

"Would you like coffee?"
Ar mhaith leat caife?
[ur wah lyat kaf-ay]

"Would y'all like cookies?"
Ar mhaith libh brioscaí?
[ur wah liv bris-kee]

"Would we like the apples?"
Ar mhaith linn na h-úlla?
[ur wah leeng nuh hool-uh]

"Would Patricia like a sandwich?"
Ar mhaith le Pádraigín ceapaire?
[ur wah leh paw-druh-geen kya-puh-ruh]

"Would the child like milk?"
Ar mhaith leis an bpáiste bainne?
[ur wah lesh un baw-stchuh bon-yuh]

"Would the friends like tea?"
Ar mhaith leis na cairde tae?
[ur wah lesh nuh kahr-juh tay]

Wouldn't You Like It?

To ask what people wouldn't like, you switch the word "**ba**" [buh] with its negative question form "**nár**" [nawr]. For example:

"You <u>would</u> like cookies."
<u>Ba</u> mhaith leat brioscaí.
[buh wah lyat bris-kee]

"<u>Wouldn't</u> you like cookies?"
<u>Nár</u> mhaith leat brioscaí?
[nawr wah lyat bris-kee]

Examples

"Wouldn't you like an sandwich?"
Nár mhaith leat ceapaire?
[nawr wah lyat kya-puh-ruh]

"Wouldn't y'all like apples?"
Nár mhaith libh úlla?
[nawr wah liv ool-uh]

"Wouldn't she like the cookie?"
Nár mhaith léi an briosca?
[nawr wah lay-ih un bris-kuh]

"Wouldn't Brian like milk?"
Nár mhaith le Brian bainne?
[nawr wah leh bree-uhn bon-yuh]

"Wouldn't the secretary like a salad?"
Nár mhaith leis an rúnaí sailéad?
[nawr wah lesh un roo-nee sal-ayd]

"Wouldn't the students like coffee?"
Nár mhaith leis na daltaí caife?
[nawr wah lesh nuh dahl-tee kaf-ay]

Lesson 162 – Answering About What You Would Like

When answering a question in Irish, you use the positive or negative form of the verb. In this case, repeating the verb means repeating the entire *verbal phrase*. To answer "yes" to an "**ar mhaith**" [ur wah] or "**nár mhaith**" [nawr wah] question, you say:

"Yes."
Ba mhaith.
[buh wah]

To answer "no" to a "**ar mhaith**" [ur wah] or "**nár mhaith**" [nawr wah] question, you say:

"No."
Níor mhaith.
[neer wah]

Once again, you can follow this with a complete sentence, but don't forget to repeat the *verbal phrase* which means "yes" or "no."

Examples

"Would you like an apple?"
Ar mhaith leat úll?
[ur wah lyat ool]

"Yes. I would like one."
Ba mhaith. Ba mhaith liom ceann.
[buh wah. buh wah lyum kyawn]

"Would he like tea?"
Ar mhaith leis tae?
[ur wah lesh tay]

"No. He wouldn't like tea."
Níor mhaith. Níor mhaith leis tae.
[neer wah. neer wah lesh tay]

"Wouldn't they like cookies?"
Nár mhaith leo brioscaí?
[nawr wah lyo bris-kee]

"Yes. They would like cookies."
Ba mhaith. Ba mhaith leo brioscaí.
[buh wah. buh wah lyo bris-kee]

"Wouldn't Patricia like coffee?"
Nár mhaith le Pádraigin caife?
[nawr wah leh paw-druh-geen kaf-ay]

"No. She would like water."
Níor mhaith. Ba mhaith léi uisce.
[neer wah. buh wah lay-ih ish-kuh]

Conversation

Now we'll practice talking about what people would like with a conversation.

Pádraigín:
"Brian, would you like anything?"
A Bhriain, ar mhaith leat aon rud?
[uh vree-uhn, ur wah lyat ayn ruhd]

Brian:
"Yes. I would like tea, please."
Ba mhaith. Ba mhaith liom tae, le do thoil.
[buh wah. buh wah lyum tay, leh duh hull]

Pádraigín:
"Here you are!"
Seo duit!
[shuh ghitch]

Brian:
"Thank you."
Go raibh maith agat.
[guh ruh mah ah-gut]

Pádraigín:
"You're welcome."
Tá fáilte romhat.
[taw fawl-tchuh roet]

"Would Noreen like tea, too?"
Ar mhaith le Noirín tae, freisin?
[ur wah leh nor-een tay, fresh-in]

Brian:
"No. But she would like cookies and milk."
Níor mhaith. Ach ba mhaith léi brioscaí agus bainne.
[neer wah. akh buh wah lay-ih bris-kee ah-gus bon-yuh]

Pádraigín:
"Would Liam like cookies and milk?"
Ar mhaith le Liam brioscaí agus bainne?
[ur wah leh lee-um bris-kee ah-gus bon-yuh]

Brian:
"No."
Níor mhaith.
[neer wah]

Pádraigín:
"Wouldn't he like anything?"
Nár mhaith leis rud ar bith?
[nawr wah lesh ruhd air bih]

Brian:
"No. He's fine."
Níor mhaith. Tá sé go breá.
[neer wah. taw shay guh braw]

Lesson 163 — What Would You Like?

To ask, "What would you like?" in Irish, all you have to do is add the word "**céard**" [kayrd], "what," in front of the positive statement.

"What would you like?"
Céard ba mhaith leat?
[kayrd buh wah lyat]

Examples

"What would y'all like?"
Céard ba mhaith libh?
[kayrd buh wah liv]

"We would like tea."
Ba mhaith linn tae.
[buh wah leeng tay]

"What would Patricia like?"
Céard ba mhaith le Pádraigín?
[kayrd buh wah leh paw-druh-geen]

"She would like a salad."
Ba mhaith léi sailéad.
[buh wah lay-ih sal-ayd]

"What would the children like?"
Céard ba mhaith leis na páistí?
[kayrd buh wah lesh nuh paw-stchee]

"They would like sugar."
Ba mhaith leo siúcra.
[buh wah lyo shoo-kruh]

Conversation

Let's practice asking what people would like with a conversation.

Brian:
"What would you like, Patricia?"
Céard ba mhaith leat, a Phádraigín?
[kayrd buh wah lyat, uh faw-druh-geen]

Pádraigín:
"I would like tea, please."
Ba mhaith liom tae, le do thoil.
[buh wah lyum tay, leh duh hull]

Brian:
"Okay."
Ceart go leor.
[kyart guh leeyor]

"And what would the students like?"
Agus céard ba mhaith leis na daltaí?
[ah-gus kayrd buh wah lesh nuh dahl-tee]

Pádraigín:
"They would like coffee."
Ba mhaith leo caife.
[buh wah lyo kaf-ay]

Brian:
"Would y'all like milk and sugar?"
Ar mhaith libh bainne agus siúcra?
[ur wah liv bon-yuh ah-gus shoo-kruh]

Pádraigín:
"Yes, thank you."
Ba mhaith, go raibh maith agat.
[buh wah, guh ruh mah ah-gut]

Brian:
"And what would the teacher like?"
Agus céard ba mhaith leis an múinteoir?
[ah-gus kayrd buh wah lesh un moon-chor]

Pádraigín:
"He would like water."
Ba mhaith leis uisce.
[buh wah lesh ish-kuh]

Lesson 164 – I Like It

Rather than expressing what you *would* like, sometimes you just want to say what you *do* like. To state a liking, all you have to do is take the sentence for what you would like, and change "**ba**" [buh] and "**mhaith**" [wah] into their regular forms, "**is**" [iss] and "**maith**" [mah].

To say that you like something in Irish, you say:

"I like X."
Is maith liom X.
[iss mah lyum ...]

This loosely translates as, "X is good with me."

Let's take a look at a sentence saying what you *would* like and one saying what you *do* like to compare:

"I <u>would like</u> coffee."
<u>Ba mhaith</u> liom caife.
[buh wah lyum kaf-ay]

"I <u>like</u> coffee."
<u>Is maith</u> liom caife.
[iss mah lyum kaf-ay]

Examples

Now let's look at some sample sentences that say what someone likes.

"I like coffee."
Is maith liom caife.
[iss mah lyum kaf-ay]

"You like tea."
Is maith leat tae.
[iss mah lyat tay]

"He likes maps."
Is maith leis léarscáileanna.
[iss mah lesh layr-skoyl-uh-nuh]

"She likes the beach."
Is maith léi an trá.
[iss mah lay-ih un traw]

"We like these cookies."
Is maith linn na brioscaí seo.
[iss mah leeng nuh bris-kee shuh]

"Y'all like apples."
Is maith libh úlla.
[iss mah liv ool-uh]

"They like the hotel."
Is maith leo an t-óstán.
[iss mah lyo un toess-tawn]

"Brian likes the book."
Is maith le Brian an leabhar.
[iss mah leh bree-uhn un lyow-er]

"The man likes the chair."
Is maith leis an bhfear an chathaoir.
[iss mah lesh un var un khah-heer]

"The secretaries like that restaurant."
Is maith leis na rúnaithe an bhialann sin.
[iss mah lesh nuh roo-nee-heh un vee-uh-luhn shin]

Lesson 165 – I Like Doing Things

You can like activities as well as things. To talk about what you like doing, you use the same kind of "like" sentence we learned in the previous lesson, only you use a phrase in the *progressive tense* instead of a noun.

In Irish, you make the progressive tense by saying "**ag**" [ehg], "at," and then a verbal noun. (See Lesson 33 for more about the progressive tense.) Because you're talking about what you like "to" do, you also use a phrase for "to be" before the progressive tense. While in English you can say simply, "I like swimming," in Irish you state more precisely that you like "*to be* swimming."

To say "to be" in this sense, you say, "**a bheith**" [uh veh]. So, to say that you like doing something, you say:

"I like X-ing."
Is maith liom a bheith ag X.
[iss mah lyum uh veh ehg ...]

Vocabulary

Here are some activities that people can like doing. You've seen a few of these before and some are new.

"learning"	"swimming"	"travelling"	"cooking"
ag foghlaim	**ag snámh**	**ag taisteal**	**ag cócaireacht**
[ehg foe-lum]	[ehg snawv]	[ehg tash-tuhl]	[ehg ko-kuh-rahkht]

"running"	"dancing"	"reading"	"shopping"
ag rith	**ag rince**	**ag léamh**	**ag siopadóireacht**
[ehg rih]	[ehg ring-kuh]	[ehg lay-uv]	[ehg shuh-puh-doy-rahkht]

Examples

Let's take a look at some sentences talking about what people like to do:

"I like learning."
Is maith liom a bheith ag foghlaim.
[iss mah lyum uh veh ehg foe-lum]

"They like running."
Is maith leo a bheith ag rith.
[iss mah lyo uh veh ehg rih]

"Patricia likes swimming."
Is maith le Pádraigín a bheith ag snámh.
[iss mah leh paw-druh-geen uh veh ehg snawv]

"The people like dancing."
Is maith leis na daoine a bheith ag rince.
[iss mah lesh nuh dee-nuh uh veh ehg ring-kuh]

"We like travelling."
Is maith linn a bheith ag taisteal.
[iss mah leeng uh veh ehg tash-tuhl]

"The doctors like reading."
Is maith leis na dochtúirí a bheith ag léamh.
[iss mah lesh nuh dokh-toor-ee uh veh ehg lay-uv]

"The mechanic likes cooking."
Is maith leis an meicneoir a bheith ag cócaireacht.
[iss mah lesh un mek-nyor uh veh ehg ko-kuh-rahkht]

"The friends like shopping."
Is maith leis na cairde a bheith ag siopadóireacht.
[iss mah lesh nuh kahr-juh uh veh ehg shuh-puh-doy-rahkht]

Lesson 166 – I Don't Like Things

To say what you don't like, all you have to do is say a "like" sentence using the negative form of "**is**" [iss], which is "**ní**" [nee].

"I don't like X."
Ní maith liom X.
[nee mah lyum ...]

Examples

"I don't like coffee."
Ní maith liom caife.
[nee mah lyum kaf-ay]

"He doesn't like swimming."
Ní maith leis a bheith ag snámh.
[nee mah lesh uh veh ehg snawv]

"We don't like that store."
Ní maith linn an siopa sin.
[nee mah leeng un shuhp-uh shin]

"They don't like cooking."
Ní maith leo a bheith ag cócaireacht.
[nee mah lyo uh veh ehg ko-kuh-rahkht]

"Patricia doesn't like running."
Ní maith le Pádraigín a bheith ag rith.
[nee mah leh paw-druh-geen uh veh ehg rih]

"The musician doesn't like tea."
Ní maith leis an gceoltóir tae.
[nee mah lesh un gyoel-tor tay]

"The boys don't like shopping."
Ní maith leis na buachaillí a bheith ag siopadóireacht.
[nee mah lesh nuh boo-uh-khulee uh veh ehg shuh-puh-doy-rahkht]

Lesson 167 – Asking About What You Like

To ask about what people like, you use the positive question form of "**is**" [iss], which is "**an**" [un].

"Do you like X?"
An maith leat X?
[un mah lyat ...]

Examples

"Do you like tea?"
An maith leat tae?
[un mah lyat tay]

"Does she like cookies?"
An maith léi brioscaí?
[un mah lay-ih bris-kee]

"Do y'all like travelling?"
An maith libh a bheith ag taisteal?
[un mah liv uh veh ehg tash-tuhl]

"Do doctors like apples?"
An maith le dochtúirí úlla?
[un mah leh dokh-toor-ee ool-uh]

"Does Brian like cooking?"
An maith le Brian a bheith ag cócaireacht?
[un mah leh bree-uhn uh veh ehg ko-kuh-rahkht]

"Does the cat like milk?"
An maith leis an gcat bainne?
[un mah lesh un got bon-yuh]

"Do the men like dancing?"
An maith leis na fir ag rince?
[un mah lesh nuh fihr ehg ring-kuh]

"Do the boys and girls like fruit?"
An maith leis na buachaillí agus cailíní torthaí?
[un mah lesh nuh boo-uh-khulee ah-gus kall-yeen-ee tor-hee]

Don't You Like It?

To ask about what people don't like, you use the negative question form of "**is**" [iss], which is "**nach**" [nahkh].

"Don't you like X?"
Nach maith leat X?
[nahkh mah lyat ...]

Examples

"Don't you like cookies?"
Nach maith leat brioscaí?
[nahkh mah lyat bris-kee]

"Doesn't he like reading?"
Nach maith leis a bheith ag léamh?
[nahkh mah lesh uh veh ehg lay-uv]

"Don't y'all like the park?"
Nach maith libh an pháirc?
[nahkh mah liv un fawrk]

"Don't they like swimming?"
Nach maith leo a bheith ag snámh?
[nahkh mah lyo uh veh ehg snawv]

"Doesn't Patricia like shopping?"
Nach maith le Pádraigín a bheith ag siopadóireacht?
[nahkh mah leh paw-druh-geen uh veh ehg shuh-puh-doy-rahkht]

"Doesn't the dog like running?"
Nach maith leis an madra a bheith ag rith?
[nahkh mah lesh un mah-druh uh veh ehg rih]

"Don't the women like tea?"
Nach maith leis na mná tae?
[nahkh mah lesh nuh mraw tay]

Lesson 168 – Answering About What You Like

When you answer a question in Irish, you use the positive or negative form of the verb or verbal phrase. To answer "yes" to an "**an maith**" [un mah] or "**nach maith**" [nahkh mah] question, you say:

"Yes."
Is maith.
[iss mah]

To answer "no" to an "**an maith**" [un mah] or "**nach maith**" [nahkh mah] question, you say:

"No."
Ní maith.
[nee mah]

As always, you can follow this with a complete sentence, but don't forget to repeat the verbal phrase for "yes" or "no."

Examples

Let's take a look at some questions about liking things with some answers.

"Do you like running?"
An maith leat a bheith ag rith?
[un mah lyat uh veh ehg rih]

"Yes, I like running."
Is maith. Is maith liom a bheith ag rith.
[iss mah. iss mah lyum uh veh ehg rih]

"No, I don't like running."
Ní maith. Ní maith liom a bheith ag rith.
[nee mah. nee mah lyum uh veh ehg rih]

"No. I like dancing."
Ní maith. Is maith liom a bheith ag rince.
[nee mah. iss mah lyum uh veh ehg ring-kuh]

"Doesn't he like coffee?"
Nach maith leis caife?
[nahkh mah lesh kaf-ay]

"Yes, he likes coffee."
Is maith. Is maith leis caife.
[iss mah. iss mah lesh kaf-ay]

"No, he doesn't like coffee."
Ní maith. Ní maith leis caife.
[nee mah. nee mah lesh kaf-ay]

"No. He likes tea."
Ní maith. Is maith leis tae.
[nee mah. iss mah lesh tay]

Conversation

Now we'll practice talking about what people like with a conversation.

Pádraigín:
"Do you like salad?"
An maith leat sailéad?
[un mah lyat sal-ayd]

Brian:
"No, I don't like salad."
Ní maith. Ní maith liom sailéad.
[nee mah. nee mah lyum sal-ayd]

"But I do like cookies."
Ach is maith liom brioscaí.
[akh iss mah lyum bris-kee]

Pádraigín:
"Do you like cooking?"
An maith leat a bheith ag cócaireacht?
[un mah lyat uh veh ehg ko-kuh-rahkht]

Brian:
"Yes. I like cooking."
Is maith. Is maith liom a bheith ag cócaireacht.
[iss mah. iss mah lyum uh veh ehg ko-kuh-rahkht]

Pádraigín:

"Don't the children like cooking, too?"

Nach maith leis na páistí a bheith ag cócaireacht, freisin?

[nahkh mah lesh nuh paw-stchee uh veh ehg ko-kuh-rahkht, fresh-in]

Brian:

"No. They like reading."

Ní maith. Is maith leo a bheith ag léamh.

[nee mah. iss mah lyo uh veh ehg lay-uv]

Lesson 169 – What Do You Like?

To ask someone, "What do you like?", you add the word "**céard**" [kayrd], "what," in front of the positive statement.

"What do you like?"
Céard is maith leat?
[kayrd iss mah lyat]

Examples

"What do they like?"
Céard is maith leo?
[kayrd iss mah lyo]

"They like apples."
Is maith leo úlla.
[iss mah lyo ool-uh]

"What does Brian like?"
Céard is maith le Brian?
[kayrd iss mah leh bree-uhn]

"He likes learning."
Is maith leis a bheith ag foghlaim.
[iss mah lesh uh veh ehg foe-lum]

"What does the engineer like?"
Céard is maith leis an innealtóir?
[kayrd iss mah lesh un in-yil-tor]

"She likes maps."
Is maith léi léarscáileanna.
[iss mah lay-ih layr-skoyl-uh-nuh]

Conversation

Let's practice asking what people like with a conversation.

Brian:
"What does Noreen like?"
Céard is maith le Noirín?
[kayrd iss mah leh nor-een]

Pádraigín:
"She likes the beach."
Is maith léi an trá.
[iss mah lay-ih un traw]

Brian:
"And what does Liam like?"
Agus céard is maith le Liam?
[ah-gus kayrd iss mah leh lee-um]

Pádraigín:
"He likes the beach, but he also likes the park."
Is maith leis an trá, ach is maith leis an pháirc, freisin.
[iss mah lesh un traw, akh iss mah lesh un fawrk, fresh-in]

Brian:
"Do Noreen and Liam like travelling?"
An maith le Noirín agus Liam a bheith ag taisteal?
[un mah leh nor-een ah-gus lee-um uh veh ehg tash-tuhl]

Pádraigín:
"No. They don't like travelling."
Ní maith. Ní maith leo a bheith ag taisteal.
[nee mah. nee mah lyo uh veh ehg tash-tuhl]

Brian:
"What do they like?"
Céard is maith leo?
[kayrd iss mah lyo]

Pádraigín:
"They like running."
Is maith leo a bheith ag rith.
[iss mah lyo uh veh ehg rih]

Lesson 170 – I Love Things

Sometimes, you don't just like a thing – you love it! To express that you love something, you take the sentence for what you like, and switch out "**maith**" [mah], "good," for the word "**breá**" [braw], which means "fine" or "lovely."

To say that you love something, you say:

"I love X."
Is breá liom X.
[iss braw lyum ...]

Note that this phrase is used to indicate a strong liking for a thing, rather than affectionate love. (See Lesson 155 to review the expression we learned for affectionate love).

Examples

"I love cookies."
Is breá liom brioscaí.
[iss braw lyum bris-kee]

"You love that chair."
Is breá leat an chathaoir sin.
[iss braw lyat un khah-heer shin]

"He loves dancing."
Is breá leis a bheith ag rince.
[iss braw lesh uh veh ehg ring-kuh]

"She loves sugar."
Is breá léi siúcra.
[iss braw lay-ih shoo-kruh]

"We love these plates."
Is breá linn na plátaí seo.
[iss braw leeng nuh plaw-tee shuh]

"Y'all love shopping."
Is breá libh a bheith ag siopadóireacht.
[iss braw liv uh veh ehg shuh-puh-doy-rahkht]

"They love the land."
Is breá leo an tír.
[iss braw lyo un tcheer]

"Patricia loves swimming."
Is breá le Pádraigín a bheith ag snámh.
[iss braw leh paw-druh-geen uh veh ehg snawv]

"The dentist loves apples."
Is breá leis an bhfiaclóir úlla.
[iss braw lesh un vee-uh-klor ool-uh]

"The students love learning."
Is breá leis na daltaí a bheith ag foghlaim.
[iss braw lesh nuh dahl-tee uh veh ehg foe-lum]

I Don't Love It

To talk about what people don't love, you use the negative form of "**is**" [iss], which is "**ní**" [nee].
To say that you don't love something, you say:

"I don't love X."
Ní breá liom X.
[nee braw lyum ...]

Examples

"She doesn't love coffee."
Ní breá léi caife.
[nee braw lay-ih kaf-ay]

"We don't love cooking."
Ní breá linn a bheith ag cócaireacht.
[nee braw leeng uh veh ehg ko-kuh-rahkht]

"Brian doesn't love apples."
Ní breá le Brian úlla.
[nee braw leh bree-uhn ool-uh]

"The secretaries don't love running."
Ní breá leis na rúnaithe a bheith ag rith.
[nee braw lesh nuh roo-nee-heh uh veh ehg rih]

Lesson 171 – Asking About What You Love

To ask about what people love, you simply switch the word "**is**" [iss] for its question form, "**an**" [un].

"Do you love X?"
An breá leat X?
[un braw lyat ...]

Examples

"Do you love tea?"
An breá leat tae?
[un braw lyat tay]

"Do they love salad?"
An breá leo sailéad?
[un braw lyo sal-ayd]

"Does Liam love swimming?"
An breá le Liam a bheith ag snámh?
[un braw leh lee-um uh veh ehg snawv]

"Do the servers love the restaurant?"
An breá leis na freastalaithe an bhialann?
[un braw lesh nuh fras-tuh-lee-huh un vee-uh-luhn]

Don't You Love It?

To ask about what people don't love, you switch "**is**" [iss] with its negative question form, "**nach**" [nahkh].

"Don't you love X?"
Nach breá leat X?
[nahkh braw lyat ...]

Examples

"Don't y'all love apples?"
Nach breá libh úlla?
[nahkh braw liv ool-uh]

"Doesn't he love reading?"
Nach breá leis a bheith ag léamh?
[nahkh braw lesh uh veh ehg lay-uv]

"Doesn't Noreen love coffee?"
Nach breá le Noirín caife?
[nahkh braw leh nor-een kaf-ay]

"Doesn't the child love milk?"
Nach breá leis an bpáiste bainne?
[nahkh braw lesh un baw-stchuh bon-yuh]

Lesson 172 – Answering About What You Love

When answering a question in Irish, you use the positive or negative form of the verb or verbal phrase. To answer "yes" or "no" to an "**an breá**" [un braw] or "**nach breá**" [nahkh braw] question, you say:

"Yes."	"No."
Is breá.	**Ní breá.**
[iss braw]	[nee braw]

Examples

Let's take a look at some questions about loving things with some answers.

"Does she love dancing?"
An breá léi a bheith ag rince?
[un braw lay-ih uh veh ehg ring-kuh]

"Yes, she loves dancing."
Is breá. Is breá léi a bheith ag rince.
[iss braw. iss braw lay-ih uh veh ehg ring-kuh]

"No. She doesn't love dancing."
Ní breá. Ní breá léi a bheith ag rince.
[nee braw. nee braw lay-ih uh veh ehg ring-kuh]

"No. She loves cooking."
Ní breá. Is breá léi a bheith ag cócaireacht.
[nee braw. iss braw lay-ih uh veh ehg ko-kuh-rahkht]

"Don't they love boxes?"
Nach breá leo boscaí?
[nahkh braw lyo bus-kee]

"Yes, they love boxes."
Is breá. Is breá leo boscaí.
[iss braw. iss braw lyo bus-kee]

"No. They don't love boxes."
Ní breá. Ní breá leo boscaí.
[nee braw. nee braw lyo bus-kee]

"No. They love keys."
Ní breá. Is breá leo eochracha.
[nee braw. iss braw lyo ukh-rukh-uh]

Conversation

Now we'll practice talking about what people love with a conversation.

Pádraigín:
"Don't you love cookies!"
Nach breá leat brioscaí!
[nahkh braw lyat bris-kee]

Brian:
"Yes. I love cookies."
Is breá. Is breá liom brioscaí.
[iss braw. iss braw lyum bris-kee]

"Do you love tea?"
An breá leat tae?
[un braw lyat tay]

Pádraigín:
"I like tea, but I don't love it."
Is maith liom tae, ach ní breá liom é.
[iss mah lyum tay, akh nee braw lyum ay]

Brian:
"Do you love milk and cookies?"
An breá leat bainne agus brioscaí?
[un braw lyat bon-yuh ah-gus bris-kee]

Pádraigín:
"Yes! I love them!"
Is breá! Is breá liom iad!
[iss braw! iss braw lyum ee-ud]

Brian:
"Me, too!"
Mise, freisin!
[mih-shuh, fresh-in]

Lesson 173 – What Do You Love?

To ask, "What do you love?" in Irish, you add the word "**céard**" [kayrd], "what," in front of the positive statement.

"What do you love?"
Céard is breá leat?
[kayrd iss braw lyat]

Examples

"What do you love?"
Céard is breá leat?
[kayrd iss braw lyat]

"I love cars."
Is breá liom carranna.
[iss braw lyum kahr-uh-nuh]

"What does Brian love?"
Céard is breá le Brian?
[kayrd iss braw leh bree-uhn]

"He loves salad."
Is breá leis sailéad.
[iss braw lesh sal-ayd]

"What do the teachers love?"
Céard is breá leis na múinteoirí?
[kayrd iss braw lesh nuh moon-chor-ee]

"They love to read."
Is breá leo a bheith ag léamh.
[iss braw lyo uh veh ehg lay-uv]

Conversation

Let's practice asking what people love with a conversation.

Brian:
"What do the sisters love?"
Céard is breá leis na deirfiúracha?
[kayrd iss braw lesh nuh drih-foor-uh-khuh]

Pádraigín:

"They love dancing."

Is breá leo a bheith ag rince.

[iss braw lyo uh veh ehg ring-kuh]

Brian:

"And what do the brothers love?"

Agus céard is breá leis na deartháireacha?

[ah-gus kayrd iss braw lesh nuh dreh-har-uh-khuh]

Pádraigín:

"They love swimming."

Is breá leo a bheith ag snámh.

[iss braw lyo uh veh ehg snawv]

Brian:

' Do the sisters love swimming, too?"

An breá leis na deirfiúracha a bheith ag snámh, freisin?

[un braw lesh nuh drih-foor-uh-khuh uh veh ehg snawv, fresh-in]

Pádraigín:

"They like swimming, but they don't love it."

Is maith leo a bheith ag snámh, ach ní breá leo é.

[iss mah lyo uh veh ehg snawv, akh nee braw lyo ay]

Lesson 174 – I Hate Things

Sometimes, there are things that you don't love, or don't even like at all. To say that you hate something, all you have to do is take the sentence for what you like, and switch out the word "**maith**" [mah] for "**fuath**" [foo-uh], which means "hate" or "hatred."

To say that you hate something, you say:

"I hate X."
Is fuath liom X.
[iss foo-uh lyum ...]

Examples

"I hate cookies."
Is fuath liom brioscaí.
[iss foo-uh lyum bris-kee]

"You hate running."
Is fuath leat a bheith ag rith.
[iss foo-uh lyat uh veh ehg rih]

"He hates that bicycle."
Is fuath leis an rothar sin.
[iss foo-uh lesh un ruh-her shin]

"She hates waiting."
Is fuath léi a bheith ag fanacht.
[iss foo-uh lay-ih uh veh ehg faw-nahkht]

"We hate this table."
Is fuath linn an bord seo.
[iss foo-uh leeng un bord shuh]

"Y'all hate coffee."
Is fuath libh caife.
[iss foo-uh liv kaf-ay]

"They hate working."
Is fuath leo a bheith ag obair.
[iss foo-uh lyo uh veh ehg uh-ber]

"Brian hates apples."
Is fuath le Brian úlla.
[iss foo-uh leh bree-uhn ool-uh]

"The mechanic hates running."
Is fuath leis an meicneoir a bheith ag rith.
[iss foo-uh lesh un mek-nyor uh veh ehg rih]

"The boys hate tea."
Is fuath leis na buachaillí tae.
[iss foo-uh lesh nuh boo-uh-khulee tay]

I Don't Hate It

To talk about what you don't hate, you switch "**is**" [iss] for its negative form, which is "**ní**" [nee].

"I don't hate X."
Ní fuath liom X.
[nee foo-uh lyum ...]

Examples

"He doesn't hate travelling."
Ní fuath leis a bheith ag taisteal.
[nee foo-uh lesh uh veh ehg tash-tuhl]

"They don't hate milk."
Ní fuath leo bainne.
[nee foo-uh lyo bon-yuh]

"Patricia doesn't hate salad."
Ní fuath le Pádraigín sailéad.
[nee foo-uh leh paw-druh-geen sal-ayd]

"The student doesn't hate cooking."
Ní fuath leis an dalta a bheith ag cócaireacht.
[nee foo-uh lesh un dahl-tuh uh veh ehg ko-kuh-rahkht]

Lesson 175 – Asking About What You Hate

To ask about what people hate, you use the question form of "**is**" [iss], which is "**an**" [un].

"Do you hate X?"
An fuath leat X?
[un foo-uh lyat ...]

Examples

"Do you hate tea?"
An fuath leat tae?
[un foo-uh lyat tay]

"Does she hate fruit?"
An fuath léi torthaí?
[un foo-uh lay-ih tor-hee]

"Do y'all hate cooking?"
An fuath libh a bheith ag cócaireacht?
[un foo-uh liv uh veh ehg ko-kuh-rahkht]

"Does Brian hate sugar?"
An fuath le Brian siúcra?
[un foo-uh leh bree-uhn shoo-kruh]

"Do the secretaries hate waiting?"
An fuath leis na rúnaithe a bheith ag fanacht?
[un foo-uh lesh nuh roo-nee-heh uh veh ehg faw-nahkht]

Don't You Hate It?

To ask what people don't hate, you use the negative question form of "**is**" [iss], which is "**nach**" [nahkh].

"Don't you hate X?"
Nach fuath leat X?
[nahkh foo-uh lyat ...]

Examples

"Don't you hate coffee?"
Nach fuath leat caife?
[nahkh foo-uh lyat kaf-ay]

"Doesn't he hate walking?"
Nach fuath leis a bheith ag siúl?
[nahkh foo-uh lesh uh veh ehg shool]

"Don't we hate that restaurant?"
Nach fuath linn an bhialann sin?
[nahkh foo-uh leeng un vee-uh-luhn shin]

"Don't Brian and Patricia hate apples?"
Nach fuath le Brian agus Pádraigín úlla?
[nahkh foo-uh leh bree-uhn ah-gus paw-druh-geen ool-uh]

"Doesn't the dog hate salad?"
Nach fuath leis an madra sailéad?
[nahkh foo-uh lesh un mah-druh sal-ayd]

Lesson 176 – Answering About What You Hate

When you answer a question in Irish, you use the positive or negative form of the verb or verbal phrase. To answer "yes" or "no" to an "**an fuath**" [un foo-uh] or "**nach fuath**" [nahkh foo-uh] question, you say:

"Yes."	"No."
Is fuath.	**Ní fuath.**
[iss foo-uh]	[nee foo-uh]

Examples

Let's take a look at some questions about hating things with some answers.

"Does he hate tea?"
An fuath leis tae?
[un foo-uh lesh tay]

"Yes, he hates tea."
Is fuath. Is fuath leis tae.
[iss foo-uh. iss foo-uh lesh tay]

"No. He doesn't hate tea."
Ní fuath. Ní fuath leis tae.
[nee foo-uh. nee foo-uh lesh tay]

"No. He hates milk."
Ní fuath. Is fuath leis bainne.
[nee foo-uh. iss foo-uh lesh bon-yuh]

"Don't y'all hate cooking?"
Nach fuath libh a bheith ag cócaireacht?
[nahkh foo-uh liv uh veh ehg ko-kuh-rahkht]

"Yes, we hate cooking."
Is fuath. Is fuath linn a bheith ag cócaireacht.
[iss foo-uh. iss foo-uh leeng uh veh ehg ko-kuh-rahkht]

"No. We don't hate cooking."
Ní fuath. Ní fuath linn a bheith ag cócaireacht.
[nee foo-uh. nee foo-uh leeng uh veh ehg ko-kuh-rahkht]

"No. We hate shopping."
Ní fuath. Is fuath linn a bheith ag siopadóireacht.
[nee foo-uh. iss foo-uh leeng uh veh ehg shuh-puh-doy-rahkht]

Lesson 177 – What Do You Hate?

To ask, "What do you hate?" in Irish, you add the word "**céard**" [kayrd], "what," in front of the positive statement.

"What do you hate?"
Céard is fuath leat?
[kayrd iss foo-uh lyat]

Examples

"What do you hate?"
Céard is fuath leat?
[kayrd iss foo-uh lyat]

"I hate talking."
Is fuath liom a bheith ag caint.
[iss foo-uh lyum uh veh ehg kyintch]

"What does Patricia hate?"
Céard is fuath le Pádraigín?
[kayrd iss foo-uh leh paw-druh-geen]

"She hates sugar."
Is fuath léi siúcra.
[iss foo-uh lay-ih shoo-kruh]

"What does the man hate?"
Céard is fuath leis an bhfear?
[kayrd iss foo-uh lesh un var]

"He hates coffee."
Is fuath leis caife.
[iss foo-uh lesh kaf-ay]

Conversation

Now we'll practice talking about what people hate with a conversation.

Pádraigín:
"The sons hate tea."
Is fuath leis na mic tae.
[iss foo-uh lesh nuh mik tay]

Brian:
"What do the daughters hate?"
Céard is fuath leis na h-iníonacha?
[kayrd iss foo-uh lesh nuh hin-yeen-ih-khuh]

Pádraigín:
"They hate coffee."
Is fuath leo caife.
[iss foo-uh lyo kaf-ay]

Brian:
"Doesn't the mother hate coffee, too?"
Nach fuath leis an máthair caife, freisin?
[nahkh foo-uh lesh un maw-her kaf-ay, fresh-in]

Pádraigín:
"No, she hates milk."
Ní fuath. Is fuath léi bainne.
[nee foo-uh. iss foo-uh lay-ih bon-yuh]

Brian:
"Does she hate cookies?"
An fuath léi brioscaí?
[un foo-uh lay-ih bris-kee]

Pádraigín:
"No. She loves cookies!"
Ní fuath. Is breá léi brioscaí!
[nee foo-uh. iss braw lay-ih bris-kee]

Lesson 178 – I Prefer Things

There are times when you may like many things, and want to express that you prefer one over another. To say that you prefer something in Irish, you simply take the sentence for what you like, and switch out the word "**maith**" [mah] for "**fearr**" [fawr], which means "better."

To say that you prefer something, you say:

"I prefer X."
Is fearr liom X.
[iss fawr lyum ...]

Examples

"I prefer coffee."
Is fearr liom caife.
[iss fawr lyum kaf-ay]

"You prefer walking."
Is fearr leat a bheith ag siúl.
[iss fawr lyat uh veh ehg shool]

"He prefers these tables."
Is fearr leis na boird seo.
[iss fawr lesh nuh bweerj shuh]

"She prefers fruit."
Is fearr léi torthaí.
[iss fawr lay-ih tor-hee]

"We prefer learning."
Is fearr linn a bheith ag foghlaim.
[iss fawr leeng uh veh ehg foe-lum]

"Y'all prefer eating."
Is fearr libh a bheith ag ithe.
[iss fawr liv uh veh ehg ih-huh]

"They prefer reading."
Is fearr leo a bheith ag léamh.
[iss fawr lyo uh veh ehg lay-uv]

"Patricia prefers listening."
Is fearr le Pádraigín a bheith ag éisteacht.
[iss fawr leh paw-druh-geen uh veh ehg aysh-tahkht]

"The secretary prefers that cup."
Is fearr leis an rúnaí an cupán sin.
[iss fawr lesh un roo-nee un kuh-pawn shin]

"The children prefer presents."
Is fearr leis na páistí bronntanais.
[iss fawr lesh nuh paw-stchee brun-tun-ish]

I Don't Prefer It

To talk about what you don't prefer, you switch "**is**" [iss] for its negative form, "**ní**" [nee].

"I don't prefer X."
Ní fearr liom X.
[nee fawr lyum ...]

Examples

"I don't prefer running."
Ní fearr liom a bheith ag rith.
[nee fawr lyum uh veh ehg rih]

"Y'all don't prefer tea."
Ní fearr libh tae.
[nee fawr liv tay]

"Brian doesn't prefer sugar."
Ní fearr le Brian siúcra.
[nee fawr leh bree-uhn shoo-kruh]

"The servers don't prefer those dishes."
Ní fearr leis na freastalaithe na soithí sin.
[nee fawr lesh nuh fras-tuh-lee-huh nuh suh-hee shin]

Lesson 179 – Asking About What You Prefer

To ask about what someone prefers, you use the question form of "**is**" [iss], which is "**an**" [un].

"Do you prefer X?"
An fearr leat X?
[un fawr lyat ...]

Examples

"Do you prefer cooking?"
An fearr leat a bheith ag cócaireacht?
[un fawr lyat uh veh ehg ko-kuh-rahkht]

"Does he prefer tea?"
An fearr leis tae?
[un fawr lesh tay]

"Do they prefer the park?"
An fearr leo an pháirc?
[un fawr lyo un fawrk]

"Does Brian prefer salad?"
An fearr le Brian sailéad?
[un fawr leh bree-uhn sal-ayd]

"Does the cat prefer water?"
An fearr leis an gcat uisce?
[un fawr lesh un got ish-kuh]

Don't You Prefer It?

To ask about what someone doesn't prefer, you switch "**is**" [iss] with its negative question form, "**nach**" [nahkh].

"Don't you prefer X?"
Nach fearr leat X?
[nahkh fawr lyat ...]

Examples

"Don't you prefer apples?"
Nach fearr leat úlla?
[nahkh fawr lyat ool-uh]

"Doesn't he prefer this pen?"
Nach fearr leis an peann seo?
[nahkh fawr lesh un pyawn shuh]

"Don't y'all prefer that window?"
Nach fearr libh an fhuinneog sin?
[nahkh fawr liv un in-yoeg shin]

"Doesn't Patricia prefer travelling?"
Nach fearr le Pádraigín a bheith ag taisteal?
[nahkh fawr leh paw-druh-geen uh veh ehg tash-tuhl]

"Doesn't the boy prefer the dog?"
Nach fearr leis an mbuachaill an madra?
[nahkh fawr lesh un moo-uh-khil un mah-druh]

Lesson 180 – Answering About What You Prefer

When you answer a question in Irish, you use the positive or negative form of the verb or verbal phrase. To answer "yes" or "no" to an "**an fearr**" [un fawr] or "**nach fearr**" [nahkh fawr] question, you say:

"Yes."	"No."
Is fearr.	**Ní fearr.**
[iss fawr]	[nee fawr]

Examples

Let's take a look at some questions about preferring things with some answers.

"Do they prefer reading?"
An fearr leo a bheith ag léamh?
[un fawr lyo uh veh ehg lay-uv]

"Yes, they prefer reading."
Is fearr. Is fearr leo a bheith ag léamh.
[iss fawr. iss fawr lyo uh veh ehg lay-uv]

"No. They don't prefer reading."
Ní fearr. Ní fearr leo a bheith ag léamh.
[nee fawr. nee fawr lyo uh veh ehg lay-uv]

"No. They prefer listening."
Ní fearr. Is fearr leo a bheith ag éisteacht.
[nee fawr. iss fawr lyo uh veh ehg aysh-tahkht]

"Doesn't the woman prefer coffee?"
Nach fearr leis an mbean caife?
[nahkh fawr lesh un man kaf-ay]

"Yes. She prefers coffee."
Is fearr. Is fearr léi caife.
[iss fawr. iss fawr lay-ih kaf-ay]

"No. She doesn't prefer coffee."
Ní fearr. Ní fearr léi caife.
[nee fawr. nee fawr lay-ih kaf-ay]

"No. She prefers water."
Ní fearr. Is fearr léi uisce.
[nee fawr. iss fawr lay-ih ish-kuh]

Lesson 181 – What Do You Prefer?

To ask, "What do you prefer?" in Irish, you add the word "**céard**" [kayrd], "what," in front of the positive statement.

"What do you prefer?"
Céard is fearr leat?
[kayrd iss fawr lyat]

Examples

"What do y'all prefer?"
Céard is fearr libh?
[kayrd iss fawr liv]

"We prefer fruit."
Is fearr linn torthaí.
[iss fawr leeng tor-hee]

"What do Patricia and Brian prefer?"
Céard is fearr le Pádraigín agus Brian?
[kayrd iss fawr leh paw-druh-geen ah-gus bree-uhn]

"They prefer talking."
Is fearr leo a bheith ag caint.
[iss fawr lyo uh veh ehg kyintch]

"What does the engineer prefer?"
Céard is fearr leis an innealtóir?
[kayrd iss fawr lesh un in-yil-tor]

"She prefers coffee."
Is fearr léi caife.
[iss fawr lay-ih kaf-ay]

Conversation

Now we'll practice talking about what people prefer with a conversation.

Brian:
"Do you like milk?"
An maith leat bainne?
[un mah lyat bon-yuh]

Pádraigín:
"Yes. Milk's okay."
Is maith. Tá bainne ceart go leor.
[iss mah. taw bon-yuh kyart guh leeyor]

Brian:
"What do you prefer?"
Céard is fearr leat?
[kayrd iss fawr lyat]

Pádraigín:
"I prefer coffee."
Is fearr liom caife.
[iss fawr lyum kaf-ay]

Brian:
"Do the secretaries prefer coffee, too?"
An fearr leis na rúnaithe caife, freisin?
[un fawr lesh nuh roo-nee-heh kaf-ay, fresh-in]

Pádraigín:
"No. They prefer tea."
Ní fearr. Is fearr leo tae.
[nee fawr. iss fawr lyo tay]

Brian:
"I also prefer tea."
Is fearr liom tae, freisin.
[iss fawr lyum tay, fresh-in]

Lesson 182 – Expressing "To Own"

We've already learned that Irish doesn't use an exclusive verb to express "having" something. Similarly, Irish doesn't use an exclusive verb to express "owning" something, either. In Irish, you say that something is "with" you, indicating that it belongs to you. It may or may not be "at" you at the moment, but you still own it.

Making A Simple Sentence Using the "Own" Expression

When saying what you "have" in Irish, you use a form of the verb "**tá**" [taw]. However, since ownership is a stronger concept, when you say that you "own" something in Irish, you use the other verb for "to be," "**is**" [iss].

To make an "own" sentence, you start with the verb, "**is**" [iss], then a form of "**le**" [leh], "with," followed by the thing being owned.

An important distinction is that the "**is**" [iss] plus "**le**" [leh] expression is only used with *definite nouns*. To talk about owning something indefinite, you go back to the expression for having things, which is "**tá**" [taw] plus "**ag**" [ehg].

Both of these expressions can be translated into English with the word "own." However, the "**is**" [iss] plus "**le**" [leh] expression can also be translated with the possessive words, "mine," "yours," "theirs," etc. For example, you can say, "I own the car," or "The car is mine."

Examples

"I own the car."
Is liom an carr.
[iss lyum un kahr]

"She owns the store."
Is léi an siopa.
[iss lay-ih un shuhp-uh]

"The book is Brian's."
Is le Brian an leabhar.
[iss leh bree-uhn un lyow-er]

"The friends own the hotel."
Is leis na cairde an t-óstán.
[iss lesh nuh kahr-juh un toess-tawn]

Owning This or That

When you're talking about what's being owned, you often want to be very specific about which thing you're referring to. Therefore, this expression is often used with the words for "this" and "that." As we learned before, to express "this" or "that," all you need to do is use the definite article, and then put "**seo**" [shuh] or "**sin**" [shin] after the noun.

Examples

"I own this car."
Is liom an carr seo.
[iss lyum un kahr shuh]

"He owns that bicycle."
Is leis an rothar sin.
[iss lesh un ruh-her shin]

"That is Patricia's key."
Is le Pádraigín an eochair sin.
[iss leh paw-druh-geen un ukh-er shin]

"The daughter owns these lands."
Is leis an iníon na tíortha seo.
[iss lesh un in-yeen nuh tcheer-huh shuh]

Lesson 183 – Asking and Answering Questions About Ownership

You can use any of the forms of "**is**" [iss] with this expression, including negatives and questions. When answering an ownership question, you use the positive or negative form of the verb, along with the appropriate form of "**le**" [leh].

Examples

Let's take a look at some questions with matching answers to get a better idea of how the answers are made.

"Do you own that car?"
An leat an carr sin?
[un lyat un kahr shin]

"Yes."	"No."
Is liom.	**Ní liom.**
[iss lyum]	[nee lyum]

"Doesn't she own this car?"
Nach léi an carr seo?
[nahkh lay-ih un kahr shuh]

"Yes."	"No."
Is léi.	**Ní léi.**
[iss lay-ih]	[nee lay-ih]

"Don't they own these cars?"
Nach leo na carranna seo?
[nahkh lyo nuh kahr-uh-nuh shuh]

"Yes."	"No."
Is leo.	**Ní leo.**
[iss lyo]	[nee lyo]

"Does Brian own those cars?"
An le Brian na carranna sin?
[un leh bree-uhn nuh kahr-uh-nuh shin]

"Yes."	"No."
Is leis.	**Ní leis.**
[iss lesh]	[nee lesh]

You can also answer with a full sentence. Just remember to repeat the verbal phrase using the positive or negative form of "**is**" [iss] and the appropriate form of "**le**" [leh].

"Do you own this bicycle?"
An leat an rothar seo?
[un lyat un ruh-her shuh]

"Yes, I own this bike."
Is liom. Is liom an rothar seo.
[iss lyum. iss lyum un ruh-her shuh]

"No, I don't own this bike."
Ní liom. Ní liom an rothar seo.
[nee lyum. nee lyum un ruh-her shuh]

"No. Patricia owns this bike."
Ní liom. Is le Pádraigín an rothar seo.
[nee lyum. iss leh paw-druh-geen un ruh-her shuh]

Lesson 184 – Emphatics with Ownership

Many times, when you're indicating who owns something, you want to be emphatic about who it belongs to. You can use the emphatic forms of the prepositional pronouns for this.

Vocabulary

Here are the emphatic forms for the preposition pronouns of "**le**" [leh]:

"with *me*"
liomsa
[lyum-suh]

"with *us*"
linne
[leeng-uh]

"with *you*"
leatsa
[lyat-suh]

"with *y'all*"
libhse
[liv-shuh]

"with *him*"
leisean
[lesh-un]

"with *them*"
leosan
[lyo-sun]

"with *her*"
léise
[lay-ih-shuh]

Examples

Here are some examples using the emphatic forms of "**le**" [leh] to show ownership. Notice that these emphatic sentences are often translated into English with the possessive words.

"It's *mine*!"
Is liomsa é!
[iss lyum-suh ay]

"That's not *yours*!"
Ní leatsa é sin!
[nee lyat-suh ay shin]

"Is this *his* car?"
An leisean an carr seo?
[un lesh-un un kahr shuh]

"Doesn't *she* own the store?"
Nach léise an siopa?
[nahkh lay-ih-shuh un shuhp-uh]

"*We* own these computers."
Is linne na ríomhairí seo.
[ss leeng-uh nuh ree-ver-ee shuh]

"Are these apples *y'all's*?"
An libhse na h-úlla seo?
[un liv-shuh nuh hool-uh shuh]

"That's *their* box."
Is leosan an bosca sin.
[iss lyo-sun un bus-kuh shin]

Lesson 185 – Who Owns It?

When asking about owning a thing, you may not know who owns it at all. To ask who owns something without using any names or nouns, you can say:

"Who owns it?"
Cé leis é?
[kay lesh ay]

As we've seen before with other question words, there's no form of the verb "**is**" [iss] in this question. The question word "**cé**" [kay] "who," implies the verb "is." You'll also notice that the *masculine* "with," "**leis**" [lesh], is used. Since you don't know if the person who owns something is male or female, you just default to the *masculine* form of the prepositional pronoun.

Answering "Who Owns It?"

To answer a "Who owns it?" question, all you have to do is say a simple statement with "**is**" [iss] and "**le**" [leh]. You don't even have to say a phrase for "yes" or "no" first, because you weren't asked about a specific owner.

Examples

"Who owns it?"
Cé leis é?
[kay lesh ay]

"Brian owns it."
Is le Brian é.
[iss leh bree-uhn ay]

"Who owns these?"
Cé leis iad seo?
[kay lesh ee-ud shuh]

"The teacher owns those."
Is leis an múinteoir iad sin.
[iss lesh un moon-chor ee-ud shin]

"Who owns this bag?"
Cé leis an mála seo?
[kay lesh un maw-luh shuh]

"That's *my* bag."
Is liomsa an mála sin.
[iss lyum-suh un maw-luh shin]

Conversation

Now we'll practice talking about ownership with a conversation.

Pádraigín:
"Whose box is this?"
Cé leis an bosca seo?
[kay lesh un bus-kuh shuh]

Brian:
"That's Noreen's box."
Is le Noirín an bosca sin.
[iss leh nor-een un bus-kuh shin]

Pádraigín:
"Are these her dishes?"
An léi na soithí seo?
[un lay-ih nuh suh-hee shuh]

Brian:
"No. Those are Liam's."
Ní léi. Is le Liam iad sin.
[nee lay-ih. iss leh lee-um ee-ud shin]

Pádraigín:
"Doesn't Liam own the restaurant?"
Nach le Liam an bhialann?
[nahkh leh lee-um un vee-uh-luhn]

Brian:
"Yes, he owns it."
Is leis. Is leisean í.
[iss lesh. iss lesh-un ee]

Lesson 186 – Regular Verbs in Irish

You've learned a lot of Irish! So far, we've been making sentences using the two verbs for "to be": "**tá**" [taw] and "**is**" [iss]. These are very useful verbs, and you can express a lot with them.

But Irish has lots of other verbs, too! Also, Irish has only eleven irregular verbs, which isn't very many at all. Most verbs follow standard patterns, though, so we'll take a look at some samples first, and then go over the handful of irregular verbs later.

Please note that this will not be a comprehensive study of verbs. The purpose of this and following lessons is to familiarize you with things that you'll see as you continue learning and speaking Irish. We'll be going over a variety of topics to give you a good groundwork from which you can build new concepts. Also, simply being aware of what's out there can be very helpful, in and of itself.

The Command Form

Irish doesn't use an *infinitive form*, such as "to be," "to do," etc. Irish verbs start off in what's called their *root form*. This is the same as their *command form*, which is how you say a verb when giving an order.

When you give a command in Irish, you don't have to use any pronouns. However, Irish does distinguish between a singular "you" and a plural "you," so there is a form for giving commands to one person and a different form for giving commands to more than one person.

Singular Commands

We'll start learning some regular verbs in Irish by looking at them in their *singular command form*. This is also their *root form*, which is how you'll find them in most dictionaries.

Vocabulary

"take"	"walk"	"listen"
tóg	**siúil**	**éist**
[toeg]	[shoo-ihl]	[aysht]

"buy"	"run"	"write"
ceannaigh	**rith**	**scríobh**
[kya-nee]	[rih]	[shkree-uv]

"drink"	"look"	"speak"
ól	**féach**	**labhair**
[oel]	[fay-ukh]	[lau-wer]

Examples

A verb's *root form* is the same as a command to one person. Here are a few singular commands:

"Listen!"
Éist!
[aysht]

"Look!"
Féach!
[fay-ukh]

"Run!"
Rith!
[rih]

Lesson 187 – Plural Commands

To give a command to more than one person, you add the endings "**-igí**" [ih-gee] or "**-aigí**" [uh-gee] to the end of the root form. Sometimes, before you put the plural ending on, the root verb will drop its ending, or drop a vowel from its ending, or even add a vowel to its ending. There are patterns to these changes, but we won't go into all of the details here.

Verbs are categorized into groups called *conjugations*. That means that verbs from one group follow different patterns than verbs from the other group. In Irish, there are two verb groups, and the eleven irregular verbs.

Vocabulary

Here are the plural command forms of our sample verbs:

"(y'all) take"
tógaigí
[toeg-uh-gee]

"(y'all) walk"
siúlaigí
[shool-uh-gee]

"(y'all) listen"
éistigí
[aysht-ih-gee]

"(y'all) buy"
ceannaígí
[kya-nuh-gee]

"(y'all) run"
rithigí
[rih-hih-gee]

"(y'all) write"
scríobhaigí
[shkree-uv-uh-gee]

"(y'all) drink"
ólaigí
[oel-uh-gee]

"(y'all) look"
féachaigí
[fay-ukh-uh-gee]

"(y'all) speak"
labhraígí
[lau-wruh-gee]

Examples

Let's take a look at some singular commands and their plural commands to compare:

"Listen!" (to one person)
Éist!
[aysht]

"Listen!" (to many people)
Éistigí!
[aysht-ih-gee]

"Drink!" (to one person)
Ól!
[oel]

"Drink!" (to many people)
Ólaigí!
[oel-uh-gee]

"Walk!" (to one person)
Siúil!
[shoo-ihl]

"Walk!" (to many people)
Siúlaigí!
[shool-uh-gee]

Lesson 188 – Negative Commands

To make a command negative in Irish, all you have to do is put the word "**ná**" [naw] in front of the command. "**Ná**" [naw] translates as "don't." This is used both when you're talking to one person, and to more than one person. It causes no change to the word after it, but, if the verb begins with a vowel, you put an "**h-**" in front of the verb so that it's easier to say.

Note that there are no question forms for commands. You're not asking; you're telling!

Examples

Let's take a look at some positive commands and some negative commands to compare:

"Walk!"
Siúil!
[shoo-ihl]

"Don't walk!"
Ná siúil!
[naw shoo-ihl]

"Take!"
Tógaigí!
[toeg-uh-gee]

"Don't take!"
Ná tógaigí!
[naw toeg-uh-gee]

"Drink!"
Ól!
[oel]

"Don't drink!"
Ná h-ól!
[naw hoel]

Lesson 189 – Being More Specific with Commands

Sometimes, you'll need to be more specific about what you want, especially when giving a command. You can say, "Buy!", but you'd be more likely to say, "Buy it!", or even, "Buy it now while supplies last!"

To modify a command, all you have to do is add words after the verb. You can have any number or any kind of words after a command, but often you'll just say something simple, like "it," or a noun.

When saying "he," "she," or "they" after a command, make sure to use "**é**" [ay], "**í**" [ee], or "**iad**" [ee-ud] respectively. These are the *object pronouns* that we learned in Lesson 100.

Examples

Let's take a look at a few sentences that use commands with nouns or pronouns after them.

"Take it."
Tóg é.
[toeg ay]

"Buy them."
Ceannaigh iad.
[kya-nee ee-ud]

"Drink this coffee."
Ólaigí an caife seo.
[oel-uh-gee un kaf-ay shuh]

"Don't take those ones."
Ná tóg na cinn sin.
[naw toeg nuh keen shin]

"Buy my apples!"
Ceannaígí m'úlla!
[kya-nuh-gee mool-uh]

"Don't drink the water!"
Ná h-ól an t-uisce!
[naw hoel un tish-kuh]

Lesson 190 – Saying When You Want Something Done

When you give a command, sometimes you want to be specific about when you want it to happen. You can use a time word or phrase like, "today," or "right now," to expand your command. The time word comes right after the verb, or the verb and noun. If you use a pronoun for "it" or "they," the pronoun gets pushed to the end of the sentence, and is said after the time phrase.

Vocabulary

Here are some time words and phrases:

"now"	"later"	"today"
anois	**níos déanaí**	**inniu**
[uh-nish]	[nees jay-nee]	[in-yoo]

"right now"		"tomorrow"
anois díreach		**amárach**
[uh-nish jee-rahkh]		[uh-maw-rahkh]

Examples

"Take the boxes tomorrow."
Tóg na boscaí amárach.
[toeg nuh bus-kee uh-maw-rahkh]

"Don't buy them right now."
Ná ceannaigh anois díreach iad.
[naw kya-nee uh-nish jee-rahkh ee-ud]

"Drink the milk today."
Ól an bainne inniu.
[oel un bon-yuh in-yoo]

"Walk to the park later."
Siúlaigí go dtí an pháirc níos déanaí.
[shool-uh-gee guh jee un fawrk nees jay-nee]

"Run there right now!"
Rith ansin anois díreach!
[rih un-shin uh-nish jee-rahkh]

"Look now."
Féach anois.
[fay-ukh uh-nish]

"Listen right now!"
Éist anois díreach!
[aysht uh-nish jee-rahkh]

"Write it later."
Scríobh níos déanaí é.
[shkree-uv nees jay-nee ay]

"Don't speak now."
Ná labhraígí anois.
[naw lau-wruh-gee uh-nish]

Lesson 191 – Saying Where You Want Something Done

You can use location words to be more specific when you give commands. These can be as simple as "here" and "there," or phrases like the ones we learned with "on," "under," and "in" (see Lessons 39-46 and Lessons 137-147). Similar to time words, location words and phrases come right after the verb, or the verb and noun. If you use a pronoun for "it" or "they," the pronoun gets pushed to the end of the sentence, and is said after the location phrase.

Examples

Let's take a look at some examples showing different kinds of location words and phrases you can use with commands.

"Buy it here."
Ceannaigh anseo é.
[kya-nee un-shuh ay]

"Don't walk under it."
Ná siúil faoi.
[naw shoo-ihl fwee]

"Run to the wedding!"
Rith chuig an mbainis!
[rih khig un man-ish]

"Look inside the box."
Féach isteach sa bhosca.
[fay-ukh iss-tchahkh suh wuss-kuh]

"Don't write on that thing!"
Ná scríobhaigí ar an rud sin!
[naw shkree-uv-uh-gee air un ruhd shin]

Lesson 192 – Words That Pair with Verbs

Some verbs are often paired with other words to expand or clarify their meanings. These helper words are usually prepositions. For example, you can "speak," but you can also "speak *to*" someone.

Vocabulary

Here is a list of words that are often paired with some of the sample verbs:

"look at"
féach ar
[fay-ukh air]

"listen to"
éist le
[aysht leh]

"speak to"
labhair le
[lau-wer leh]

Notice that the prepositions used in Irish don't always match the prepositions used in the English translations. This is common when translating between languages.

Examples

Let's look at some sentences that use these verbs with their helper prepositions. The same pattern we learned for each preposition still applies.

"Look at it."
Féach air.
[fay-ukh air]

"Look at the cookies."
Féach ar na brioscaí.
[fay-ukh air nuh bris-kee]

"Listen to them."
Éist leo.
[aysht lyo]

"Listen to y'all's teacher."
Éistigí le bhur múinteoir.
[aysht-ih-gee leh woor moon-chor]

"Speak to me."
Labhair liom.
[lau-wer lyum]

"Speak to the secretary."
Labhair leis an rúnaí.
[lau-wer lesh un roo-nee]

Lesson 193 – The Past Tense for Regular Verbs

To put a *regular verb* in the *past tense*, all you have to do is *soften* the first letter of the *root form*. If the verb starts with a vowel, you put a "**d'**" (d+apostrophe) in front of it, instead. If the verb starts with the letter "**f**," which will become silent when *softened*, then you treat it like a vowel, and both *soften* the "**f**" and add "**d'**" (d+apostrophe) to the front. If the verb starts with a letter or letter combination that can't be *softened*, you leave it the way it is. Even if a verb stays unchanged, you'll usually be able to tell the difference between commands and past sentences by context.

Vocabulary

Here are our sample verbs in their past tense forms:

"took"	"walked"	"listened"
thóg	**shiúil**	**d'éist**
[hoeg]	[hyoo-ihl]	[jaysht]

"bought"	"ran"	"wrote"
cheannaigh	**rith**	**scríobh**
[khya-nee]	[rih]	[shkree-uv]

"drank"	"looked"	"spoke"
d'ól	**d'fhéach**	**labhair**
[doel]	[jay-ukh]	[lau-wer]

Examples

Making sentences with regular verbs is just like making sentences with "**tá**" [taw]. You say the verb, then a noun or pronoun, and finish it in any number of ways.

"He took the bag."
Thóg sé an mála.
[hoeg shay un maw-luh]

"She bought the car."
Cheannaigh sí an carr.
[khya-nee shee un kahr]

"We drank the tea."
D'ól muid an tae.
[doel mwidj un tay]

"I walked to the beach."
Shiúil mé go dtí an trá.
[shyoo-ihl may guh jee un traw]

"They ran outside."
Rith siad amach.
[rih shee-ud uh-mahkh]

"You looked at the bicycle."
D'fhéach tú ar an rothar.
[ay-ukh too air un ruh-her]

"We listened to the musicians."
D'éist muid leis na ceoltóirí.
[aysht mwidj lesh nuh kyoel-tor-ee]

"Y'all wrote a book."
Scríobh sibh leabhar.
[shkree-uv shiv lyow-er]

"I spoke to some man."
Labhair mé le fear éigin.
[lau-wer may leh far ay-gihn]

Lesson 194 – Negative and Questions for the Past Tense

As we saw before with "**tá**" [taw] and "**is**" [iss], Irish verbs have four forms in most tenses: positive, negative, question, and negative question.

Negative Statements in the Past

To make a negative statement in the past tense with a regular verb, all you have to do is say "**níor**" [neer] in front of it, then *soften* the first letter of the root form. (The extra rules about vowels and silent letters when working with positive statements don't apply here.)

Examples

"I didn't take it."
Níor thóg mé é.
[neer hoeg may ay]

"He didn't buy the cookies."
Níor cheannaigh sé na broiscaí.
[neer khya-nee shay nuh bris-kee]

"They didn't drink coffee."
Níor ól siad caife.
[neer oel shee-ud kaf-ay]

"Y'all didn't walk to the hotel."
Níor shiúil sibh go dtí an t-óstán.
[neer hyoo-ihl shiv guh jee un toess-tawn]

"The women didn't run to the store"
Níor rith na mná go dtí an siopa.
[neer rih nuh mraw guh jee un shuhp-uh]

"The engineer didn't look at it."
Níor fhéach an t-innealtóir air.
[neer ay-ukh un tin-yil-tor air]

"The children didn't listen to him."
Níor éist na páistí leis.
[neer aysht nuh paw-stchee lesh]

"Patricia didn't write that."
Níor scríobh Pádraigín é sin.
[neer shkree-uv paw-druh-geen ay shin]

"We didn't speak to them."
Níor labhair muid leo.
[neer lau-wer mwidj lyo]

Questions in the Past

To make a question in the past tense with a regular verb, all you have to do is say "**ar**" [ur] in front of it, then *soften* the first letter of the root form.

Examples

"Did you take the bag?"
Ar thóg tú an mála?
[ur hoeg too un maw-luh]

"Did someone buy the shop?"
Ar cheannaigh duine éigin an siopa?
[ur khya-nee din-uh ay-gihn un shuhp-uh]

"Did y'all drink tea?"
Ar ól sibh tae?
[ur oel shiv tay]

"Did they walk to the restaurant?"
Ar shiúil siad go dtí an bhialann?
[ur hyoo-ihl shee-ud guh jee un vee-uh-luhn]

"Did y'all run?"
Ar rith sibh?
[ur rih shiv]

"Did she look at them?"
Ar fhéach sí orthu?
[ur ay-ukh shee or-huh]

"Did the mechanic listen to you?"
Ar éist an meicneoir leat?
[ur aysht un mek-nyor lyat]

"Did Brian write on the boxes?"
Ar scríobh Brian ar na boscaí?
[ur shkree-uv bree-uhn air nuh bus-kee]

"Did a dentist speak to the child?"
Ar labhair fiaclóir leis an bpáiste?
[ur lau-wer fee-uh-klor lesh un baw-stchuh]

Negative Questions in the Past

To make a negative question in the past tense with a regular verb, you say "**nár**" [nar] in front of it, then *soften* the first letter of the root form.

Examples

"Didn't I take my coat?"
Nár thóg mé mo chóta?
[nar hoeg may muh kho-tuh]

"Didn't he buy your bicycle?"
Nár cheannaigh sé do rothar?
[nar khya-nee shay duh ruh-her]

"Didn't the cat drink the milk?"
Nár ól an cat an bainne?
[nar oel un kot un bon-yuh]

"Didn't the children walk home?"
Nár shiúil na páistí abhaile?
[nar hyoo-ihl nuh paw-stchee uh-wah-lyuh]

"Didn't the girl run inside?"
Nár rith an cailín isteach?
[nar rih un kall-yeen iss-tchahkh]

"Didn't the boy look in the book?"
Nár fhéach an buachaill sa leabhar?
[nar ay-ukh un boo-uh-khil suh lyow-er]

"Didn't you listen to the engineer?"
Nár éist tú leis an innealtóir?
[nar aysht too lesh un in-yil-tor]

"Didn't the teacher write it?"
Nár scríobh an múinteoir é?
[nar shkree-uv un moon-chor ay]

"Didn't Patricia and Brian speak to the servers?"
Nár labhair Pádraigín agus Brian leis na freastalaithe?
[nar lau-wer paw-druh-geen ah-gus bree-uhn lesh nuh fras-tuh-lee-huh]

"Yes" or "No" in the Past

To answer "yes" or "no" in the past tense with a regular verb, you reply with the positive or negative statement form of the verb you were asked. You can always expand your answer by adding a full sentence after the "yes" or "no."

Examples

"Did you buy milk?"
Ar cheannaigh tú bainne?
[ur khya-nee too bon-yuh]

"Yes."   "No."
Cheannaigh.   **Níor cheannaigh.**
[khya-nee]   [neer khya-nee]

"Didn't the students walk to the store?"
Nár shiúil na daltaí go dtí an siopa?
[nar hyoo-ihl nuh dahl-tee guh jee un shuhp-uh]

"Yes. They walked to the store."
Shiúil. Shiúil siad go dtí an siopa.
[hyoo-ihl. hyoo-ihl shee-ud guh jee un shuhp-uh]

"No. They walked to the restaurant."
Níor shiúil. Shiúil siad go dtí an bhialann.
[neer hyoo-ihl. hyoo-ihl shee-ud guh jee un vee-uh-luhn]

Lesson 195 – The Present Tense for Regular Verbs

We learned before that verbs are categorized into groups called *conjugations*. When putting regular verbs into the present tense, verbs from one group will act differently than verbs from the other group. Still, there are some general guidelines to keep in mind as you continue learning and speaking Irish.

Adding Endings

In the present tense, most verbs will add some kind of an ending. The *present tense* endings are "**-ann**" [uhn] or "**-eann**" [uhn], and "**-íonn**" [ee-uhn] or "**-aíonn**" [ee-uhn]. Sometimes the root verb will drop its ending, or drop a vowel from its ending, or even add a vowel to its ending, before you put the present tense ending on it.

Once again, this is not a comprehensive study on regular verbs, but these are good guidelines to keep in mind. Also, being aware of how these endings look and sound might help you determine if an unfamiliar word is some kind of verb in the present tense. At least that's a start you can go to the dictionary with.

Vocabulary

Here are our sample verbs in their present tense forms:

"takes"	"walks"	"listens"
tógann	**siúlann**	**éisteann**
[toeg-uhn]	[shoo-luhn]	[aysht-uhn]

"buys"	"runs"	"writes"
ceannaíonn	**ritheann**	**scríobhann**
[kya-nee-uhn]	[rih-uhn]	[shkree-uv-uhn]

"drinks"	"looks"	"speaks"
ólann	**féachann**	**labhraíonn**
[oel-uhn]	[fay-ukh-uhn]	[lau-wree-uhn]

Examples

Let's take a look at some sentences that use regular verbs in the present tense. The simple present tense is used to express habitual actions, so you can use the extra words you learned with "**bíonn**" [bee-uhn] (see Lesson 90) to expand and clarify present tense sentences.

"She takes one every day."
Tógann sí ceann gach lá.
[toeg-uhn shee kyawn gahkh law]

"I buy coffee from time to time."
Ceannaíonn mé caife ó am go h-am.
[kya-nee-uhn may kaf-ay oe ahm guh hahm]

"He drinks tea."
Ólann sé tae.
[oel-uhn shay tay]

"They walk to the park."
Siúlann siad go dtí an pháirc.
[shoo-luhn shee-ud guh jee un fawrk]

"The doctor runs often."
Ritheann an dochtúir go minic.
[rih-uhn un dokh-toor guh min-ik]

"Patricia rarely looks at it."
Féachann Pádraigín air go h-annamh.
[fay-ukh-uhn paw-druh-geen air guh hah-nuv]

"They listen to me now and again."
Éisteann siad liom anois agus arís.
[aysht-uhn shee-ud lyum uh-nish ah-gus uh-reesh]

"The boy usually writes in his book."
Scríobhann an buachaill ina leabhar de ghnáth.
[shkree-uv-uhn un boo-uh-khil ihn-uh lyow-er deh ghuh-naw]

"Y'all's father always speaks to y'all's teachers."
Labhraíonn bhur n-athair le bhur múinteoirí i gcónaí.
[lau-wree-uhn woor nah-her leh woor moon-chor-ee ih go-nee]

Lesson 196 – Negative and Questions for the Present Tense

As we've learned before, Irish verbs have four forms in most tenses: positive, negative, question, and negative question.

Negative Statements in the Present

To make a negative statement in the present tense with a regular verb, you say "**ní**" [nee] in front of it, then *soften* the first letter of the conjugated form.

Examples

"That man doesn't take the boxes."
Ní thógann an fear sin na boscaí.
[nee hoeg-uhn un far shin nuh bus-kee]

"The servers don't buy the plates."
Ní cheannaíonn na freastalaithe na plátaí.
[nee khya-nee-uhn nuh fras-tuh-lee-huh nuh plaw-tee]

"The doctor doesn't drink coffee."
Ní ólann an dochtúir caife.
[nee oel-uhn un dokh-toor kaf-ay]

"The boys don't walk home."
Ní shiúlann na buachaillí abhaile.
[nee hyoo-luhn nuh boo-uh-khulee uh-wah-lyuh]

"She doesn't run often."
Ní ritheann sí go minic.
[nee rih-uhn shee guh min-ik]

"Our secretary doesn't look in the boxes."
Ní fhéachann ár rúnaí sna boscaí.
[nee ay-ukh-uhn awr roo-nee snuh bus-kee]

"The child doesn't listen."
Ní éisteann an páiste.
[nee aysht-uhn un paw-stchuh]

"The doctor doesn't write well."
Ní scríobhann an dochtúir go maith.
[nee shkree-uv-uhn un dokh-toor guh mah]

"The engineers don't speak to the secretaries."
Ní labhraíonn na h-innealtóirí leis na rúnaithe.
[nee lau-wree-uhn nuh hin-yil-tor-ee lesh nuh roo-nee-heh]

Questions in the Present

To make a question in the present tense with a regular verb, all you have to do is say "**an**" [un] in front of it, then *eclipse* the first letter of the conjugated form.

Examples

"Do you always take it?"
An dtógann tú é i gcónaí?
[un doeg-uhn too ay ih go-nee]

"Does he usually buy drinks for the musicians?"
An gceannaíonn sé deochanna do na ceoltóirí de ghnáth?
[un gya-nee-uhn shay jawkh-uh-nuh duh nuh kyoel-tor-ee deh ghuh-naw]

"Does Brian drink tea?"
An ólann Brian tae?
[un oel-uhn bree-uhn tay]

"Does your wife walk to the beach?"
An siúlann do bhean chéile go dtí an trá?
[un shoo-luhn duh van khay-leh guh jee un traw]

"Does her husband run from time to time?"
An ritheann a fear céile ó am go h-am?
[un rih-uhn uh far kay-leh oe ahm guh hahm]

"Does the teacher look in her book?"
An bhféachann an múinteoir ina leabhar?
[un vay-ukh-uhn un moon-chor ihn-uh lyow-er]

"Does the woman listen to you?"
An éisteann an bhean leat?
[un aysht-uhn un van lyat]

"Does he write often?"
An scríobhann sé go minic?
[un shkree-uv-uhn shay guh min-ik]

"Do the mechanics speak to the engineer?"
An labhraíonn na meicneoirí leis an innealtóir?
[un lau-wree-uhn nuh mek-nyor-ee lesh un in-yil-tor]

Negative Questions in the Present

To make a negative question in the present tense with a regular verb, you say "**nach**" [nahkh] in front of it, then *eclipse* the first letter of the conjugated form. If the verb begins with a vowel, you put "**n-**" in front of the conjugated form.

Examples

"Don't they usually take those things?"
Nach dtógann siad na rudaí sin de ghnáth?
[nahkh doeg-uhn shee-ud nuh ruh-dee shin deh ghuh-naw]

"Doesn't Patricia always buy a sandwich?"
Nach gceannaíonn Pádraigín ceapaire i gcónaí?
[nahkh gya-nee-uhn paw-druh-geen kya-puh-ruh ih go-nee]

"Don't the servers drink water from time to time?"
Nach n-ólann na freastalaithe uisce ó am go h-am?
[nahkh noel-uhn nuh fras-tuh-lee-huh ish-kuh oe ahm guh hahm]

"Doesn't y'all's friend walk home?"
Nach siúlann bhur gcara abhaile?
[nahkh shoo-luhn woor gahr-uh uh-wah-lyuh]

"Don't the boys always run?"
Nach ritheann na buachaillí i gcónaí?
[nahkh rih-uhn nuh boo-uh-khulee ih go-nee]

"Don't they look at a map often?"
Nach bhféachann siad ar léarscáil go minic?
[nahkh vay-ukh-uhn shee-ud air layr-skoyl guh min-ik]

"Doesn't a teacher listen to the students?"
Nach n-éisteann múinteoir leis na daltaí?
[nahkh naysht-uhn moon-chor lesh nuh dahl-tee]

"Doesn't your daughter write every day?"
Nach scríobhann d'iníon gach lá?
[nahkh shkree-uv-uhn din-yeen gahkh law]

"Doesn't her sister speak to her from time to time?"
Nach labhraíonn a deirfiúr léi ó am go h-am?
[nahkh lau-wree-uhn uh drih-foor lay-ih oe ahm guh hahm]

"Yes" or "No" in the Present

To answer "yes" or "no" in the present tense with a regular verb, you reply with the appropriate positive or negative statement form of the verb you were asked. Remember that you can always expand your answer by adding a full sentence after the "yes" or "no."

Examples

"Do the women run in the park?"
An ritheann na mná sa pháirc?
[un rih-uhn nuh mraw suh fawrk]

"Yes. They run in the park."
Ritheann. Ritheann siad sa pháirc
[rih-uhn. rih-uhn shee-ud suh fawrk]

"Doesn't he drink coffee?"
Nach n-ólann sé caife?
[nahkh noel-uhn shay kaf-ay]

"No. He only drinks tea."
Ní ólann. Ní ólann sé ach tae.
[nee oel-uhn. nee oel-uhn shay akh tay]

Lesson 197 – The Future Tense for Regular Verbs

Putting verbs in the future tense is like using the present tense. Once again, regular verbs from the two verb groups act differently, but they follow some general guidelines.

Adding Endings

In the future tense, most verbs will add some kind of an ending. The *future tense* endings are "**-faidh**" [ee] or "**-fidh**" [ee], and "**-óidh**" [oe-ee] or "**-eoidh**" [oe-ee]. Again, sometimes the root verb will drop its ending, or drop a vowel from its ending, or add a vowel to its ending, before you put the future tense ending on it.

Once again, this is not a comprehensive study on regular verbs, but being aware of how these endings look and sound might help you identify verbs in the future tense.

Vocabulary

Here are our sample verbs in their future tense forms:

"will take"	"will walk"	"will listen"
tógfaidh	**siúlfaidh**	**éistfidh**
[toe-gee]	[shool-ee]	[aysht-ee]
"will buy"	"will run"	"will write"
ceannóidh	**rithfidh**	**scríobhfaidh**
[kya-noe-ee]	[rih-hee]	[shkree-uv-ee]
"will drink"	"will look"	"will speak"
ólfaidh	**féachfaidh**	**labhróidh**
[oel-ee]	[fay-ukh-ee]	[lau-wroe-ee]

Examples

"I will take a pen."
Tógfaidh mé peann.
[toe-gee may pyawn]

"We will buy ten."
Ceannóidh muid deich gcinn.
[kya-noe-ee mwidj jeh geen]

"She will drink a drink."
Ólfaidh sí deoch.
[oel-ee shee jawkh]

"The students will walk to the movie."
Siúlfaidh na daltaí chuig an scannán.
[shool-ee nuh dahl-tee khig un skuh-nawn]

"The dog will run home."
Rithfidh an madra abhaile.
[rih-hee un mah-druh uh-wah-lyuh]

"The doctor will look in his bag."
Féachfaidh an dochtúir ina mhála.
[fay-ukh-ee un dokh-toor ihn-uh wah-luh]

"My friends and I will listen to the musicians."
Éistfidh mé agus mo chairde leis na ceoltóirí.
[aysht-ee may ah-gus muh khahr-juh lesh nuh kyoel-tor-ee]

"The secretary will write it."
Scríobhfaidh an rúnaí é.
[shkree-uv-ee un roo-nee ay]

"*You* will speak to the engineer."
Labhróidh tusa leis an innealtóir.
[lau-wroe-ee tuh-suh lesh un in-yil-tor]

Lesson 198 – Negative and Questions for the Future Tense

Verbs in Irish have four forms in most tenses: positive, negative, question, and negative question.

Negative Statements in the Future

To make a negative statement in the future tense with a regular verb, you say "**ní**" [nee] in front of it, then *soften* the first letter of the conjugated form.

Examples

"The child won't take a coat."
Ní thógfaidh an páiste cóta.
[nee hoe-gee un paw-stchuh ko-tuh]

"She won't buy any cookies."
Ní cheannóidh sí aon bhrioscaí.
[nee khya-noe-ee shee ayn vris-kee]

"*I* won't drink it."
Ní ólfaidh mise é.
[nee oel-ee mih-shuh ay]

"The mechanic won't walk to the store."
Ní shiúlfaidh an meicneoir go dtí an siopa.
[nee hyool-ee un mek-nyor guh jee un shuhp-uh]

"The man won't run."
Ní rithfidh an fear.
[nee rih-hee un far]

"The girl won't look in the box."
Ní fhéachfaidh an cailín sa bhosca.
[nee ay-ukh-ee un kall-yeen suh wuss-kuh]

"They won't listen to me."
Ní éistfidh siad liom.
[nee aysht-ee shee-ud lyum]

"That student won't write in her book."
Ní scríobhfaidh an dalta sin ina leabhar.
[nee shkree-uv-ee un dahl-tuh shin ihn-uh lyow-er]

"The doctor won't speak to y'all."
Ní labhróidh an dochtúir libh.
[nee lau-wroe-ee un dokh-toor liv]

Questions in the Future

To make a question in the future tense with a regular verb, you say "**an**" [un] in front of it, then *eclipse* the first letter of the conjugated form.

Examples

"Will the servers take the drinks?"
An dtógfaidh na freastalaithe na deochanna?
[un doe-gee nuh fras-tuh-lee-huh nuh jawkh-uh-nuh]

"Will your friend buy the shoes?"
An gceannóidh do chara na bróga?
[un gya-noe-ee duh khahr-uh nuh bro-guh]

"Will the girls drink the milk?"
An ólfaidh na cailíní an bainne?
[un oel-ee nuh kall-yeen-ee un bon-yuh]

"Will we walk home tonight?"
An siúlfaidh muid abhaile anocht?
[un shool-ee mwidj uh-wah-lyuh uh-nahkht]

"Will you run to the beach?"
An rithfidh tú go dtí an trá?
[un rih-hee too guh jee un traw]

"Will y'all look under the table?"
An bhféachfaidh sibh faoin mbord?
[un vay-ukh-ee shiv fween mord]

"Will he listen to *you*?"
An éistfidh sé leatsa?
[un aysht-ee shay lyat-suh]

"Will the woman write it on the boxes?"
An scríobhfaidh an bhean ar an mboscaí é?
[un shkree-uv-ee un van air un muss-kee ay]

"Will your son speak to him tomorrow?"
An labhróidh do mhac leis amárach?
[un lau-wroe-ee duh wahk lesh uh-maw-rahkh]

Negative Questions in the Future

To make a negative question in the future tense with a regular verb, you say "**nach**" [nahkh] in front of it, then *eclipse* the first letter of the conjugated form. If the verb begins with a vowel, you put "**n-**" in front of the conjugated form.

Examples

"Won't you take a cookie?"
Nach dtógfaidh tú briosca?
[nahkh doe-gee too bris-kuh]

"Won't Brian buy one?"
Nach gceannóidh Brian ceann?
[nahkh gya-noe-ee bree-uhn kyawn]

"Won't he drink it?"
Nach n-ólfaidh sé é?
[nahkh noel-ee shay ay]

"Won't the boys walk to the park?"
Nach siúlfaidh na buachaillí go dtí an pháirc?
[nahkh shool-ee nuh boo-uh-khulee guh jee un fawrk]

"Won't they run there?"
Nach rithfidh siad ann?
[nahkh rih-hee shee-ud on]

"Won't the mechanic look at it?"
Nach bhféachfaidh an meicneoir air?
[nahkh vay-ukh-ee un mek-nyor air]

"Won't the woman listen to the doctors?"
Nach n-éistfidh an bhean leis na dochtúirí?
[nahkh naysht-ee un van lesh nuh dokh-toor-ee]

"Won't the engineer write the book?"
Nach scríobhfaidh an t-innealtóir an leabhar?
[nahkh shkree-uv-ee un tin-yil-tor un lyow-er]

"Won't his wife speak tomorrow night?"
Nach labhróidh a bhean chéile oíche amárach?
[nahkh lau-wroe-ee uh van khay-leh ee-khuh uh-maw-rahkh]

"Yes" or "No" in the Future

To answer "yes" or "no" in the future tense with a regular verb, you reply with the positive or negative statement form of the verb you were asked. You can always expand your answers by adding a full sentence after the "yes" or "no."

Examples

"Will she buy the shirt?"
An gceannóidh sí an léine?
[un gya-noe-ee shee un lay-nuh]

"No. She will buy the dress."
Ní cheannóidh. Ceannóidh sí an gúna.
[nee khya-noe-ee. kya-noe-ee shee un goo-nuh]

"Won't we walk to the hotel?"
Nach siúlfaidh muid go dtí an t-óstán?
[nahkh shool-ee mwidj guh jee un toess-tawn]

"Yes. We will walk there."
Siúlfaidh. Siúlfaidh muid ann.
[shool-ee. shool-ee mwidj on]

Lesson 199 – Irregular Verbs

There are only eleven irregular verbs in Irish. That's not many at all, especially when compared to many other languages. The good news is that you've learned a lot about one of them already. The verb we've been referring to as "**tá**" [taw] is technically the present tense form of the irregular verb "**bí**" [bee].

The not so good news is that, as in many other languages, very common verbs tend to be irregular verbs. Also, as the name "irregular" indicates, there are no general guidelines between them, so you'll need to study them each individually.

Vocabulary

Here is a full list of all of the irregular verbs in Irish:

"say"	"hear"	"see"	"come"
abair	**clois**	**feic**	**tar**
[ah-ber]	[klish]	[fek]	[tar]

"bear, bring"	"do, make"	"eat"	"go"
beir	**déan**	**ith**	**téigh**
[baer]	[jayn]	[ih]	[tchay]

"be"	"get"	"give"	
bí	**faigh**	**tabhair**	
[bee]	[fai]	[toor]	

The Command Form

Luckily, as irregular as these verbs might be, the root form is still the command form. As we learned before, when you give a command, you don't use any pronouns. Also, as Irish distinguishes between a singular "you" and a plural "you," there is a form when addressing one person and a form for addressing more than one person.

Singular Commands

The singular command form is the same as the root form in the list above.

Examples

Let's take a look at some examples of commands using some of the irregular verbs. Remember that commands can be expanded by adding nouns, pronouns, or other phrases after the verb.

"Say it."
Abair é.
[ah-ber ay]

"Be good!"
Bí maith!
[bee mah]

"Do it."
Déan é.
[jayn ay]

"Get your coat."
Faigh do chóta.
[fai duh kho-tuh]

"Eat the salad."
Ith an sailéad.
[ih un sal-ayd]

"Give it to me."
Tabhair dom é.
[toor dum ay]

"Come here."
Tar anseo.
[tar un-shuh]

"Go home."
Téigh abhaile.
[tchay uh-wah-lyuh]

Plural Commands

To give a command to more than one person, you usually add the endings "**-igí**" [ih-gee] or "**-aigí**" [uh-gee] to the end of the root form. For some irregular verbs, the root word will change before you put the plural ending on.

Vocabulary

Here are the plural command forms for all of the irregular verbs:

"(y'all) say"
abraigí
[ah-bruh-gee]

"(y'all) hear"
cloisigí
[klish-ih-gee]

"(y'all) see"
feicigí
[fek-ih-gee]

"(y'all) come"
tagaigí
[tah-guh-gee]

"(y'all) bear, (y'all) bring"
beirigí
[baer-ih-gee]

"(y'all) do, (y'all) make"
déanaigí
[jayn-uh-gee]

"(y'all) eat"
ithigí
[ih-hih-gee]

"(y'all) go"
téigí
[tchay-gee]

"(y'all) be"
bígí
[bee-gee]

"(y'all) get"
faighigí
[fai-ih-gee]

"(y'all) give"
tugaigí
[tug-uh-gee]

Examples

Let's look at some examples of commands to several people using some of the irregular verbs.

"Say something."
Abraigí rud éigin.
[ah-bruh-gee ruhd ay-gihn]

"Be good!"
Bígí maith!
[bee-gee mah]

"Do it."
Déanaigí é.
[jayn-uh-gee ay]

"Get the boxes."
Faighigí na boscaí.
[fai-ih-gee nuh bus-kee]

"Eat the cookies."
Ithigí na brioscaí.
[ih-hih-gee nuh bris-kee]

"Give the apples to them."
Tugaigí na h-úlla dóibh.
[tug-uh-gee nuh hool-uh doe-iv]

"Come home."
Tagaigí abhaile.
[tah-guh-gee uh-wah-lyuh]

"Go to the meeting."
Téigí chuig an gcruinniú.
[tchay-gee khig un grin-nyew]

Lesson 200 – Negative Irregular Commands

As with the regular verbs, to make a command negative, all you have to do is put the word "ná" [naw] in front of the command. This is the same whether you're speaking to one person, or more than one person. If the verb begins with a vowel, you add an "h-" in front of it to make it easier to say. Once again, note that there are no question forms for commands.

Examples

"Don't say anything."
Ná h-abair rud ar bith.
[naw hah-ber ruhd air bih]

"Don't do it now."
Ná déan anois é.
[naw jayn uh-nish ay]

"Don't eat that sandwich."
Ná h-ith an ceapaire sin.
[naw hih un kya-puh-ruh shin]

"Don't give these plates to him."
Ná tugaigí na plátaí seo dó.
[naw tug-uh-gee nuh plaw-tee shuh doe]

"Don't come to the restaurant."
Ná tar go dtí an bhialann.
[naw tar guh jee un vee-uh-luhn]

"Don't go there."
Ná téigí ansin.
[naw tchay-gee un-shin]

Lesson 201 – Words That Pair with Irregular Verbs

As we learned in Lesson 192, some verbs are often paired with prepositions to expand or clarify their meanings . This is true for some of the irregular verbs, as well. For example, you can "give," but you can also "give *to*" someone.

Vocabulary

Here is a list of words that are often paired with some of the irregular verbs:

"say to"
abair le
[ah-ber leh]

"catch"
beir ar
[baer air]

"give to"
tabhair do
[toor duh]

Examples

Let's look at some sentences using these irregular verbs with their helper prepositions. The same pattern we learned for each preposition still applies.

"Say something to the teacher."
Abair rud éigin leis an múinteoir.
[ah-ber ruhd ay-gihn lesh un moon-chor]

"Say it to her."
Abair léi é.
[ah-ber lay-ih ay]

"Catch the bag."
Beir ar an mála.
[baer air un maw-luh]

"Catch it."
Beir air.
[baer air]

"Give the map to him."
Tabhair an léarscáil dó.
[toor un layr-skoyl doe]

"Give it to him."
Tabhair dó í.
[toor doe ee]

Notice that in the sentences above, when you use a noun as your *object* (the thing affected by the action), it comes before the preposition. When you use a pronoun as the object, it goes after the preposition. This is a common pattern in Irish.

Lesson 202 – The Past Tense of Irregular Verbs

As stated in the name, irregular verbs don't follow regular patterns. Therefore, rather than give general guidelines, below you will find all of the past tense forms of the irregular verbs spelled out.

Once again, this is not a comprehensive study on irregular verbs. This is more of a reference to aid you in your further studies of Irish.

Abair – "Say"

"said"
dúirt
[doo-urtch]

"didn't say"
ní dúirt
[nee doo-urtch]

"did say?"
an ndúirt
[un noo-urtch]

"didn't say?"
nach ndúirt
[nahkh noo-urtch]

Beir – "Bear", "Bring"

"bore, brought"
rug
[rug]

"didn't bear, didn't bring"
níor rug
[neer rug]

"did bear?, did bring?"
ar rug
[ur rug]

"didn't bear?, didn't bring?"
nár rug
[nawr rug]

Bí – "Be"

"was"
bhí
[vee]

"wasn't"
ní raibh
[nee rev]

"was?"
an raibh
[un rev]

"wasn't?"
nach raibh
[nahkh rev]

Clois – "Hear"

"heard"
chuala
[khoo-uh-luh]

"didn't hear"
níor chuala
[neer khoo-uh-luh]

"did hear?"
ar chuala
[ur khoo-uh-luh]

"didn't hear?"
nár chuala
[nar khoo-uh-luh]

Déan – "Do", "Make"

"did, made"
rinne
[rin-yuh]

"didn't, didn't make"
ní dhearna
[nee yarn-uh]

"did?, did make?"
an ndearna
[un nyarn-uh]

"didn't?, didn't make?"
nach ndearna
[nahkh nyarn-uh]

Faigh – "Get"

"got"
fuair
[foo-ihr]

"didn't get"
ní bhfuair
[nee woo-ihr]

"did get?"
an bhfuair
[un woo-ihr]

"didn't get?"
nach bhfuair
[nahkh woo-ihr]

Feic – "See"

"saw"
chonaic
[khuh-nik]

"didn't see"
ní fhaca
[nee ah-kuh]

"did see?"
an bhfaca
[un wah-kuh]

"didn't see?"
nach bhfaca
[nahkh wah-kuh]

Ith – "Eat"

"ate"
d'ith
[djih]

"didn't eat"
níor ith
[neer ih]

"did eat?"
ar ith
[ur ih]

"didn't eat?"
nár ith
[nar ih]

Tabhair – "Give"

"gave"
thug
[hug]

"didn't give"
níor thug
[neer hug]

"did give?"
ar thug
[ur hug]

"didn't give?"
nár thug
[nar hug]

Tar – "Come"

"came"
tháinig
[haw-nihg]

"didn't come"
níor tháinig
[neer haw-nihg]

"did come?"
ar tháinig
[ur haw-nihg]

"didn't come?"
nár tháinig
[nar haw-nihg]

Téigh – "Go"

"went"
chuaigh
[khoo-ee]

"didn't go"
ní dheachaigh
[nee yah-khee]

"did go?"
an ndeachaigh
[un nyah-khee]

"didn't go?"
nach ndeachaigh
[nahkh nyah-khee]

Examples

Let's look at some sample sentences that use the irregular verbs in their past tense forms. Making sentences with irregular verbs is just like making sentences with any other verb. You start with the verb, then say a noun or pronoun, and then finish it in any number of ways.

"I said it."
Dúirt mé é.
[doo-urtch may ay]

"She didn't catch it."
Níor rug sí air.
[neer rug shee air]

"Was he there?"
An raibh sé ann?
[un rev shay on]

"Didn't y'all hear the news?"
Nár chuala sibh an scéal?
[nar khoo-uh-luh shiv un shkayl]

"A child made it."
Rinne páiste é.
[rin-yuh paw-stchuh ay]

"The teacher didn't make it."
Ní dhearna an múinteoir é.
[nee yarn-uh un moon-chor ay]

"Did we get the boxes?"
An bhfuair muid na boscaí?
[un woo-ihr mwidj nuh bus-kee]

"I saw them."
Chonaic mé iad.
[khuh-nik may ee-ud]

"Did *he* see them?"
An bhfaca seisean iad?
[un wah-kuh shesh-in ee-ud]

"Didn't they eat any apples?"
Nár ith siad aon úlla?
[nar ih shee-ud ayn ool-uh]

"The engineer gave the book to her."
Thug an t-innealtóir an leabhar di.
[hug un tin-yil-tor un lyow-er jih]

"Patricia didn't come to the party last night."
Níor tháinig Pádraigín chuig an gcóisir aréir.
[neer haw-nihg paw-druh-geen khig un goe-sher uh-rayr]

"The women went to the hotel."
Chuaigh na mná go dtí an t-óstán.
[khoo-ee nuh mraw guh jee un toess-tawn]

"Did the men go to the beach?"
An ndeachaigh na fir go dtí an trá?
[un nyah-khee nuh fihr guh jee un traw]

Lesson 203 – The Present Tense of Irregular Verbs

Once again, rather than give general guidelines for the irregular verbs, here are all of the present tense forms of the irregular verbs spelled out. This is for your reference and future study as you increase your skills in Irish.

Abair – "Say"

"says"
deir
[djair]

"doesn't say"
ní deir
[nee djair]

"does say?"
an ndeir
[un nyair]

"doesn't say?"
nach ndeir
[nahkh nyair]

Beir – "Bear", "Bring"

"bears, brings"
beireann
[baer-uhn]

"doesn't bear, doesn't bring"
ní bheireann
[nee vaer-uhn]

"does bear?, does bring?"
an mbeireann
[un maer-uhn]

"doesn't bear?, doesn't bring?"
nach mbeireann
[nahkh maer-uhn]

Bí – "Be"

"is"
bíonn
[bee-uhn]

"isn't"
ní bhíonn
[nee vee-uhn]

"is?"
an mbíonn
[un me-uhn]

"isn't?"
nach mbíonn
[nahkh me-uhn]

Clois – "Hear"

"hears"
cloiseann
[klish-uhn]

"doesn't hear"
ní chloiseann
[nee khlish-uhn]

"does hear?"
an gcloiseann
[un glish-uhn]

"doesn't hear?"
nach gcloiseann
[nahkh glish-uhn]

Déan – "Do", "Make"

"does, makes"
déanann
[jay-nuhn]

"doesn't, doesn't make"
ní dhéanann
[nee yay-nuhn]

"does?, does make?"
an ndéanann
[un nyay-nuhn]

"doesn't?, doesn't make?
nach ndéanann
[nahkh nyay-nuhn]

Faigh – "Get"

"gets"
faigheann
[fai-uhn]

"doesn't get"
ní fhaigheann
[nee ai-uhn]

"does get?"
an bhfaigheann
[un wai-uhn]

"doesn't get?"
nach bhfaigheann
[nahkh wai-uhn]

Feic – "See"

"sees"
feiceann
[fek-uhn]

"doesn't see"
ní fheiceann
[nee ek-uhn]

"does see?"
an bhfeiceann
[un vek-uhn]

"doesn't see?"
nach bhfeiceann
[nahkh vek-uhn]

Ith – "Eat"

"eats"
itheann
[ih-huhn]

"doesn't eat"
ní itheann
[nee ih-huhn]

"does eat?"
an itheann
[un ih-huhn]

"doesn't eat?"
nach n-itheann
[nahkh nih-huhn]

Tabhair – "Give"

"gives"
tugann
[tug-uhn]

"doesn't give"
ní thugann
[nee hug-uhn]

"does give?"
an dtugann
[un dug-uhn]

"doesn't give?"
nach dtugann
[nahkh dug-uhn]

Tar – "Come"

"comes"
tagann
[tah-guhn]

"doesn't come"
ní thagann
[nee hah-guhn]

"does come?"
an dtagann
[un dah-guhn]

"doesn't come?"
nach dtagann
[nahkh dah-guhn]

Téigh – "Go"

"goes"
téann
[tchay-uhn]

"doesn't go"
ní théann
[nee hay-uhn]

"does go?"
an dtéann
[un djay-uhn]

"doesn't go?"
nach dtéann
[nahkh djay-uhn]

Examples

Let's look at some sample sentences that use the irregular verbs in their present tense forms. Making sentences with irregular verbs is just like making sentences with any other verb. You start with the verb, then say a noun or pronoun, and then finish it in any number of ways.

"He doesn't usually say anything."
Ní deir sé aon rud de ghnáth.
[nee djair shay ayn ruhd deh ghuh-naw]

"Does the student bring her book with her?"
An mbeireann an dalta a leabhar léi?
[un maer-uhn un dahl-tuh uh lyow-er lay-ih]

"Aren't the days beautiful here?"
Nach mbíonn na laethanta go h-álainn anseo?
[nahkh me-uhn nuh lay-hen-tuh guh haw-ling un-shuh]

"The dog hears very well."
Cloiseann an madra an-mhaith.
[klish-uhn un mah-druh on wah]

"We don't do this often."
Ní dhéanann muid é seo go minic.
[nee yay-nuhn mwidj ay shuh guh min-ik]

"Does the cat get milk?"
An bhfaigheann an cat bainne?
[un wai-uhn un kot bon-yuh]

"Don't the servers see the boxes?"
Nach bhfeiceann na freastalaithe na boscaí?
[nahkh vek-uhn nuh fras-tuh-lee-huh nuh bus-kee]

"The doctor eats salad."
Itheann an dochtúir sailéad.
[ih-huhn un dokh-toor sal-ayd]

"The musicians don't usually give it to them."
Ní thugann na ceoltóirí dóibh é de ghnáth.
[nee hug-uhn nuh kyoel-tor-ee doe-iv ay deh ghuh-naw]

"Do you come here often?"
An dtagann tú anseo go minic?
[un dah-guhn too un-shuh guh min-ik]

"Don't y'all's daughters go to the beach now and again?"
Nach dtéann bhur n-iníonacha go dtí an trá anois agus arís?
[nahkh djay-uhn woor nin-yeen-ih-khuh guh jee un traw uh-nish ah-gus uh-reesh]

Lesson 204 – The Future Tense of Irregular Verbs

For your reference and future study of Irish, here are all of the future tense forms of the irregular verbs spelled out.

Abair – "Say"

"will say"
déarfaidh
[djair-ee]

"won't say"
ní déarfaidh
[nee yair-ee]

"will say?"
an ndéarfaidh
[un nyair-ee]

"won't say?"
nach ndéarfaidh
[nahkh nyair-ee]

Beir – "Bear", "Bring"

"will bear, will bring"
béirfaidh
[baer-ee]

"won't bear, won't bring"
ní bhéirfaidh
[nee vaer-ee]

"will bear?, will bring?"
an mbéirfaidh
[un maer-ee]

"won't bear?, won't bring?"
nach mbéirfaidh
[nahkh maer-ee]

Bí – "Be"

"will be"
beidh
[bay]

"won't be"
ní bheidh
[nee vay]

"will be?"
an mbeidh
[un may]

"won't be?"
nach mbeidh
[nahkh may]

Clois – "Hear"

"will hear"
cloisfidh
[klish-ee]

"won't hear"
ní chloisfidh
[nee khlish-ee]

"will hear?"
an gcloisfidh
[un glish-ee]

"won't hear?"
nach gcloisfidh
[nahkh glish-ee]

Déan – "Do", "Make"

"will do, will make"
déanfaidh
[jay-nee]

"won't do, won't make"
ní dhéanfaidh
[nee yay-nee]

"will do?, will make?"
an ndéanfaidh
[un nyay-nee]

"won't do?, won't make?"
nach ndéanfaidh
[nahkh nyay-nee]

Faigh – "Get"

"will get"
gheobhaidh
[yoe-ee]

"won't get"
ní bhfaighidh
[nee wai-yee]

"will get?"
an bhfaighidh
[un wai-yee]

"won't get?"
nach bhfaighidh
[nahkh wai-yee]

Feic – "See"

"will see"
feicfidh
[fek-ee]

"won't see"
ní fheicfidh
[nee ek-ee]

"will see?"
an bhfeicfidh
[un vek-ee]

"won't see?"
nach bhfeicfidh
[nahkh vek-ee]

Ith – "Eat"

"will eat"
íosfaidh
[ee-see]

"won't eat"
ní íosfaidh
[nee ee-see]

"will eat?"
an íosfaidh
[un ee-see]

"won't eat?"
nach n-íosfaidh
[nahkh nee-see]

Tabhair – "Give"

"will give"
tabharfaidh
[toor-ee]

"won't give"
ní thabharfaidh
[nee hoor-ee]

"will give?"
an dtabharfaidh
[un doo-ree]

"won't give?"
nach dtabharfaidh
[nahkh doo-ree]

Tar – "Come"

"will come"
tiocfaidh
[tchuhk-ee]

"won't come"
ní thiocfaidh
[nee hyuhk-ee]

"will come?"
an dtiocfaidh
[un djuhk-ee]

"won't come?"
nach dtiocfaidh
[nahkh djuhk-ee]

Téigh – "Go"

"will go"
rachaidh
[rah-khee]

"won't go"
ní rachaidh
[nee rah-khee]

"will go?"
an rachaidh
[un rah-khee]

"won't go?"
nach rachaidh
[nahkh rah-khee]

Examples

Let's look at some sample sentences that use the irregular verbs in their future tense forms. Making sentences with irregular verbs is just like making sentences with any other verb. You start with the verb, then say a noun or pronoun, and then finish it in any number of ways.

"Will Brian say something to them?"
An ndéarfaidh Brian rud éigin leo?
[un nyair-ee bree-uhn ruhd ay-gihn lyo]

"Won't she catch it?"
Nach mbéirfaidh sí air?
[nahkh maer-ee shee air]

"It will be wet tomorrow."
Beidh sé fliuch amárach.
[bay shay flyukh uh-maw-rahkh]

"The mechanic won't hear you."
Ní chloisfidh an meicneoir tú.
[nee khlish-ee un mek-nyor too]

"Will *you* do it for the child?"
An ndéanfaidh tusa don pháiste é?
[un nyay-nee tuh-suh duhn faw-stchuh ay]

"The secretary will get a computer for us."
Gheobhaidh an rúnaí ríomhaire duinn.
[yoe-ee un roo-nee ree-ver-uh doo-een]

"Won't the dentist get one?"
Nach bhfaighidh an fiaclóir ceann?
[nahkh wai-yee un fee-uh-klor kyawn]

"We'll see."
Feicfidh muid.
[fek-ee mwidj]

"The girl won't eat them."
Ní íosfaidh an cailín iad.
[nee ee-see un kall-yeen ee-ud]

"Will y'all take this with y'all?"
An dtabharfaidh sibh é seo libh?
[un doo-ree shiv ay shuh liv]

"Won't the cat come out of the box?"
Nach dtiocfaidh an cat amach as an mbosca?
[nahkh djuhk-ee un kot uh-mahkh oss un muss-kuh]

"My mother and I will go to the wedding."
Rachaidh mé féin agus mo mháthair chuig an mbainis.
[rah-khee may fayn ah-gus muh waw-her khig un man-ish]

Lesson 205 – Connecting Sentences with "And"

An easy way to increase the variety of what you can say in Irish is to connect short sentences together to make longer ones. The simplest way to do this is to use the word "and," "**agus**" [ah-gus]. All you have to do is say one sentence, then "and," then another sentence.

When you connect sentences using "**agus**" [ah-gus], no changes occur to the word following it. Also, you can connect as many sentences as you like this way. You can say a whole lot this way, but just be careful not to make too many run-on sentences!

Examples

Let's take a look at some short sentences, then connect them to make a longer sentence using "and," "**agus**" [ah-gus], to see how this works.

"I'm well."
Tá mé go maith.
[taw may guh mah]

"I'm happy."
Tá áthas orm.
[taw aw-huss or-um]

"I'm well, <u>and</u> I'm happy."
Tá mé go maith, <u>agus</u> tá áthas orm.
[taw may guh mah, ah-gus taw aw-huss or-um]

"He's a doctor."
Is dochtúir é.
[iss dokh-toor ay]

"He's in a hurry."
Tá deifir air.
[taw jef-fer air]

"He's a doctor, <u>and</u> he's in a hurry."
Is dochtúir é, <u>agus</u> tá deifir air.
[iss dokh-toor ay, ah-gus taw jef-fer air]

"She was hungry."
Bhí ocras uirthi.
[vee uhk-russ ur-hee]

"She ate an apple."
D'ith sí úll.
[djih shee ool]

"She was hungry, <u>and</u> she ate and apple."
Bhí ocras uirthi, <u>agus</u> d'ith sí úll.
[vee uhk-russ ur-hee, ah-gus djih shee ool]

Notice that you can use "and" to connect sentences that use any verb in any tense. Because "**agus**" [ah-gus] doesn't change the words around it, you simply say the sentences the same way you would if you were saying them by themselves.

Lesson 206 – Connecting Sentences with "But"

Another easy way to connect sentences and expand the variety of your Irish is to use the word "but," **ach** [akh]. Just like you learned with "and," connecting sentences with "but" is simple. You say one sentence, then "but," then another sentence. The word "**ach**" [akh] causes no changes to the word following it.

Examples

Let's take a look at some sentences, then connect them using "but," **ach** [akh], to see how this works.

"I'm cold."
Tá mé fuar.
[taw may foo-uhr]

"I'm okay."
Tá mé ceart go leor.
[taw may kyart guh leeyor]

"I'm cold, but I'm okay."
Tá mé fuar, ach tá mé ceart go leor.
[taw may foo-uhr, akh taw may kyart guh leeyor]

"He's a doctor."
Is dochtúir é.
[iss dokh-toor ay]

"He's not in a hurry right now."
Níl deifir air anois díreach.
[neel jef-fer air uh-nish jee-rahkh]

"He's a doctor, but he's not in a hurry right now."
Is dochtúir é, ach níl deifir air anois díreach.
[iss dokh-toor ay, akh neel jef-fer air uh-nish jee-rahkh]

"The apple wasn't very big."
Ní raibh an t-úll ró-mhór.
[nee rev un tool roe wor]

"She ate it."
D'ith sí é.
[djih shee ay]

"The apple wasn't very big, <u>but</u> she ate it."
Ní raibh an t-úll ró-mhór, <u>ach</u> d'ith sí é.
[nee rev un tool roe wor, akh djih shee ay]

Notice that you can use "**ach**" [akh] to connect sentences using any verb in any tense.

Lesson 207 – Connecting Sentences with "Because"

You can increase the variety of your Irish sentences even more by using the word "because," "**mar**" [mar]. You simply say one sentence, then "because," then another sentence. When you connect sentences using "**mar**" [mar], "because," no change occurs to the word following it.

Examples

Let's take a look at some sentences, then connect them using "because," "**mar**" [mar], to see how this works.

"I'm happy."
Tá áthas orm.
[taw aw-huss or-um]

"I'm not cold."
Níl mé fuar.
[neel may foo-uhr]

"I'm happy, <u>because</u> I'm not cold."
Tá áthas orm, <u>mar</u> níl mé fuar.
[taw aw-huss or-um, mar neel may foo-uhr]

"He's in a hurry."
Tá deifir air.
[taw jef-fer air]

"He's a doctor."
Is dochtúir é.
[iss dokh-toor ay]

"He's in a hurry, <u>because</u> he's a doctor."
Tá deifir air, <u>mar</u> is dochtúir é.
[taw jef-fer air, mar iss dokh-toor ay]

"She won't be hungry."
Ní bheidh ocras uirthi.
[nee vay uhk-russ ur-hee]

"She ate an apple."
D'ith sí úll.
[djih shee ool]

"She won't be hungry, <u>because</u> she ate an apple."
Ní bheidh ocras uirthi, <u>mar</u> d'ith sí úll.
[nee vay uhk-russ ur-hee, mar djih shee ool]

Notice that you can use "**mar**" [mar] to connect sentences using any verb in any tense.

Lesson 208 – Mixing and Matching to Connect Sentences

Not only can you make sentences longer with "**agus**" [ah-gus], "**ach**" [akh], and "**mar**" [mar], you can even string several simple sentences together by using each several times, or by mixing them into the same sentence.

Examples

Let's take a look at some sets of sentences, then connect them using "**agus**" [ah-gus], "**ach**" [akh], "**mar**" [mar], or all three to see how this works.

"I'm happy."
Tá áthas orm.
[taw aw-huss or-um]

"I like cookies."
Is maith liom broiscaí.
[iss mah lyum bris-kee]

"I have a cookie."
Tá broisca agam.
[taw bris-kuh ah-gum]

"I'm happy, <u>because</u> I like cookies, <u>and</u> I have a cookie."
Tá áthas orm, <u>mar</u> is maith liom broiscaí, <u>agus</u> tá broisca agam.
[taw aw-huss or-um, mar iss mah lyum bris-kee, ah-gus taw bris-kuh ah-gum]

"She's usually working."
Bíonn sí ag obiar de ghnáth.
[bee-uhn shee ehg uh-ber deh ghuh-naw]

"The weather is wet."
Tá an aimsir fliuch.
[taw un am-sheer flyukh]

"It is eleven o'clock at night."
Tá sé a h-aon deag a chlog san oíche.
[taw shay uh hayn jayug uh khluhg sun ee-khuh]

"She's usually working, <u>but</u> the weather is wet, <u>and</u> it is eleven o'clock at night."
Bíonn sí ag obiar de ghnáth, <u>ach</u> tá an aimsir fliuch, <u>agus</u> tá sé a h-aon deag a chlog san oíche.
[bee-uhn shee ehg uh-ber deh ghuh-naw, akh taw un am-sheer flyukh, ah-gus taw shay uh hayn jayug uh khluhg sun ee-khuh]

"They bought water."
Cheannaigh siad uisce.
[khya-nee shee-ud ish-kuh]

"They didn't drink it."
Níor ól siad é.
[neer oel shee-ud ay]

"They weren't thirsty."
Ní raibh tart orthu.
[nee rev tart or-huh]

"They bought water, <u>but</u> they didn't drink it, <u>because</u> they weren't thirsty."
Cheannaigh siad uisce, <u>ach</u> níor ól siad é, <u>mar</u> ní raibh tart orthu.
[khya-nee shee-ud ish-kuh, akh neer oel shee-ud ay, mar nee rev tart or-huh]

"I like coffee."
Is maith liom caife.
[iss mah lyum kaf-ay]

"I went to the restaurant."
Chuaigh mé go dtí an bhialann.
[khoo-ee may guh jee un vee-uh-luhn]

"I didn't drink anything."
Níor ól mé aon rud.
[neer oel may ayn ruhd]

"I was sick."
Bhí mé tinn.
[vee may tcheen]

"I like coffee, <u>and</u> I went to the restaurant, <u>but</u> I didn't drink anything, <u>because</u> I was sick."
Is maith liom caife, <u>agus</u> chuaigh mé go dtí an bhialann, <u>ach</u> níor ól mé aon rud, <u>mar</u> bhí mé tinn.
[iss mah lyum kaf-ay, ah-gus khoo-ee may guh jee un vee-uh-luhn, akh neer oel may ayn ruhd, mar vee may tcheen]

Lesson 209 – Connecting Sentences with "That"

Another way you can connect sentences is by using "that." This is the *conjunction* "that," the one that joins sentences, as opposed to the one that refers to distant or specific objects, such as, "that table," or "That's my friend." In English, we can drop out the joining word "that" in a sentence, though it's still implied. In Irish, you always say "that" when connecting sentences this way.

Also, there's more than one way to say the conjunction "that." Irish makes a distinction between when the following sentence is positive, and when the following sentence is negative. The patterns we're learning here work with almost all verbs. The copula, "**is**" [iss], is a special linking verb, so it has a slightly different pattern. We'll cover how to say "that" with "**is**" [iss] in the next lesson.

The Negative "That"

The forms that are used with negative "that" sentences are easy to remember, because they're the same words you'd use to start a negative question. For example, if a verb uses the word "**nach**" [nahkh] to start a negative question, you use the same word, "**nach**" [nahkh], for the negative "that." If you were using a past tense verb that uses "**nár**" [nawr] for negative questions, then you'd also use "**nár**" [nawr] for the negative "that."

When a verb comes after "**nach**" [nahkh], it gets eclipsed. When a verb comes after "**nár**" [nawr], it gets softened.

While irregular verbs also follow this rule, some of them will use a special form after "that." This is called the *dependent form* of the verb. It's the same form you see in questions, if the irregular verb isn't following the patterns of regular verbs. For example, the dependent form of "**bí**" [bee] in the present tense is "**bhfuil**" [will].

Examples

Let's take a look at some sets of sentences to see how using the negative "that," or "that not," works in action.

"I'm sorry."
Tá brón orm.
[taw broen or-um]

"You are not well."
Níl tú go maith.
[neel too guh mah]

"I'm sorry <u>that</u> you <u>are not</u> well."
Tá brón orm <u>nach bhfuil</u> tú go maith.
[taw broen or-um nahkh will too guh mah]

"My friend said..."
Dúirt mo chara...
[doo-urtch muh khahr-uh]

"He won't be coming."
Ní bheidh sé ag teacht.
[nee vay shay ehg tchakht]

"My friend said <u>that</u> he <u>won't be</u> coming."
Dúirt mo chara <u>nach mbeidh</u> sé ag teacht.
[doo-urtch muh khahr-uh nahkh may shay ehg tchakht]

"I saw..."
Chonaic mé...
[khuh-nik may]

"She didn't eat the sandwich."
Níor ith sí an ceapaire.
[neer ih shee un kya-puh-ruh]

"I saw <u>that</u> she <u>didn't eat</u> the sandwich."
Chonaic mé <u>nár ith</u> sí an ceapaire.
[khuh-nik may nawr ih shee un kya-puh-ruh]

"Did y'all say...?"
An ndúirt sibh...?
[un noo-urtch shiv]

"Y'all won't take the box."
Ní thógfaidh sibh an bosca.
[nee hoeg-ee shiv un bus-kuh]

"Did y'all say <u>that</u> y'all <u>won't take</u> the box?"
An ndúirt sibh <u>nach dtógfaidh</u> sibh an bosca?
[un noo-urtch shiv nahkh doeg-ee shiv un bus-kuh]

"Weren't they happy?"
Nach raibh áthas orthu?
[nahkh rev aw-huss or-huh]

"The party wasn't outside."
Ní raibh an chóisir amuigh.
[nee rev un khoe-sher uh-muh]

"Weren't they happy <u>that</u> the party <u>wasn't</u> outside?"
Nach raibh áthas orthu <u>nach raibh</u> an chóisir amuigh?
[nahkh rev aw-huss or-huh nahkh rev un khoe-sher uh-muh]

The Positive "That"

Making positive "that" sentences is similar to making negative ones. The positive forms of "that" are "**go**" [guh] and "**gur**" [gur]. These match up with the negative forms, "**nach**" [nahkh] and "**nár**" [nawr]. For a verb that uses "**nach**" [nahkh], the positive "that" is "**go**" [guh]. For a verb that uses "**nár**" [nawr], the positive "that" is "**gur**" [gur].

When a verb comes after "**go**" [guh], it gets eclipsed. When a verb comes after "**gur**" [gur], it gets softened. Irregular verbs that have a dependent form will also use it after "**go**" [guh] and "**gur**" [gur].

TIP!   The forms of the conjunction "that" pair like this:

"**go**" [guh] and "**nach**" [nahkh] – both eclipse
"**gur**" [gur] and "**nár**" [nawr] – both soften

Most verbs in most tenses use "**go**" [guh] and "**nach**" [nahkh]. You can tell which set to use by looking at the verb's negative question form. This will also show you what an irregular verb's dependent form is. Also notice that "**gur**" [gur] and "**nár**" [nawr] both end in the letter "r," which can help you remember that they're paired.

Examples

Let's take a look at some sets of sentences using the positive "that" to see how this works in action.

"I'm happy."
Tá áthas orm.
[taw aw-huss or-um]

"You are happy."
Tá áthas ort.
[taw aw-huss ort]

"I'm happy <u>that</u> you <u>are</u> happy."
Tá áthas orm <u>go bhfuil</u> áthas ort.
[taw aw-huss or-um guh will aw-huss ort]

"His friend said..."
Dúirt a chara...
[doo-urtch uh khahr-uh]

"He will be coming."
Beidh sé ag teacht.
[bay shay ehg tchakht]

"His friend said <u>that</u> he <u>will be</u> coming."
Dúirt a chara <u>go mbeidh</u> sé ag teacht.
[doo-urtch uh khahr-uh guh may shay ehg tchakht]

"I see…"
Feiceann mé…
[fek-in may]

"She bought a bicycle."
Cheannaigh sí rothar.
[khya-nee shee ruh-her]

"I see _that_ she _bought_ a bicycle."
Feiceann mé <u>gur cheannaigh</u> sí rothar.
[fek-in may gur khya-nee shee ruh-her]

"Did Brian say…?"
An ndúirt Brian…?
[an noo-urtch bree-uhn]

"The weather was too hot."
Bhí an aimsir ró-the.
[vee un am-sheer roe heh]

"Did Brian say _that_ the weather _was_ too hot?"
An ndúirt Brian <u>go raibh</u> an aimsir ró-the?
[an noo-urtch bree-uhn guh rev un am-sheer roe heh]

"Didn't the engineer hear…?"
Nár chuala an t-innealtóir…?
[nawr khoo-uh-luh un tin-yil-tor]

"Y'all will take the boxes."
Tógfaidh sibh na boscaí.
[toeg-ee shiv nuh bus-kee]

"Didn't the engineer hear _that_ y'all _will take_ the boxes?"
Nár chuala an t-innealtóir <u>go dtógfaidh</u> sibh na boscaí?
[nawr khoo-uh-luh un tin-yil-tor guh doeg-ee shiv nuh bus-kee]

Lesson 210 – Connecting "Is" Sentences with "That"

When you use "that" with the copula "**is**" [iss], the pattern is slightly different. Like the irregular verbs, it uses its dependent forms, and that's all it uses. You don't have to put anything else in front of them to indicate "that."

For "**is**" [iss], the positive "that" is "**gur**" [gur]. If the word that comes after "**gur**" [gur] starts with a vowel, it becomes "**gurb**" [gur-uhb]. The negative "that" is "**nach**" [nahkh]. These forms don't cause any softening or eclipsing to the following word.

Examples

Let's take a look at some sets of sentences using "that" with "**is**" [iss] to see how this works.

"She said..."
Dúirt sí..."
[doo-urtch shee]

"It's a key."
Is eochair í.
[iss ukh-er ee]

"She said <u>that</u> it <u>is</u> a key."
Dúirt sí <u>gurb</u> eochair í."
[doo-urtch shee gur-uhb ukh-er ee]

"We heard..."
Chuala muid...
[khoo-uh-luh mwidj]

"He's not a dentist."
Ní fiaclóir é.
[nee fee-uh-klor ay]

"We heard <u>that</u> he <u>isn't</u> a dentist."
Chuala muid <u>nach</u> fiaclóir é.
[khoo-uh-luh mwidj nahkh fee-uh-klor ay]

"I see..."
Feiceann mé...
[fek-in may]

"Y'all like cookies."
Is maith libh brioscaí.
[iss mah liv bris-kee]

"I see that y'all like cookies."
Feiceann mé gur maith libh brioscaí.
[fek-in may gur mah liv bris-kee]

"They said..."
Dúirt siad...
[doo-urtch shee-ud]

"You don't prefer cooking."
Ní fearr leat a bheidh ag cócaireacht.
[nee fawr lyat uh vay ehg ko-kuh-rahkht]

"They said that you don't prefer cooking."
Dúirt siad nach fearr leat a bheidh ag cócaireacht.
[doo-urtch shee-ud nahkh fawr lyat uh vay ehg ko-kuh-rahkht]

"He says..."
Deir sé...
[djair shay]

"They own that car."
Is leo an carr sin.
[iss lyo un kahr shin]

"He says that they own that car."
Deir sé gur leo an carr sin.
[djair shay gur lyo un kahr shin]

"Didn't you hear...?"
Nár chuala tú...?
[nawr khoo-uh-luh too]

"She's from Scotland."
Is as Albain í.
[iss oss all-uh-bin ee]

"Didn't you hear that she is from Scotland?"
Nár chuala tú gurb as Albain í?
[nawr khoo-uh-luh too gur-uhb oss all-uh-bin ee]

Lesson 211 – A Little About Attributive Adjectives

The easiest way to describe things in Irish using adjectives is to make a simple "**tá**" [taw] sentence. Adjectives can also work with nouns to describe them directly. These are called *attributive adjectives*, because they state an attribute of the noun without using a verb to connect them.

When an adjective and a noun work together as a team, the adjective will change to match the noun. How the adjective changes also depends on what kind of adjective it is. Like nouns, adjectives are categorized into groups called *declensions*. That means that adjectives from one group follow different patterns than adjectives from other groups. There are four adjective groups in Irish.

Most adjectives come after the noun, and can change differently depending on whether the noun is masculine, feminine, singular, or plural. Because there are too many patterns to cover here, this lesson will only introduce you to these concepts so that you are aware of them as you continue to learn and speak Irish.

Examples

Let's take a look at some sentences that use adjectives teamed up with nouns.

"This is the good pen."
Seo é an peann maith.
[shuh ay un pyawn mah]

"It's not a good shirt."
Ní léine mhaith í.
[nee lay-nuh wah ee]

"Aren't they good musicians!"
Nach ceoltóirí maithe iad!
[nahkh kyoel-tor-ee mah-huh ee-ud]

"They are good men."
Is fir mhaithe iad.
[iss fihr wah-huh ee-ud]

"He has a big box for you."
Tá bosca mór aige duit.
[taw bus-kuh mor ehg-uh ditch]

"It's a big window."
Is fuinneog mhór í.
[iss fwin-yoeg wor ee]

"They bought the big apples."
Cheannaigh siad na h-úlla móra.
[khya-nee shee-ud nuh hool-uh mor-uh]

"Look at the young boy."
Féach ar an mbuachaill óg.
[fay-ukh air un moo-uh-khil oeg]

"The young girl is running."
Tá an cailín óg ag rith.
[taw un kall-yeen oeg ehg rih]

"Do they have young children?"
An bhfuil páistí óga acu?
[un will paw-stchee oeg-uh ah-kuh]

"We drank cold milk."
D'ól muid bainne fuar.
[doel mwidj bon-yuh foo-uhr]

"He would like a cold glass."
Ba mhaith leis gloine fhuar.
[buh wah lesh glih-nyuh oo-uhr]

"I hate the cold nights."
Is fuath liom na h-oícheanta fuara.
[iss foo-uh lyum nuh hee-khen-tuh foo-uhr-uh]

A Few Common Exceptions

There are a few adjectives which come before the noun. These adjectives attach themselves directly to the front of the noun, and also soften the noun. While there aren't many exceptions, a couple of them are fairly common.

Vocabulary

The following adjectives come before nouns:

"bad"	"old"
droch	**sean**
[druhkh]	[shan]

Note that "**sean**" [shan] will not soften words that begin with a "**d**," "**t**," or "**s**."

Examples

"It's not a <u>bad</u> car."
Ní <u>drochcharr</u> é.
[nee druhkh-khahr ay]

"It's an <u>old</u> car."
Is <u>seancharr</u> é.
[iss shan-khahr ay]

"Is it an <u>old</u> door?"
An <u>seandoras</u> é?
[un shan-dor-us ay]

Lesson 212 – The Genitive Case

One last thing that's good to know about Irish is something called the *genitive case*. The *genitive case* is used to show a relationship between two nouns without using a verb to connect them.

In English, we often use the word "of" for this purpose. For example, in the phrase, "a cup of coffee," the word "of" connects the cup and the coffee. We also use the genitive case in English without the word "of." For example, when you say, "the food's taste," you're talking about "the taste *of* the food," the connection between the food and the taste.

Though we use this concept a lot in English, it's much more common in Irish. Also, instead of using "of" between two nouns, Irish changes the form of the last noun into the *genitive case*. Irish will also use the *genitive case* in phrases where English does not.

Some nouns will change only slightly, some will change a lot, and some won't seem to change at all. There are several patterns involved, but they are too intricate to explain here. At this stage, it's best to simply learn the *genitive* forms as you encounter them. A dictionary that shows a noun's *genitive* form will be very helpful to you as you continue learning and speaking Irish.

You can say a lot in Irish without the *genitive case*. Everything you've learned so far is very practical and completely common. Still, the *genitive case* can be sprinkled into any kind of sentence, so it's something you should be aware of when expanding your knowledge of Irish.

When The *Genitive Case* Is Used

Here is a list of general situations when the *genitive case* is used in Irish. Some of these may seem logical to an English speaker, and some will seem surprising, because Irish uses a turn of phrase that English doesn't to express certain ideas. Once again, this is an overview to get your feet wet in this very useful concept.

When You'd Say "Of" in English

The *genitive case* is used to show when one thing is "of" another thing.

Examples

"a glass"	"a kind"	"a woman, a lady"
gloine (f.)	**cineál** (m.)	**bean** (f.)
[glih-nyuh]	[kin-yal]	[ban]
"beer"	"music"	"the house"
beoir (f.)	**ceol** (m.)	**an teach** (m.)
[byor]	[kyoel]	[un tchahkh]
"a glass of beer"	"a kind of music"	"lady of the house"
gloine beorach	**cineál ceoil**	**bean an tí**
[glih-nyuh byor-akh]	[kin-yal kyoe-ihl]	[ban un tchee]

When Saying A Lot, A Little, Some, Etc.

You use the *genitive case* when you're talking about a quantity of something.

Examples

"a lot"	"a little"	"a portion, some"
mórán (m.)	**beagán** (m.)	**cuid** (f.)
[mor-awn]	[byuh-gawn]	[kidj]
"money"	"bread"	"work"
airgead (m.)	**arán** (m.)	**obair** (f.)
[air-ih-gud]	[uh-rawn]	[uh-ber]
"a lot of money"	"a little bread"	"some work"
mórán airgid	**beagán aráin**	("a portion of work")
[mor-awn air-ih-gidj]	[byuh-gawn uh-royn]	**cuid oibre**
		[kidj iy-bruh]

When Expressing a Compound Word or Concept

Some words that are compound words in English may be expressed using the *genitive case* in Irish. Also, words that are like compound words, but not actually spelled as one word, can be made with the *genitive* in Irish.

Examples

"a light"
solas (m.)
[suhl-us]

"a ring"
fáinne (m.)
[faw-nyuh]

"an office"
oifig (f.)
[if-fig]

"the sun"
an ghrian (f.)
[un ghree-un]

"keys"
eochracha (f.)
[ukh-rukh-uh]

"the mail"
an post (m.)
[un pust]

"sunlight"
("light of the sun")
solas na gréine
[suhl-us nuh gray-nyuh]

"key ring"
("ring of keys")
fáinne eochracha
[faw-nyuh ukh-rukh-uh]

"post office"
("office of the post")
oifig an phoist
[if-fig un fwisht]

Possessives with Names or Nouns

When you use a person's name or a noun to show possession, you use the *genitive case*. In English, we use an "'s" (apostrophe+s), or an "s'" (s+apostrophe) in this case.

Examples

"a house"
teach (m.)
[tchahkh]

"toys"
bréagáin (m.)
[bray-goyn]

"a license"
ceadúnas (m.)
[kya-doon-us]

"Patricia"
Pádraigín
[paw-druh-geen]

"the child"
an páiste (m.)
[un paw-stchuh]

"a driver"
tiománaí (m.)
[tchih-maw-nee]

"Patricia's house"
teach Phádraigín
[tchahkh faw-druh-geen]

"the child's toys"
bréagáin an pháiste
[bray-goyn un faw-stchuh]

"driver's license"
ceadúnas tiomána
[kya-doon-us tchih-maw-nuh]

When Counting People

If you include a noun when you're counting people, that noun is put into the *genitive case*.

EXAMPLES

"three" (people)
triur
[troo-ihr]

"five" (people)
cúigear
[kooih-gur]

"women"
mná
[mraw]

"men"
fir
[fihr]

"three <u>women</u>"
triur <u>ban</u>
[troo-ihr bahn]

"five <u>men</u>"
cúigear <u>fear</u>
[kooih-gur far]

With Certain Prepositions and Expressions

Some prepositions in Irish will cause the next word to use the *genitive case*. Also, some expressions will bring on the *genitive case*.

Examples

"across"
trasna
[tras-nuh]

"in front"
os comhair
[oess koe-wer]

"during"
i rith
[ih rih]

"the bridge"
an droichead (m.)
[un drih-khed]

"the fire"
an tine (f.)
[un tchih-nuh]

"the day"
an lá (m.)
[un law]

"across <u>the bridge</u>"
trasna <u>an droichid</u>
[tras-nuh un drih-khid]

"in front <u>of the fire</u>"
os comhair <u>na tine</u>
[oess koe-wer nuh tchih-nuh]

"during <u>the day</u>"
("in the course <u>of the day</u>")
i rith <u>an lae</u>
[ih rih un lay]

After a Verbal Noun

As we learned in Lesson 33, Irish uses a verbal noun with the preposition "**ag**" [ehg], "at," where English uses "-ing" at the ends of words. Because of this, the Irish progressive tense translates as "at doing," rather than just "doing." When you're more specific about what you're doing, you have to say you're "at the doing *of*" something. This is why verbal nouns bring on the *genitive case* in Irish.

Examples

"eating"
ag ithe
[ehg ih-huh]

"making"
ag deanamh
[ehg jay-nuv]

"writing"
ag scríobh
[ehg shkree-uv]

"an apple"
úll (m.)
[ool]

"cars"
carranna
[kahr-uh-nuh]

"a letter"
litir (f.)
[lih-tcher]

"eating <u>an apple</u>"
ag ithe <u>úill</u>
[ehg ih-huh oo-ihl]

"making <u>cars</u>"
ag deanamh <u>carranna</u>
[ehg jay-nuv kahr-uh-nuh]

"writing <u>a letter</u>"
ag scríobh <u>litreach</u>
[ehg shkree-uv lih-tchrakh]

Appendix – The Irish Alphabet

The Alphabet

There are 18 letters in the Irish alphabet: 5 vowels and 13 consonants. Irish has its own version of the Latin script called the Irish Script, which is designed to handle all of the sounds of the spoken Irish language. Most of the material that learners will see is written in the Roman Script, the same one we use in English, so that's what we use throughout this book.

The phonetics given below are a guide to get you started. They are not hard and fast rules of how each letter must be pronounced. Every language has exceptions and variations, and even individual speakers vary how they pronounce the same word at different times.

Vowels

The five vowels in Irish are: **a, e, i, o, u**. Vowels can be said with both a short sound and a long sound. The long sound is indicated by a long stroke above the letter. This is called a "**fada**" [fah-duh], which means "long" in Irish. The long vowels are written like this: **á, é, í, ó, ú**.

The vowels are also grouped into two types: broad vowels and slender vowels. The broad vowels in Irish are "**a**," "**o**," and "**u**," and the slender vowels are "**e**" and "**i**." Whether a vowel is broad or slender affects the pronunciation of the consonants next to it. This is true in English, too, but there are many more exceptions to English pronunciations.

Let's take a look at a sentence in English to see how broad and slender letters work. For example, you could say, "Call me on my cell." Notice that the words "call" and "cell" are spelled almost exactly the same, but the letter "c" is pronounced very differently in each. In the word "call," the "c" is next to an "a," which is a broad vowel, and will cause the consonant to make a hard "k" sound. In the word "cell," the "c" is next to an "e," which is a slender vowel, and will cause the consonant to make a slender "s" sound. That's how broad and slender vowels can affect the consonants around them.

Irish uses a spelling convention to keep pronunciation consistent – "**leathan le leathan agus caol le caol**" [lah-hin leh lah-hin ah-gus keel leh keel], which means, "broad with broad and slender with slender." This means that a consonant should only be touching one kind of vowel, broad or slender, so you know which way to pronounce the consonant. That's why you may see what look like "extra" vowels around a consonant; they are there to show you how to say the consonant.

Below is a list of vowels, and roughly how they sound, when said with a short sound or a long sound ("**fada**" [fah-duh]).

a – [uh] as in "up"

á – [aw] as in "paw"

e – [eh] as in "bet"

é – [ay] as in "hay"

i – [ih] as in "it"

í – [ee] as in "free"

o – [uh] as in "up"

ó – [oe] as in "toe"

u – [uh] as in "up"

ú – [oo] as in "too"

Consonants

The thirteen consonants in Irish are: **b, c, d, f, g, h, l, m, n, p, r, s, t**. How each consonant is pronounced is affected by the vowels that surround it. As we learned in the "Vowels" section, broad vowels can make a consonant sound one way, and slender vowels can make a consonant sound another way. Some consonants sound the same with either kind of vowel.

Below is a list of consonants, and roughly how they sound, when they're said with broad vowels or slender vowels.

b – *broad*: [b] as in "ball"

b – *slender*: [b] as in "bill"

c – *broad*: [k] as in "cot"

c – *slender*: [ky] as in "cube"

d – *broad*: [d] as in "dot"

d – *slender*: [dj] as in "edge"

f – *broad*: [f] as in "fawn"

f – *slender*: [f] as in "fee"

g – *broad*: [g] as in "got"

g – *slender*: [gy] as in "regular"

h – *broad*: [h] as in "hall"

h – *slender*: [h] as in "heel"

l – *broad*: [l] as in "law"

l – *slender*: [ly] as in "folio"

m – *broad*: [m] as in "mop"

m – *slender*: [m] as in "mitt"

n – *broad*: [n] as in "no"

n – *slender*: [n] as in "knee"

p – *broad*: [p] as in "paw"

p – *slender*: [p] as in "pill"

r – *broad*: [r] as in "raw"

r – *slender*: [r] as in "reel"

s – *broad*: [s] as in "saw"

s – *slender*: [sh] as in "sheep"

t – *broad*: [t] as in "top"

t – *slender*: [tch] as in "itch"

<u>Softening and Eclipsis</u>

The sounds of consonants in Irish can be changed by *softening* them or *eclipsing* them. Some consonants can be affected by both of these changes, and some can be affected by only one. The letters "**l**," "**n**," and "**r**" cannot be softened or eclipsed. The letter "**h**" rarely appears without another consonant, and is also not softened or eclipsed.

Softening

One of the ways a consonant can change in Irish is for its sound to become softer. This is called "**séimhiú**" [shay-voo], or *softening*. Sometimes, you will see this referred to by the linguistic terms "lenition" or "aspiration." To represent this softer sound, Irish puts an "**h**" after the consonant to show that it's being changed. Most consonants can be softened, but some cannot.

Below is a list of consonants that can be softened, and roughly how they sound when said with a broad vowel or a slender vowel.

bh – *broad*: [w] as in "water"
bh – *slender*: [v] as in "vapor"
ch – *broad*: [kh] as in "Bach"
ch – *slender*: [khy] like "Bach"
dh – *broad*: [gh] like the guttural "g" in "rogue"
dh – *slender*: [y] as in "you"
fh – *broad*: silent
fh – *slender*: silent
gh – *broad*: [gh] like the guttural "g" in "rogue"
gh – *slender*: [y] as in "you"
mh – *broad*: [w] as in "water"
mh – *slender*: [v] as in "vapor"
ph – *broad*: [f] as in "fawn"
ph – *slender*: [fy] as in "fuel"
sh – *broad*: [h] as in "hall"
sh – *slender*: [hy] as in "huge"
th – *broad*: [h] as in "hall"
th – *slender*: [hy] as in "huge"

The following "**s**" letter combinations cannot be softened: **sc, sf, sm, sp, st**.

When a word that causes softening ends in the letter "**n**," and the word after it begins with the letter "**d**" or "**t**," the "**d**" or the "**t**" does not get softened.

Eclipsis

One of the ways a consonant can change in Irish is when its sound is *eclipsed* by another sound. This is called "**urú**" [uh-roo], or *eclipsis*. This means that a new letter is put before the consonant, and this new sound takes over for the original sound. Some consonants can be eclipsed, and some cannot. Each consonant that can be eclipsed is always eclipsed by a specific letter.

Below is a list of consonants that can be eclipsed, and which letters eclipse them.

b – mb

c – gc

d – nd

f – bhf

g – ng

p – bp

t – dt

Once a letter is eclipsed, you say the sound of the eclipsing letter. The only exception is "**g**," which becomes "**ng**" when eclipsed. In this case, the "g" sound is only partially eclipsed, so "**ng**" is said [ing] as in "thing."

Note that the letter "**f**" is eclipsed by a softened "**b**," which is written as two letters, "**bh**."

The letter "**s**" follows its own rules. While it doesn't technically get eclipsed, it will sometimes be prefixed by the letter "**t**." Even though this sounds like eclipsis, it is not considered eclipsis because this generally happens when the "**s**" word should be softened. The following "**s**" letter combinations do not take a "**t**" in front of them: **sc, sf, sm, sp, st**.

Glossary – English to Irish

"a little" **beagán** [byuh-gawn] (masculine) (Lesson 212)
"a lot" **mórán** [mor-awn] (masculine) (Lesson 212)
"across" **trasna** [tras-nuh] (Lesson 212)
"after" **tar éis** [tar aysh] (Lesson 51)
"alone" **amháin** [uh-woyn] (Lesson 53)
"always" **i gcónaí** [ih go-nee] (Lesson 90)
"America" **Meiriceá** [mair-ih-kaw] (masculine) (Lesson 147)
"and" **agus** [ah-gus] (Lesson 1)
"anger" **fearg** [far-ihg] (feminine) (Lesson 140)
"any" **aon** [ayn] (Lesson 64)
"apple" **úll** [ool] (masculine) (Lesson 26)
"apples" **úlla** [ool-uh] (masculine) (Lesson 159)
"at" **ag** [ehg] (Lesson 28)
"at all" **ar bith** [air bih] (Lesson 66)
"at her" **aici** [ehk-ee] (Lesson 29)
"at him" **aige** [ehg-uh] (Lesson 29)
"at length / really" **ar fad** [air fahd] (Lesson 68)
"at me" **agam** [ah-gum] (Lesson 29)
"at night" **san oíche** [sun ee-khuh] (Lesson 50)
"at them" **acu** [ah-kuh] (Lesson 29)
"at us" **againn** [ah-geen] (Lesson 29)
"at y'all" **agaibh** [ah-giv] (Lesson 29)
"at you" **agat** [ah-gut] (Lesson 29)
"Australia" **an Astráil** [un aws-trawyil] (feminine) (Lesson 147)
"bad" **droch** [druhkh] (Lesson 211)
"bad" **go dona** [guh dun-uh] (Lesson 1)
"bag" **mála** [maw-luh] (masculine) (Lesson 32)
"bathroom" **leithreas** [leh-hruss] (masculine) (Lesson 38)
"be" **bí** [bee] (Lesson 199)
"beach" **trá** [traw] (feminine) (Lesson 41)
"bear / bring" **beir** [baer] (Lesson 199)
"beautiful" **go h-álainn** [guh haw-ling] (Lesson 9)
"because" **mar** [mar] (Lesson 207)
"beer" **beoir** [byor] (feminine) (Lesson 212)
"before" **roimh** [riv] (Lesson 51)
"better" **fearr** [fawr] (Lesson 178)
"bicycle" **rothar** [ruh-her] (masculine) (Lesson 32)
"big" **mór** [mor] (Lesson 9)
"black" **dubh** [duhv] (Lesson 141)
"blue" **gorm** [gor-um] (Lesson 141)
"book" **leabhar** [lyow-er] (masculine) (Lesson 32)
"box" **bosca** [bus-kuh] (masculine) (Lesson 25)

"boxes" **boscaí** [bus-kee] (masculine) (Lesson 64)
"boy" **buachaill** [boo-uh-khil] (masculine) (Lesson 103)
"boys" **buachaillí** [boo-uh-khulee] (masculine) (Lesson 103)
"bread" **arán** [uh-rawn] (masculine) (Lesson 212)
"bridge" **droichead** [drih-khed] (masculine) (Lesson 212)
"broad" **leathan** [lah-hin] (Appendix)
"brother" **deartháir** [dreh-har] (masculine) (Lesson 126)
"brothers" **deartháireacha** [dreh-har-uh-khuh] (masculine) (Lesson 126)
"brown" **donn** [duhn] (Lesson 141)
"brush" **scuab** [skoo-uhb] (feminine) (Lesson 102)
"brushes" **scuaba** [skoo-uh-buh] (feminine) (Lesson 102)
"but" **ach** [akh] (Lesson 67)
"buy" **ceannaigh** [kya-nee] (Lesson 186)
"Canada" **Ceanada** [kya-nuh-duh] (masculine) (Lesson 147)
"car" **carr** [kahr] (masculine) (Lesson 54)
"cars" **carranna** [kahr-uh-nuh] (masculine) (Lesson 146)
"cat" **cat** [kot] (masculine) (Lesson 155)
"chair" **cathaoir** [kah-heer] (feminine) (Lesson 16)
"chairs" **cathaoireacha** [kah-heer-ih-khuh] (feminine) (Lesson 19)
"child" **páiste** [paw-stchuh] (masculine) (Lesson 103)
"children" **páistí** [paw-stchee] (masculine) (Lesson 103)
"China" **an tSín** [un tcheen] (feminine) (Lesson 147)
"clean" **glan** [glon] (Lesson 18)
"cloudy" **scamallach** [skom-uh-lahkh] (Lesson 12)
"coat" **cóta** [ko-tuh] (masculine) (Lesson 138)
"coffee" **caife** [kaf-ay] (masculine) (Lesson 159)
"cold" **fuar** [foo-uhr] (Lesson 12)
"cold (sickness)" **slaghdán** [sly-dawn] (masculine) (Lesson 139)
"color" **dath** [dah] (masculine) (Lesson 141)
"come" **tar** [tar] (Lesson 199)
"coming" **ag teacht** [ehg tchakht] (Lesson 36)
"computer" **ríomhaire** [ree-ver-uh] (masculine) (Lesson 102)
"computers" **ríomhairí** [ree-ver-ee] (masculine) (Lesson 102)
"cookie" **briosca** [bris-kuh] (masculine) (Lesson 159)
"cookies" **brioscaí** [bris-kee] (masculine) (Lesson 159)
"cooking" **ag cócaireacht** [ehg ko-kuh-rahkht] (Lesson 165)
"cup" **cupán** [kuh-pawn] (masculine) (Lesson 54)
"dancing" **ag rince** [ehg ring-kuh] (Lesson 165)
"daughter" **iníon** [in-yeen] (feminine) (Lesson 126)
"daughters" **iníonacha** [in-yeen-ih-khuh] (feminine) (Lesson 126)
"day" **lá** [law] (masculine) (Lesson 12)
"days" **laethanta** [lay-hen-tuh] (masculine) (Lesson 94)
"dentist" **fiaclóir** [fee-uh-klor] (masculine) (Lesson 104)
"dentists" **fiaclóirí** [fee-uh-klor-ee] (masculine) (Lesson 104)
"dirty" **salach** [sahl-ahkh] (Lesson 18)

"dish" **soitheach** [suh-hahkh] (masculine) (Lesson 106)
"dishes" **soithí** [suh-hee] (masculine) (Lesson 106)
"do / make" **déan** [jayn] (Lesson 199)
"doctor" **dochtúir** [dokh-toor] (masculine) (Lesson 43)
"doctors" **dochtúirí** [dokh-toor-ee] (masculine) (Lesson 104)
"dog" **madra** [mah-druh] (masculine) (Lesson 155)
"doing" **ag déanamh** [ehg jay-nuv] (Lesson 37)
"door" **doras** [dor-us] (masculine) (Lesson 16)
"doors" **doirse** [deer-shuh] (masculine) (Lesson 19)
"doubt" **amhras** [ow-russ] (masculine) (Lesson 140)
"dress" **gúna** [goo-nuh] (masculine) (Lesson 138)
"drink" **deoch** [jawkh] (feminine) (Lesson 22)
"drink" **ól** [oel] (Lesson 186)
"drinking" **ag ól** [ehg oel] (Lesson 34)
"drinks" **deochanna** [jawkh-uh-nuh] (feminine) (Lesson 22)
"driver" **tiománaí** [tchih-maw-nee] (masculine) (Lesson 212)
"dry" **tirim** [tchih-ruhm] (Lesson 12)
"during" **i rith** [ih rih] (Lesson 212)
"eat" **ith** [ih] (Lesson 199)
"eating" **ag ithe** [ehg ih-huh] (Lesson 34)
"eclipse" **urú** [uh-roo] (masculine) (Lesson 24)
"eight" **ocht** [awkht] (Lesson 48)
"eight people" **ochtar** [awkh-tur] (Lesson 61)
"eighteen" **ocht déag** [awkht jayug] (Lesson 48)
"eighty" **ochtó** [awkh-toe] (Lesson 48)
"eleven" **aon déag** [ayn jayug] (Lesson 48)
"engineer" **innealtóir** [in-yil-tor] (masculine) (Lesson 104)
"engineers" **innealtóirí** [in-yil-tor-ee] (masculine) (Lesson 104)
"England" **Sasana** [soss-uh-nuh] (masculine) (Lesson 147)
"English (language)" **Béarla** [baer-luh] (masculine) (Lesson 135)
"every day" **gach lá** [gahkh law] (Lesson 90)
"father" **athair** [ah-her] (masculine) (Lesson 126)
"fear" **eagla** [og-luh] (feminine) (Lesson 140)
"fifteen" **cúig déag** [kooig jayug] (Lesson 48)
"fifty" **caoga** [kay-guh] (Lesson 48)
"fine" **go breá** [guh braw] (Lesson 1)
"fire" **tine** [tchih-nuh] (feminine) (Lesson 212)
"five" **cúig** [kooig] (Lesson 48)
"five people" **cúigear** [kooih-gur] (Lesson 61)
"floor" **urlár** [oor-lawr] (masculine) (Lesson 16)
"floors" **urláir** [oor-lawyer] (masculine) (Lesson 19)
"for / to" **do** [duh] (Lesson 152)
"for her / to her" **di** [jih] (Lesson 152)
"for *her* (emphatic) / to *her* (emphatic)" **dise** [jih-shuh] (Lesson 152)
"for him / to him" **dó** [doe] (Lesson 152)

"for *him* (emphatic) / to *him* (emphatic)" **dósan** [doe-sun] (Lesson 152)

"for me / to me" **dom** [dum] (Lesson 152)

"for *me* (emphatic) / to *me* (emphatic)" **domsa** [dum-suh] (Lesson 152)

"for the (singular) / to the (singular)" **don** [duhn] (Lesson 152)

"for them / to them" **dóibh** [doe-iv] (Lesson 152)

"for *them* (emphatic) / to *them* (emphatic)" **dóibhsean** [doe-iv-shun] (Lesson 152)

"for us / to us" **dúinn** [doo-een] (Lesson 152)

"for *us* (emphatic) / to *us* (emphatic)" **dúinne** [doo-een-uh] (Lesson 152)

"for y'all / to y'all" **daoibh** [deev] (Lesson 152)

"for *y'all* (emphatic) / to *y'all* (emphatic)" **daoibhse** [deev-shuh] (Lesson 152)

"for you / to you" **duit** [ditch] (Lesson 152)

"for *you* (emphatic) / to *you* (emphatic)" **duitse** [dih-tchuh] (Lesson 152)

"fork" **gabhlóg** [gow-loeg] (feminine) (Lesson 32)

"forty" **daichead** [dah-khayd] (Lesson 48)

"four" **ceathair** [kya-her] (Lesson 48)

"four (quantity)" **ceithre** [keh-ruh] (Lesson 53)

"four people" **ceathrar** [kya-hrer] (Lesson 61)

"fourteen" **ceathair déag** [kya-her jayug] (Lesson 48)

"France" **an Fhrainc** [un rank] (feminine) (Lesson 147)

"French (language)" **Fraincis** [fran-keesh] (feminine) (Lesson 135)

"friend" **cara** [kahr-uh] (masculine) (Lesson 126)

"friends" **cairde** [kahr-juh] (masculine) (Lesson 126)

"from" **ó** [oe] (Lesson 157)

"from her" **uaithi** [wuh-hee] (Lesson 157)

"from him" **uaidh** [wy] (Lesson 157)

"from me" **uaim** [wem] (Lesson 157)

"from the (singular)" **ón** [oen] (Lesson 157)

"from them" **uathu** [wuh-huh] (Lesson 157)

"from time to time" **ó am go h-am** [oe ahm guh hahm] (Lesson 90)

"from us" **uainn** [weng] (Lesson 157)

"from y'all" **uaibh** [wev] (Lesson 157)

"from you" **uait** [wet] (Lesson 157)

"fruit" **toradh** [tor-uh] (masculine) (Lesson 106)

"fruits" **torthaí** [tor-hee] (masculine) (Lesson 106)

"Germany" **an Ghearmáin** [un yah-ruh-moyn] (feminine) (Lesson 147)

"get" **faigh** [fai] (Lesson 199)

"gift" **bronntanas** [brun-tun-us] (masculine) (Lesson 153)

"gifts" **bronntanais** [brun-tun-ish] (masculine) (Lesson 153)

"girl" **cailín** [kall-yeen] (masculine) (Lesson 103)

"girls" **cailíní** [kall-yeen-ee] (masculine) (Lesson 103)

"give" **tabhair** [toor] (Lesson 199)

"gladness" **áthas** [aw-huss] (masculine) (Lesson 140)

"glass" **gloine** [glih-nyuh] (feminine) (Lesson 32)

"go" **téigh** [tchay] (Lesson 199)

"going" **ag dul** [ehg dull] (Lesson 41)

"green" **glas** [gloss] (Lesson 141)
"grey" **liath** [lee-uh] (Lesson 141)
"half of an hour" **leathuair** [lah-hooir] (feminine) (Lesson 51)
"handsome" **dathúil** [dah-hool] (Lesson 9)
"hat" **hata** [hot-uh] (masculine) (Lesson 138)
"hatred" **fuath** [foo-uh] (Lesson 174)
"he" **é** [ay] (Lesson 100)
"*he* (emphatic)" **eisean** [esh-in] (Lesson 124)
"he" **sé** [shay] (Lesson 2)
"*he* (emphatic)" **seisean** [shesh-in] (Lesson 10)
"head" **ceann** [kyawn] (masculine) (Lesson 55)
"heads" **cinn** [keen] (masculine) (Lesson 55)
"hear" **clois** [klish] (Lesson 199)
"her" **a** [uh] (Lesson 25)
"here" **anseo** [un-shuh] (Lesson 39)
"his" **a** [uh] (Lesson 25)
"home" **baile** [ball-yeh] (maculine) (Lesson 45)
"homeward" **abhaile** [uh-wah-lyuh] (Lesson 45)
"hot" **te** [tcheh] (Lesson 12)
"hotel" **óstán** [oess-tawn] (masculine) (Lesson 41)
"house" **teach** [tchahkh] (masculine) (Lesson 212)
"hundred" **céad** [kayud] (Lesson 48)
"hunger" **ocras** [uhk-russ] (masculine) (Lesson 139)
"hurry" **deifir** [jef-fer] (feminine) (Lesson 140)
"husband" **fear céile** [far kay-leh] (masculine) (Lesson 126)
"I / me" **mé** [may] (Lesson 2)
"*I* (emphatic)" **mise** [mih-shuh] (Lesson 10)
"improvement" **biseach** [bih-shahkh] (masculine) (Lesson 139)
"in" **i** [ih] (Lesson 145)
"in" **in** [ihn] (Lesson 145)
"in (with movement)" **isteach** [iss-tchahkh] (Lesson 46)
"in front" **os comhair** [oess koe-wer] (Lesson 212)
"in her" **inti** [in-tchee] (Lesson 145)
"in him" **ann** [on] (Lesson 145)
"in me" **ionam** [un-um] (Lesson 145)
"in the" **sa** [suh] (Lesson 146)
"in the" **san** [sun] (Lesson 146)
"in the (plural)" **sna** [snuh] (Lesson 146)
"in the afternoon" **sa tráthnóna** [suh traw-no-nuh] (Lesson 50)
"in the morning" **ar maidin** [air ma-jin] (Lesson 50)
"in them" **iontu** [un-tuh] (Lesson 145)
"in us" **ionainn** [un-een] (Lesson 145)
"in y'all" **ionaibh** [un-iv] (Lesson 145)
"in you" **ionat** [un-ut] (Lesson 145)
"inside" **istigh** [iss-tchih] (Lesson 39)

"Ireland" **Éire** [air-uh] (feminine) (Lesson 147)
"Irish (language)" **Gaeilge** [gay-lih-guh] (feminine) (Lesson 135)
"is (copula)" **is** [iss] (Lesson 99)
"job" **post** [pust] (masculine) (Lesson 135)
"key" **eochair** [ukh-er] (feminine) (Lesson 16)
"keys" **eochracha** [ukh-rukh-uh] (feminine) (Lesson 19)
"kind" **cineál** [kin-yal] (masculine) (Lesson 212)
"knife" **scian** [shkee-un] (feminine) (Lesson 22)
"knives" **sceana** [shkyah-nuh] (feminine) (Lesson 22)
"knowledge" **fios** [fiss] (masculine) (Lesson 135)
"land" **tír** [tcheer] (feminine) (Lesson 22)
"lands" **tíortha** [tcheer-huh] (feminine) (Lesson 22)
"last night" **aréir** [uh-rayr] (Lesson 70)
"later" **níos déanaí** [nees jay-nee] (Lesson 190)
"laughing" **ag gáire** [ehg goy-ruh] (Lesson 34)
"learning" **ag foghlaim** [ehg foe-lum] (Lesson 34)
"letter" **litir** [lih-tcher] (feminine) (Lesson 212)
"license" **ceadúnas** [kya-doon-us] (masculine) (Lesson 212)
"light" **solas** [suhl-us] (masculine) (Lesson 212)
"listen" **éist** [aysht] (Lesson 186)
"listening" **ag éisteacht** [ehg aysh-tahkht] (Lesson 36)
"long" **fada** [fah-duh] (Appendix)
"look" **féach** [fay-ukh] (Lesson 186)
"love" **grá** [graw] (masculine) (Lesson 155)
"mail" **post** [pust] (masculine) (Lesson 212)
"man" **fear** [far] (masculine) (Lesson 103)
"map" **léarscáil** [layr-skoyl] (feminine) (Lesson 102)
"maps" **léarscáileanna** [layr-skoyl-uh-nuh] (feminine) (Lesson 102)
"mechanic" **meicneoir** [mek-nyor] (masculine) (Lesson 104)
"mechanics" **meicneoirí** [mek-nyor-ee] (masculine) (Lesson 104)
"meeting" **cruinniú** [krin-nyew] (masculine) (Lesson 43)
"men" **fir** [fihr] (masculine) (Lesson 103)
"Mexico" **Meicsiceo** [mek-shih-ko] (masculine) (Lesson 147)
"milk" **bainne** [bon-yuh] (masculine) (Lesson 159)
"million" **milliún** [mil-yoon] (Lesson 48)
"minute" **nóiméad** [no-mayd] (masculine) (Lesson 54)
"money" **airgead** [air-ih-gud] (masculine) (Lesson 212)
"mother" **máthair** [maw-her] (feminine) (Lesson 126)
"movie" **scannán** [skuh-nawn] (masculine) (Lesson 43)
"music" **ceol** [kyoel] (masculine) (Lesson 212)
"musician" **ceoltóir** [kyoel-tor] (masculine) (Lesson 104)
"musicians" **ceoltóirí** [kyoel-tor-ee] (masculine) (Lesson 104)
"my" **mo** [muh] (Lesson 25)
"new" **nua** [noo-uh] (Lesson 18)
"night" **oíche** [ee-khuh] (feminine) (Lesson 12)

"nights" **oícheanta** [ee-khen-tuh] (feminine) (Lesson 94)

"nine" **naoi** [nee] (Lesson 48)

"nine people" **naonúr** [nee-noor] (Lesson 61)

"nineteen" **naoi déag** [nee jayug] (Lesson 48)

"ninety" **nócha** [no-khuh] (Lesson 48)

"now" **anois** [uh-nish] (Lesson 50)

"now and again" **anois agus arís** [uh-nish ah-gus uh-reesh] (Lesson 90)

"o'clock" **a chlog** [uh khluhg] (Lesson 49)

"office" **oifig** [if-fig] (feminine) (Lesson 212)

"often" **go minic** [guh min-ik] (Lesson 90)

"okay" **ceart go leor** [kyart guh leeyor] (Lesson 1)

"old" **sean** [shan] (Lesson 9)

"on" **ar** [air] (Lesson 137)

"on her" **uirthi** [ur-hee] (Lesson 137)

"on him" **air** [air] (Lesson 137)

"on me" **orm** [or-um] (Lesson 137)

"on them" **orthu** [or-huh] (Lesson 137)

"on us" **orainn** [or-een] (Lesson 137)

"on y'all" **oraibh** [or-iv] (Lesson 137)

"on you" **ort** [ort] (Lesson 1)

"on *you* (emphatic)" **ortsa** [ort-suh] (Lesson 1)

"one" **aon** [ayn] (Lesson 48)

"orange" **oráiste** [or-awsh-tuh] (Lesson 141)

"our" **ár** [awr] (Lesson 25)

"out (with movement)" **amach** [uh-mahkh] (Lesson 46)

"out of" **as** [oss] (Lesson 150)

"out of her" **aisti** [ash-tchee] (Lesson 150)

"out of him" **as** [oss] (Lesson 150)

"out of me" **asam** [oss-um] (Lesson 150)

"out of them" **astu** [oss-tuh] (Lesson 150)

"out of us" **asainn** [oss-een] (Lesson 150)

"out of y'all" **asaibh** [oss-iv] (Lesson 150)

"out of you" **asat** [oss-it] (Lesson 150)

"outside" **amuigh** [uh-muh] (Lesson 39)

"pants" **bríste** [breesh-tuh] (masculine) (Lesson 138)

"park" **páirc** [pawrk] (feminine) (Lesson 41)

"party" **cóisir** [koe-sher] (feminine) (Lesson 43)

"pen" **peann** [pyawn] (masculine) (Lesson 32)

"people" **daoine** [dee-nuh] (masculine) (Lesson 64)

"person" **duine** [din-uh] (masculine) (Lesson 61)

"pink" **bándearg** [bawn-jer-uhg] (Lesson 141)

"plate" **pláta** [plaw-tuh] (masculine) (Lesson 102)

"plates" **plátaí** [plaw-tee] (masculine) (Lesson 102)

"portion / some" **cuid** [kidj] (feminine) (Lesson 212)

"purple" **corcra** [kor-kuh-ruh] (Lesson 141)

"quarter" **ceathrú** [kya-hroo] (feminine) (Lesson 51)

"question" **ceist** [kesht] (feminine) (Lesson 135)

"rarely" **go h-annamh** [guh hah-nuv] (Lesson 90)

"reading" **ag léamh** [ehg lay-uv] (Lesson 36)

"red" **dearg** [jer-uhg] (Lesson 141)

"residence" **cónaí** [koe-nee] (masculine) (Lesson 148)

"restaurant" **bialann** [bee-uh-luhn] (feminine) (Lesson 41)

"right now" **anois díreach** [uh-nish jee-rahkh] (Lesson 50)

"ring" **fáinne** [faw-nyuh] (masculine) (Lesson 26)

"run" **rith** [rih] (Lesson 186)

"running" **ag rith** [ehg rih] (Lesson 34)

"salad" **sailéad** [sal-ayd] (masculine) (Lesson 159)

"sandwich" **ceapaire** [kya-puh-ruh] (masculine) (Lesson 159)

"say" **abair** [ah-ber] (Lesson 199)

"Scotland" **Albain** [all-uh-bin] (feminine) (Lesson 147)

"secretaries" **rúnaithe** [roo-nee-heh] (masculine) (Lesson 104)

"secretary" **rúnaí** [roo-nee] (masculine) (Lesson 104)

"see" **feic** [fek] (Lesson 199)

"self" **féin** [fayn] (Lesson 1)

"server / waiter / waitress" **freastalaí** [fras-tuh-lee] (masculine) (Lesson 104)

"servers / waiters / waitresses" **freastalaithe** [fras-tuh-lee-huh] (masculine) (Lesson 104)

"seven" **seacht** [shakht] (Lesson 48)

"seven people" **seachtar** [shakh-tur] (Lesson 61)

"seventeen" **seacht déag** [shakht jayug] (Lesson 48)

"seventy" **seachtó** [shakh-toe] (Lesson 48)

"she" **í** [ee] (Lesson 100)

"*she* (emphatic)" **ise** [ish-uh] (Lesson 124)

"she" **sí** [shee] (Lesson 2)

"*she* (emphatic)" **sise** [shih-shuh] (Lesson 10)

"shirt" **léine** [lay-nuh] (feminine) (Lesson 138)

"shoe" **bróg** [broeg] (feminine) (Lesson 138)

"shoes" **bróga** [bro-guh] (feminine) (Lesson 138)

"shopping" **ag siopadóireacht** [ehg shuh-puh-doy-rahkht] (Lesson 165)

"sick" **tinn** [tcheen] (Lesson 1)

"sickness / ache" **tinneas** [tchih-nuss] (masculine) (Lesson 139)

"sister" **deirfiúr** [drih-foor] (feminine) (Lesson 126)

"sisters" **deirfiúracha** [drih-foor-uh-khuh] (feminine) (Lesson 126)

"six" **sé** [shay] (Lesson 48)

"six people" **seisear** [shesh-er] (Lesson 61)

"sixteen" **sé déag** [shay jayug] (Lesson 48)

"sixty" **seasca** [shas-kuh] (Lesson 48)

"skirt" **sciorta** [skir-tuh] (masculine) (Lesson 138)

"sleep" **codladh** [kull-uh] (masculine) (Lesson 139)

"slender" **caol** [keel] (Appendix)

"small" **beag** [bayug] (Lesson 9)

"smart / clever" **cliste** [klish-tuh] (Lesson 9)
"sock" **stoca** [stuhk-uh] (masculine) (Lesson 138)
"socks" **stocaí** [stuh-kee] (masculine) (Lesson 138)
"softening" **séimhiú** [shay-voo] (masculine) (Lesson 15)
"some" **éigin** [ay-gihn] (Lesson 63)
"sometimes" **uaireanta** [oor-en-tuh] (Lesson 90)
"son" **mac** [mahk] (masculine) (Lesson 126)
"sons" **mic** [mik] (masculine) (Lesson 126)
"sorrow" **brón** [broen] (masculine) (Lesson 140)
"Spanish (language)" **Spáinnis** [spawn-ish] (feminine) (Lesson 135)
"speak" **labhair** [lau-wer] (Lesson 186)
"spoon" **spúnóg** [spoo-noeg] (feminine) (Lesson 22)
"spoons" **spúnóga** [spoo-noeg-uh] (feminine) (Lesson 22)
"store" **siopa** [shuhp-uh] (masculine) (Lesson 41)
"story / news" **scéal** [shkayl] (masculine) (Lesson 135)
"street" **sráid** [sroyj] (feminine) (Lesson 22)
"streets" **sráideanna** [sroy-jin-uh] (feminine) (Lesson 22)
"student" **dalta** [dahl-tuh] (masculine) (Lesson 104)
"students" **daltaí** [dahl-tee] (masculine) (Lesson 104)
"sugar" **siúcra** [shoo-kruh] (masculine) (Lesson 159)
"sun" **grian** [gree-un] (feminine) (Lesson 212)
"sunny" **grianmhar** [gree-un-wer] (Lesson 12)
"surprise" **ionadh** [ee-nuh] (masculine) (Lesson 140)
"swimming" **ag snámh** [ehg snawv] (Lesson 165)
"table" **bord** [bord] (masculine) (Lesson 16)
"tables" **boird** [bweerj] (masculine) (Lesson 19)
"take" **tóg** [toeg] (Lesson 186)
"talking" **ag caint** [ehg kyintch] (Lesson 34)
"tea" **tae** [tay] (masculine) (Lesson 159)
"teacher" **múinteoir** [moon-chor] (masculine) (Lesson 104)
"teachers" **múinteoirí** [moon-chor-ee] (masculine) (Lesson 104)
"ten" **deich** [jeh] (Lesson 48)
"ten people" **deichniúr** [jeh-noor] (Lesson 61)
"that / those" **sin** [shin] (Lesson 127)
"the (singular)" **an** [un] (Lesson 15)
"the (plural)" **na** [nuh] (Lesson 15)
"The United States" **na Stáit Aontaithe** [nuh stoych ayn-tih-huh] (masculine) (Lesson 147)
"their" **a** [uh] (Lesson 25)
"there (vague location)" **ann** [on] (Lesson 40)
"there" **ansin** [un-shin] (Lesson 39)
"they" **iad** [ee-ud] (Lesson 100)
"*they* (emphatic)" **iadsan** [ee-ud-sun] (Lesson 124)
"they" **siad** [shee-ud] (Lesson 2)
"*they* (emphatic)" **siadsan** [shee-ud-sun] (Lesson 10)
"thing" **rud** [ruhd] (masculine) (Lesson 54)

"things" **rudaí** [ruh-dee] (masculine) (Lesson 64)
"thirst" **tart** [tart] (masculine) (Lesson 139)
"thirteen" **trí déag** [tree jayug] (Lesson 48)
"thirty" **tríocha** [tree-khuh] (Lesson 48)
"this / these" **seo** [shuh] (Lesson 127)
"thousand" **míle** [mee-luh] (Lesson 48)
"three" **trí** [tree] (Lesson 48)
"three people" **triúr** [troo-ihr] (Lesson 61)
"tiredness" **tuirse** [teer-shuh] (feminine) (Lesson 139)
"today" **inniu** [in-yoo] (Lesson 12)
"tomorrow" **amárach** [uh-maw-rahkh] (Lesson 80)
"tomorrow night" **oíche amárach** [ee-khuh uh-maw-rahkh] (Lesson 80)
"tonight" **anocht** [uh-nahkht] (Lesson 12)
"too / also" **freisin** [fresh-in] (Lesson 11)
"too" **ró-** [roe] (Lesson 69)
"toys" **bréagáin** [bray-goyn] (masculine) (Lesson 212)
"travelling" **ag taisteal** [ehg tash-tuhl] (Lesson 165)
"twelve" **dó dhéag** [doe yayug] (Lesson 48)
"twenty" **fiche** [fih-huh] (Lesson 48)
"twenty-eight" **fiche a h-ocht** [fih-huh uh hawkht] (Lesson 48)
"twenty-five" **fiche a cúig** [fih-huh uh kooig] (Lesson 48)
"twenty-four" **fiche a ceathair** [fih-huh uh kya-her] (Lesson 48)
"twenty-nine" **fiche a naoi** [fih-huh uh nee] (Lesson 48)
"twenty-one" **fiche a h-aon** [fih-huh uh hayn] (Lesson 48)
"twenty-seven" **fiche a seacht** [fih-huh uh shakht] (Lesson 48)
"twenty-six" **fiche a sé** [fih-huh uh shay] (Lesson 48)
"twenty-three" **fiche a trí** [fih-huh uh tree] (Lesson 48)
"twenty-two" **fiche a dó** [fih-huh uh doe] (Lesson 48)
"two" **dó** [doe] (Lesson 48)
"two (quantity)" **dhá** [ghaw] (Lesson 53)
"two people" **beirt** [baertch] (Lesson 61)
"under" **faoi** [fwee] (Lesson 143)
"under her" **fúithi** [foo-hee] (Lesson 143)
"under him" **faoi** [fwee] (Lesson 143)
"under me" **fúm** [foom] (Lesson 143)
"under the" **faoin** [fween] (Lesson 144)
"under them" **fúthu** [foo-huh] (Lesson 143)
"under us" **fúinn** [foo-een] (Lesson 143)
"under y'all" **fúibh** [foo-iv] (Lesson 143)
"under you" **fút** [foot (rhymes with "boot")] (Lesson 143)
"us / we" **muid** [mwidj] (Lesson 2)
"usually" **de ghnáth** [deh ghuh-naw] (Lesson 90)
"very" **an-** [on] (Lesson 68)
"waiting / staying" **ag fanacht** [ehg faw-nahkht] (Lesson 36)
"walk" **siúil** [shoo-ihl] (Lesson 186)

"walking" **ag siúl** [ehg shool] (Lesson 33)

"water" **uisce** [ish-kuh] (masculine) (Lesson 159)

"we / us" **muid** [mwidj] (Lesson 2)

"*we* (emphatic)" **muide** [mwidj-uh] (Lesson 10)

"weather" **aimsir** [am-sheer] (feminine) (Lesson 12)

"wedding" **bainis** [ban-ish] (feminine) (Lesson 43)

"well" **go maith** [guh mah] (Lesson 1)

"wet" **fliuch** [flyukh] (Lesson 12)

"white" **bán** [bawn] (Lesson 141)

"wife" **bean chéile** [ban khay-leh] (feminine) (Lesson 126)

"window" **fuinneog** [fwin-yoeg] (feminine) (Lesson 16)

"windows" **fuinneoga** [fwin-yoeg-uh] (feminine) (Lesson 19)

"with" **le** [leh] (Lesson 158)

"with her" **léi** [lay-ih] (Lesson 158)

"with *her* (emphatic)" **léise** [lay-ih-shuh] (Lesson 184)

"with him" **leis** [lesh] (Lesson 158)

"with *him* (emphatic)" **leisean** [lesh-un] (Lesson 184)

"with me" **liom** [lyum] (Lesson 158)

"with *me* (emphatic)" **liomsa** [lyum-suh] (Lesson 184)

"with them" **leo** [lyo] (Lesson 158)

"with *them* (emphatic)" **leosan** [lyo-sun] (Lesson 184)

"with us" **linn** [leeng] (Lesson 158)

"with *us* (emphatic)" **linne** [leeng-uh] (Lesson 184)

"with y'all" **libh** [liv] (Lesson 158)

"with *y'all* (emphatic)" **libhse** [liv-shuh] (Lesson 184)

"with you" **leat** [lyat] (Lesson 158)

"with *you* (emphatic)" **leatsa** [lyat-suh] (Lesson 184)

"woman" **bean** [ban] (feminine) (Lesson 103)

"women" **mná** [mraw] (feminine) (Lesson 103)

"wonderful" **go h-iontach** [guh hee-un-tahkh] (Lesson 1)

"work" **obair** [uh-ber] (feminine) (Lesson 212)

"working" **ag obair** [ehg uh-ber] (Lesson 34)

"worry" **imní** [im-ree] (feminine) (Lesson 140)

"write" **scríobh** [shkree-uv] (Lesson 186)

"yellow" **buí** [bwee] (Lesson 141)

"yesterday" **inné** [in-yay] (Lesson 70)

"you (plural) or y'all" **sibh** [shiv] (Lesson 2)

"*you* (plural) or *y'all* (emphatic)" **sibhse** [shiv-shuh] (Lesson 10)

"you (singular)" **tú** [too] (Lesson 1)

"*you* (emphatic)" **tusa** [tuh-suh] (Lesson 10)

"young" **óg** [oeg] (Lesson 9)

"your (plural) or y'all's" **bhur** [woor] (Lesson 25)

"your" **do** [duh] (Lesson 25)

"zero" **náid** [noyj] (Lesson 48)

Glossary – Irish to English

a [uh] "her" (Lesson 25)

a [uh] "his" (Lesson 25)

a [uh] "their" (Lesson 25)

a chlog [uh khluhg] "o'clock" (Lesson 49)

abair [ah-ber] "say" (Lesson 199)

abhaile [uh-wah-lyuh] "homeward" (Lesson 45)

ach [akh] "but" (Lesson 67)

acu [ah-kuh] "at them" (Lesson 29)

ag [ehg] "at" (Lesson 28)

ag caint [ehg kyintch] "talking" (Lesson 34)

ag cócaireacht [ehg ko-kuh-rahkht] "cooking" (Lesson 165)

ag déanamh [ehg jay-nuv] "doing" (Lesson 37)

ag dul [ehg dull] "going" (Lesson 41)

ag éisteacht [ehg aysh-tahkht] "listening" (Lesson 36)

ag fanacht [ehg faw-nahkht] "waiting / staying" (Lesson 36)

ag foghlaim [ehg foe-lum] "learning" (Lesson 34)

ag gáire [ehg goy-ruh] "laughing" (Lesson 34)

ag ithe [ehg ih-huh] "eating" (Lesson 34)

ag léamh [ehg lay-uv] "reading" (Lesson 36)

ag obair [ehg uh-ber] "working" (Lesson 34)

ag ól [ehg oel] "drinking" (Lesson 34)

ag rince [ehg ring-kuh] "dancing" (Lesson 165)

ag rith [ehg rih] "running" (Lesson 34)

ag siopadóireacht [ehg shuh-puh-doy-rahkht] "shopping" (Lesson 165)

ag siúl [ehg shool] "walking" (Lesson 33)

ag snámh [ehg snawv] "swimming" (Lesson 165)

ag taisteal [ehg tash-tuhl] "travelling" (Lesson 165)

ag teacht [ehg tchakht] "coming" (Lesson 36)

agaibh [ah-giv] "at y'all" (Lesson 29)

againn [ah-geen] "at us" (Lesson 29)

agam [ah-gum] "at me" (Lesson 29)

agat [ah-gut] "at you" (Lesson 29)

agus [ah-gus] "and" (Lesson 1)

aici [ehk-ee] "at her" (Lesson 29)

aige [ehg-uh] "at him" (Lesson 29)

aimsir [am-sheer] "weather" (feminine) (Lesson 12)

air [air] "on him" (Lesson 137)

airgead [air-ih-gud] "money" (masculine) (Lesson 212)

aisti [ash-tchee] "out of her" (Lesson 150)

Albain [all-uh-bin] "Scotland" (feminine) (Lesson 147)

amach [uh-mahkh] "out (with movement)" (Lesson 46)

amárach [uh-maw-rahkh] "tomorrow" (Lesson 80)

amháin [uh-woyn] "alone" (Lesson 53)

amhras [ow-russ] "doubt" (masculine) (Lesson 140)

amuigh [uh-muh] "outside" (Lesson 39)

an [un] "the (singular)" (Lesson 15)

an- [on] "very" (Lesson 68)

an Astráil [un aws-trawyil] "Australia" (feminine) (Lesson 147)

an Fhrainc [un rank] "France" (feminine) (Lesson 147)

an Ghearmáin [un yah-ruh-moyn] "Germany" (feminine) (Lesson 147)

an tSín [un tcheen] "China" (feminine) (Lesson 147)

ann [on] "in him" (Lesson 145)

ann [on] "there (vague location)" (Lesson 40)

anocht [uh-nahkht] "tonight" (Lesson 12)

anois [uh-nish] "now" (Lesson 50)

anois agus arís [uh-nish ah-gus uh-reesh] "now and again" (Lesson 90)

anois díreach [uh-nish jee-rahkh] "right now" (Lesson 50)

anseo [un-shuh] "here" (Lesson 39)

ansin [un-shin] "there" (Lesson 39)

aon [ayn] "any" (Lesson 64)

aon [ayn] "one" (Lesson 48)

aon déag [ayn jayug] "eleven" (Lesson 48)

ar [air] "on" (Lesson 137)

ár [awr] "our" (Lesson 25)

ar bith [air bih] "at all" (Lesson 66)

ar fad [air fahd] "at length / really" (Lesson 68)

ar maidin [air ma-jin] "in the morning" (Lesson 50)

arán [uh-rawn] "bread" (masculine) (Lesson 212)

aréir [uh-rayr] "last night" (Lesson 70)

as [oss] "out of" (Lesson 150)

as [oss] "out of him" (Lesson 150)

asaibh [oss-iv] "out of y'all" (Lesson 150)

asainn [oss-een] "out of us" (Lesson 150)

asam [oss-um] "out of me" (Lesson 150)

asat [oss-it] "out of you" (Lesson 150)

astu [oss-tuh] "out of them" (Lesson 150)

athair [ah-her] "father" (masculine) (Lesson 126)

áthas [aw-huss] "gladness" (masculine) (Lesson 140)

baile [ball-yeh] "home" (maculine) (Lesson 45)

bainis [ban-ish] "wedding" (feminine) (Lesson 43)

bainne [bon-yuh] "milk" (masculine) (Lesson 159)

bán [bawn] "white" (Lesson 141)

bándearg [bawn-jer-uhg] "pink" (Lesson 141)

beag [bayug] "small" (Lesson 9)

beagán [byuh-gawn] "a little" (masculine) (Lesson 212)

bean [ban] "woman" (feminine) (Lesson 103)

bean chéile [ban khay-leh] "wife" (feminine) (Lesson 126)

Béarla [baer-luh] "English (language)" (masculine) (Lesson 135)
beir [baer] "bear / bring" (Lesson 199)
beirt [baertch] "two people" (Lesson 61)
beoir [byor] "beer" (feminine) (Lesson 212)
bhur [woor] "your (plural) or y'all's" (Lesson 25)
bí [bee] "be" (Lesson 199)
bialann [bee-uh-luhn] "restaurant" (feminine) (Lesson 41)
biseach [bih-shahkh] "improvement" (masculine) (Lesson 139)
boird [bweerj] "tables" (masculine) (Lesson 19)
bord [bord] "table" (masculine) (Lesson 16)
bosca [bus-kuh] "box" (masculine) (Lesson 25)
boscaí [bus-kee] "boxes" (masculine) (Lesson 64)
bréagáin [bray-goyn] "toys" (masculine) (Lesson 212)
briosca [bris-kuh] "cookie" (masculine) (Lesson 159)
brioscaí [bris-kee] "cookies" (masculine) (Lesson 159)
bríste [breesh-tuh] "pants" (masculine) (Lesson 138)
bróg [broeg] "shoe" (feminine) (Lesson 138)
bróga [bro-guh] "shoes" (feminine) (Lesson 138)
brón [broen] "sorrow" (masculine) (Lesson 140)
bronntanais [brun-tun-ish] "gifts" (masculine) (Lesson 153)
bronntanas [brun-tun-us] "gift" (masculine) (Lesson 153)
buachaill [boo-uh-khil] "boy" (masculine) (Lesson 103)
buachaillí [boo-uh-khulee] "boys" (masculine) (Lesson 103)
buí [bwee] "yellow" (Lesson 141)
caife [kaf-ay] "coffee" (masculine) (Lesson 159)
cailín [kall-yeen] "girl" (masculine) (Lesson 103)
cailíní [kall-yeen-ee] "girls" (masculine) (Lesson 103)
cairde [kahr-juh] "friends" (masculine) (Lesson 126)
caoga [kay-guh] "fifty" (Lesson 48)
caol [keel] "slender" (Appendix)
cara [kahr-uh] "friend" (masculine) (Lesson 126)
carranna [kahr-uh-nuh] "cars" (masculine) (Lesson 146)
carr [kahr] "car" (masculine) (Lesson 54)
cat [kot] "cat" (masculine) (Lesson 155)
cathaoir [kah-heer] "chair" (feminine) (Lesson 16)
cathaoireacha [kah-heer-ih-khuh] "chairs" (feminine) (Lesson 19)
céad [kayud] "hundred" (Lesson 48)
ceadúnas [kya-doon-us] "license" (masculine) (Lesson 212)
Ceanada [kya-nuh-duh] "Canada" (masculine) (Lesson 147)
ceann [kyawn] "head" (masculine) (Lesson 55)
ceannaigh [kya-nee] "buy" (Lesson 186)
ceapaire [kya-puh-ruh] "sandwich" (masculine) (Lesson 159)
ceart go leor [kyart guh leeyor] "okay" (Lesson 1)
ceathair [kya-her] "four" (Lesson 48)
ceathair déag [kya-her jayug] "fourteen" (Lesson 48)

ceathrar [kya-hrer] "four people" (Lesson 61)

ceathrú [kya-hroo] "quarter" (feminine) (Lesson 51)

ceist [kesht] "question" (feminine) (Lesson 135)

ceithre [keh-ruh] "four (quantity)" (Lesson 53)

ceol [kyoel] "music" (masculine) (Lesson 212)

ceoltóir [kyoel-tor] "musician" (masculine) (Lesson 104)

ceoltóirí [kyoel-tor-ee] "musicians" (masculine) (Lesson 104)

cineál [kin-yal] "kind" (masculine) (Lesson 212)

cinn [keen] "heads" (masculine) (Lesson 55)

cliste [klish-tuh] "smart / clever" (Lesson 9)

clois [klish] "hear" (Lesson 199)

codladh [kull-uh] "sleep" (masculine) (Lesson 139)

cóisir [koe-sher] "party" (feminine) (Lesson 43)

cónaí [koe-nee] "residence" (masculine) (Lesson 148)

corcra [kor-kuh-ruh] "purple" (Lesson 141)

cóta [ko-tuh] "coat" (masculine) (Lesson 138)

cruinniú [krin-nyew] "meeting" (masculine) (Lesson 43)

cuid [kidj] "portion / some" (feminine) (Lesson 212)

cúig [kooig] "five" (Lesson 48)

cúig déag [kooig jayug] "fifteen" (Lesson 48)

cúigear [kooih-gur] "five people" (Lesson 61)

cupán [kuh-pawn] "cup" (masculine) (Lesson 54)

daichead [dah-khayd] "forty" (Lesson 48)

dalta [dahl-tuh] "student" (masculine) (Lesson 104)

daltaí [dahl-tee] "students" (masculine) (Lesson 104)

daoibh [deev] "for y'all / to y'all" (Lesson 152)

daoibhse [deev-shuh] "for *y'all* (emphatic) / to *y'all* (emphatic)" (Lesson 152)

daoine [dee-nuh] "people" (masculine) (Lesson 64)

dath [dah] "color" (masculine) (Lesson 141)

dathúil [dah-hool] "handsome" (Lesson 9)

de ghnáth [deh ghuh-naw] "usually" (Lesson 90)

déan [jayn] "do / make" (Lesson 199)

dearg [jer-uhg] "red" (Lesson 141)

deartháir [dreh-har] "brother" (masculine) (Lesson 126)

deartháireacha [dreh-har-uh-khuh] "brothers" (masculine) (Lesson 126)

deich [jeh] "ten" (Lesson 48)

deichniúr [jeh-noor] "ten people" (Lesson 61)

deifir [jef-fer] "hurry" (feminine) (Lesson 140)

deirfiúr [drih-foor] "sister" (feminine) (Lesson 126)

deirfiúracha [drih-foor-uh-khuh] "sisters" (feminine) (Lesson 126)

deoch [jawkh] "drink" (feminine) (Lesson 22)

deochanna [jawkh-uh-nuh] "drinks" (feminine) (Lesson 22)

dhá [ghaw] "two (quantity)" (Lesson 53)

di [jih] "for her / to her" (Lesson 152)

dise [jih-shuh] "for *her* (emphatic) / to *her* (emphatic)" (Lesson 152)

do [duh] "for / to" (Lesson 152)

do [duh] "your" (Lesson 25)

dó [doe] "for him / to him" (Lesson 152)

dó [doe] "two" (Lesson 48)

dó dhéag [doe yayug] "twelve" (Lesson 48)

dochtúir [dokh-toor] "doctor" (masculine) (Lesson 43)

dochtúirí [dokh-toor-ee] "doctors" (masculine) (Lesson 104)

dóibh [doe-iv] "for them / to them" (Lesson 152)

dóibhsean [doe-iv-shun] "for *them* (emphatic) / to *them* (emphatic)" (Lesson 152)

doirse [deer-shuh] "doors" (masculine) (Lesson 19)

dom [dum] "for me / to me" (Lesson 152)

domsa [dum-suh] "for *me* (emphatic) / to *me* (emphatic)" (Lesson 152)

don [duhn] "for the (singular) / to the (singular)" (Lesson 152)

donn [duhn] "brown" (Lesson 141)

doras [dor-us] "door" (masculine) (Lesson 16)

dósan [doe-sun] "for *him* (emphatic) / to *him* (emphatic)" (Lesson 152)

droch [druhkh] "bad" (Lesson 211)

droichead [drih-khed] "bridge" (masculine) (Lesson 212)

dubh [duhv] "black" (Lesson 141)

duine [din-uh] "person" (masculine) (Lesson 61)

dúinn [doo-een] "for us / to us" (Lesson 152)

dúinne [doo-een-uh] "for *us* (emphatic) / to *us* (emphatic)" (Lesson 152)

duit [ditch] "for you / to you" (Lesson 152)

duitse [dih-tchuh] "for *you* (emphatic) / to *you* (emphatic)" (Lesson 152)

é [ay] "he" (Lesson 100)

eagla [og-luh] "fear" (feminine) (Lesson 140)

éigin [ay-gihn] "some" (Lesson 63)

Éire [air-uh] "Ireland" (feminine) (Lesson 147)

eisean [esh-in] "*he* (emphatic)" (Lesson 124)

éist [aysht] "listen" (Lesson 186)

eochair [ukh-er] "key" (feminine) (Lesson 16)

eochracha [ukh-rukh-uh] "keys" (feminine) (Lesson 19)

fada [fah-duh] "long" (Appendix)

faigh [fai] "get" (Lesson 199)

fáinne [faw-nyuh] "ring" (masculine) (Lesson 26)

faoi [fwee] "under" (Lesson 143)

faoi [fwee] "under him" (Lesson 143)

faoin [fween] "under the" (Lesson 144)

féach [fay-ukh] "look" (Lesson 186)

fear [far] "man" (masculine) (Lesson 103)

fear céile [far kay-leh] "husband" (masculine) (Lesson 126)

fearg [far-ihg] "anger" (feminine) (Lesson 140)

fearr [fawr] "better" (Lesson 178)

feic [fek] "see" (Lesson 199)

féin [fayn] "self" (Lesson 1)

fiaclóir [fee-uh-klor] "dentist" (masculine) (Lesson 104)

fiaclóirí [fee-uh-klor-ee] "dentists" (masculine) (Lesson 104)

fiche [fih-huh] "twenty" (Lesson 48)

fiche a ceathair [fih-huh uh kya-her] "twenty-four" (Lesson 48)

fiche a cúig [fih-huh uh kooig] "twenty-five" (Lesson 48)

fiche a dó [fih-huh uh doe] "twenty-two" (Lesson 48)

fiche a h-aon [fih-huh uh hayn] "twenty-one" (Lesson 48)

fiche a h-ocht [fih-huh uh hawkht] "twenty-eight" (Lesson 48)

fiche a naoi [fih-huh uh nee] "twenty-nine" (Lesson 48)

fiche a sé [fih-huh uh shay] "twenty-six" (Lesson 48)

fiche a seacht [fih-huh uh shakht] "twenty-seven" (Lesson 48)

fiche a trí [fih-huh uh tree] "twenty-three" (Lesson 48)

fios [fiss] "knowledge" (masculine) (Lesson 135)

fir [fihr] "men" (masculine) (Lesson 103)

fliuch [flyukh] "wet" (Lesson 12)

Fraincis [fran-keesh] "French (language)" (feminine) (Lesson 135)

freastalaí [fras-tuh-lee] "server / waiter / waitress" (masculine) (Lesson 104)

freastalaithe [fras-tuh-lee-huh] "servers / waiters / waitresses" (masculine) (Lesson 104)

freisin [fresh-in] "too / also" (Lesson 11)

fuar [foo-uhr] "cold" (Lesson 12)

fuath [foo-uh] "hatred" (Lesson 174)

fúibh [foo-iv] "under y'all" (Lesson 143)

fúinn [foo-een] "under us" (Lesson 143)

fuinneog [fwin-yoeg] "window" (feminine) (Lesson 16)

fuinneoga [fwin-yoeg-uh] "windows" (feminine) (Lesson 19)

fúithi [foo-hee] "under her" (Lesson 143)

fúm [foom] "under me" (Lesson 143)

fút [foot (rhymes with "boot")] "under you" (Lesson 143)

fúthu [foo-huh] "under them" (Lesson 143)

gabhlóg [gow-loeg] "fork" (feminine) (Lesson 32)

gach lá [gahkh law] "every day" (Lesson 90)

Gaeilge [gay-lih-guh] "Irish (language)" (feminine) (Lesson 135)

glan [glon] "clean" (Lesson 18)

glas [gloss] "green" (Lesson 141)

gloine [glih-nyuh] "glass" (feminine) (Lesson 32)

go breá [guh braw] "fine" (Lesson 1)

go dona [guh dun-uh] "bad" (Lesson 1)

go h-álainn [guh haw-ling] "beautiful" (Lesson 9)

go h-annamh [guh hah-nuv] "rarely" (Lesson 90)

go h-iontach [guh hee-un-tahkh] "wonderful" (Lesson 1)

go maith [guh mah] "well" (Lesson 1)

go minic [guh min-ik] "often" (Lesson 90)

gorm [gor-um] "blue" (Lesson 141)

grá [graw] "love" (masculine) (Lesson 155)

grian [gree-un] "sun" (feminine) (Lesson 212)

grianmhar [gree-un-wer] "sunny" (Lesson 12)

gúna [goo-nuh] "dress" (masculine) (Lesson 138)

hata [hot-uh] "hat" (masculine) (Lesson 138)

i [ih] "in" (Lesson 145)

í [ee] "she" (Lesson 100)

i gcónaí [ih go-nee] "always" (Lesson 90)

i rith [ih rih] "during" (Lesson 212)

iad [ee-ud] "they" (Lesson 100)

iadsan [ee-ud-sun] *"they* (emphatic)" (Lesson 124)

imní [im-ree] "worry" (feminine) (Lesson 140)

in [ihn] "in" (Lesson 145)

iníon [in-yeen] "daughter" (feminine) (Lesson 126)

iníonacha [in-yeen-ih-khuh] "daughters" (feminine) (Lesson 126)

inné [in-yay] "yesterday" (Lesson 70)

innealtóir [in-yil-tor] "engineer" (masculine) (Lesson 104)

innealtóirí [in-yil-tor-ee] "engineers" (masculine) (Lesson 104)

inniu [in-yoo] "today" (Lesson 12)

inti [in-tchee] "in her" (Lesson 145)

ionadh [ee-nuh] "surprise" (masculine) (Lesson 140)

ionaibh [un-iv] "in y'all" (Lesson 145)

ionainn [un-een] "in us" (Lesson 145)

ionam [un-um] "in me" (Lesson 145)

ionat [un-ut] "in you" (Lesson 145)

iontu [un-tuh] "in them" (Lesson 145)

is [iss] "is (copula)" (Lesson 99)

ise [ish-uh] *"she* (emphatic)" (Lesson 124)

isteach [iss-tchahkh] "in (with movement)" (Lesson 46)

istigh [iss-tchih] "inside" (Lesson 39)

ith [ih] "eat" (Lesson 199)

lá [law] "day" (masculine) (Lesson 12)

labhair [lau-wer] "speak" (Lesson 186)

laethanta [lay-hen-tuh] "days" (masculine) (Lesson 94)

le [leh] "with" (Lesson 158)

leabhar [lyow-er] "book" (masculine) (Lesson 32)

léarscáil [layr-skoyl] "map" (feminine) (Lesson 102)

léarscáileanna [layr-skoyl-uh-nuh] "maps" (feminine) (Lesson 102)

leat [lyat] "with you" (Lesson 158)

leathan [lah-hin] "broad" (Appendix)

leathuair [lah-hooir] "half of an hour" (feminine) (Lesson 51)

leatsa [lyat-suh] "with *you* (emphatic)" (Lesson 184)

léi [lay-ih] "with her" (Lesson 158)

léine [lay-nuh] "shirt" (feminine) (Lesson 138)

leis [lesh] "with him" (Lesson 158)

léise [lay-ih-shuh] "with *her* (emphatic)" (Lesson 184)

leisean [lesh-un] "with *him* (emphatic)" (Lesson 184)

leithreas [leh-hruss] "bathroom" (masculine) (Lesson 38)

leo [lyo] "with them" (Lesson 158)

leosan [lyo-sun] "with *them* (emphatic)" (Lesson 184)

liath [lee-uh] "grey" (Lesson 141)

libh [liv] "with y'all" (Lesson 158)

libhse [liv-shuh] "with *y'all* (emphatic)" (Lesson 184)

linn [leeng] "with us" (Lesson 158)

linne [leeng-uh] "with *us* (emphatic)" (Lesson 184)

liom [lyum] "with me" (Lesson 158)

liomsa [lyum-suh] "with *me* (emphatic)" (Lesson 184)

litir [lih-tcher] "letter" (feminine) (Lesson 212)

mac [mahk] "son" (masculine) (Lesson 126)

madra [mah-druh] "dog" (masculine) (Lesson 155)

mála [maw-luh] "bag" (masculine) (Lesson 32)

mar [mar] "because" (Lesson 207)

máthair [maw-her] "mother" (feminine) (Lesson 126)

mé [may] "I / me" (Lesson 2)

meicneoir [mek-nyor] "mechanic" (masculine) (Lesson 104)

meicneoirí [mek-nyor-ee] "mechanics" (masculine) (Lesson 104)

Meicsiceo [mek-shih-ko] "Mexico" (masculine) (Lesson 147)

Meiriceá [mair-ih-kaw] "America" (masculine) (Lesson 147)

mic [mik] "sons" (masculine) (Lesson 126)

míle [mee-luh] "thousand" (Lesson 48)

milliún [mil-yoon] "million" (Lesson 48)

mise [mih-shuh] "*I* (emphatic)" (Lesson 10)

mná [mraw] "women" (feminine) (Lesson 103)

mo [muh] "my" (Lesson 25)

mór [mor] "big" (Lesson 9)

mórán [mor-awn] "a lot" (masculine) (Lesson 212)

muid [mwidj] "us / we" (Lesson 2)

muide [mwidj-uh] "*we* (emphatic)" (Lesson 10)

múinteoir [moon-chor] "teacher" (masculine) (Lesson 104)

múinteoirí [moon-chor-ee] "teachers" (masculine) (Lesson 104)

na [nuh] "the (plural)" (Lesson 15)

na Stáit Aontaithe [nuh stoych ayn-tih-huh] "The United States" (masculine) (Lesson 147)

náid [noyj] "zero" (Lesson 48)

naoi [nee] "nine" (Lesson 48)

naoi déag [nee jayug] "nineteen" (Lesson 48)

naonúr [nee-noor] "nine people" (Lesson 61)

níos déanaí [nees jay-nee] "later" (Lesson 190)

nócha [no-khuh] "ninety" (Lesson 48)

nóiméad [no-mayd] "minute" (masculine) (Lesson 54)

nua [noo-uh] "new" (Lesson 18)

ó [oe] "from" (Lesson 157)

ó am go h-am [oe ahm guh hahm] "from time to time" (Lesson 90)

obair [uh-ber] "work" (feminine) (Lesson 212)

ocht [awkht] "eight" (Lesson 48)

ocht déag [awkht jayug] "eighteen" (Lesson 48)

ochtar [awkh-tur] "eight people" (Lesson 61)

ochtó [awkh-toe] "eighty" (Lesson 48)

ocras [uhk-russ] "hunger" (masculine) (Lesson 139)

óg [oeg] "young" (Lesson 9)

oíche [ee-khuh] "night" (feminine) (Lesson 12)

oíche amárach [ee-khuh uh-maw-rahkh] "tomorrow night" (Lesson 80)

oícheanta [ee-khen-tuh] "nights" (feminine) (Lesson 94)

oifig [if-fig] "office" (feminine) (Lesson 212)

ól [oel] "drink" (Lesson 186)

ón [oen] "from the (singular)" (Lesson 157)

oraibh [or-iv] "on y'all" (Lesson 137)

orainn [or-een] "on us" (Lesson 137)

oráiste [or-awsh-tuh] "orange" (Lesson 141)

orm [or-um] "on me" (Lesson 137)

ort [ort] "on you" (Lesson 1)

orthu [or-huh] "on them" (Lesson 137)

ortsa [ort-suh] "on *you* (emphatic)" (Lesson 1)

os comhair [oess koe-wer] "in front" (Lesson 212)

óstán [oess-tawn] "hotel" (masculine) (Lesson 41)

páirc [pawrk] "park" (feminine) (Lesson 41)

páiste [paw-stchuh] "child" (masculine) (Lesson 103)

páistí [paw-stchee] "children" (masculine) (Lesson 103)

peann [pyawn] "pen" (masculine) (Lesson 32)

pláta [plaw-tuh] "plate" (masculine) (Lesson 102)

plátaí [plaw-tee] "plates" (masculine) (Lesson 102)

post [pust] "job" (masculine) (Lesson 135)

post [pust] "mail" (masculine) (Lesson 212)

ríomhaire [ree-ver-uh] "computer" (masculine) (Lesson 102)

ríomhairí [ree-ver-ee] "computers" (masculine) (Lesson 102)

rith [rih] "run" (Lesson 186)

ró- [roe] "too" (Lesson 69)

roimh [riv] "before" (Lesson 51)

rothar [ruh-her] "bicycle" (masculine) (Lesson 32)

rud [ruhd] "thing" (masculine) (Lesson 54)

rudaí [ruh-dee] "things" (masculine) (Lesson 64)

rúnaí [roo-nee] "secretary" (masculine) (Lesson 104)

rúnaithe [roo-nee-heh] "secretaries" (masculine) (Lesson 104)

sa [suh] "in the" (Lesson 146)

sa tráthnóna [suh traw-no-nuh] "in the afternoon" (Lesson 50)

sailéad [sal-ayd] "salad" (masculine) (Lesson 159)

salach [sahl-ahkh] "dirty" (Lesson 18)

san [sun] "in the" (Lesson 146)

san oíche [sun ee-khuh] "at night" (Lesson 50)

Sasana [soss-uh-nuh] "England" (masculine) (Lesson 147)

scamallach [skom-uh-lahkh] "cloudy" (Lesson 12)

scannán [skuh-nawn] "movie" (masculine) (Lesson 43)

scéal [shkayl] "story / news" (masculine) (Lesson 135)

sceana [shkyah-nuh] "knives" (feminine) (Lesson 22)

scian [shkee-un] "knife" (feminine) (Lesson 22)

sciorta [skir-tuh] "skirt" (masculine) (Lesson 138)

scríobh [shkree-uv] "write" (Lesson 186)

scuab [skoo-uhb] "brush" (feminine) (Lesson 102)

scuaba [skoo-uh-buh] "brushes" (feminine) (Lesson 102)

sé [shay] "he" (Lesson 2)

sé [shay] "six" (Lesson 48)

sé déag [shay jayug] "sixteen" (Lesson 48)

seacht [shakht] "seven" (Lesson 48)

seacht déag [shakht jayug] "seventeen" (Lesson 48)

seachtar [shakh-tur] "seven people" (Lesson 61)

seachtó [shakh-toe] "seventy" (Lesson 48)

sean [shan] "old" (Lesson 9)

seasca [shas-kuh] "sixty" (Lesson 48)

séimhiú [shay-voo] "softening" (masculine) (Lesson 15)

seisean [shesh-in] "*he* (emphatic)" (Lesson 10)

seisear [shesh-er] "six people" (Lesson 61)

seo [shuh] "this / these" (Lesson 127)

sí [shee] "she" (Lesson 2)

siad [shee-ud] "they" (Lesson 2)

siadsan [shee-ud-sun] "*they* (emphatic)" (Lesson 10)

sibh [shiv] "you (plural) or y'all" (Lesson 2)

sibhse [shiv-shuh] "*you* (plural) or *y'all* (emphatic)" (Lesson 10)

sin [shin] "that / those" (Lesson 127)

siopa [shuhp-uh] "store" (masculine) (Lesson 41)

sise [shih-shuh] "*she* (emphatic)" (Lesson 10)

siúcra [shoo-kruh] "sugar" (masculine) (Lesson 159)

siúil [shoo-ihl] "walk" (Lesson 186)

slaghdán [sly-dawn] "cold (sickness)" (masculine) (Lesson 139)

sna [snuh] "in the (plural)" (Lesson 146)

soitheach [suh-hahkh] "dish" (masculine) (Lesson 106)

soithí [suh-hee] "dishes" (masculine) (Lesson 106)

solas [suhl-us] "light" (masculine) (Lesson 212)

Spáinnis [spawn-ish] "Spanish (language)" (feminine) (Lesson 135)

spúnóg [spoo-noeg] "spoon" (feminine) (Lesson 22)

spúnóga [spoo-noeg-uh] "spoons" (feminine) (Lesson 22)

sráid [sroyj] "street" (feminine) (Lesson 22)

sráideanna [sroy-jin-uh] "streets" (feminine) (Lesson 22)

stoca [stuhk-uh] "sock" (masculine) (Lesson 138)

stocaí [stuh-kee] "socks" (mas.) (Lesson 138)

tabhair [toor] "give" (Lesson 1

tae [tay] "tea" (masculine) (Les 59)

tar [tar] "come" (Lesson 199)

tar éis [tar aysh] "after" (Lessor

tart [tart] "thirst" (masculine) (L 139)

te [tcheh] "hot" (Lesson 12)

teach [tchahkh] "house" (mascul Lesson 212)

téigh [tchay] "go" (Lesson 199)

tine [tchih-nuh] "fire" (feminine) on 212)

tinn [tcheen] "sick" (Lesson 1)

tinneas [tchih-nuss] "sickness / ac masculine) (Lesson 139)

tiománaí [tchih-maw-nee] "driver' sculine) (Lesson 212)

tíortha [tcheer-huh] "lands" (femin (Lesson 22)

tír [tcheer] "land" (feminine) (Lesso

tirim [tchih-ruhm] "dry" (Lesson 12

tóg [toeg] "take" (Lesson 186)

toradh [tor-uh] "fruit" (masculine) (L n 106)

torthaí [tor-hee] "fruits" (masculine) son 106)

trá [traw] "beach" (feminine) (Lesson

trasna [tras-nuh] "across" (Lesson 212)

trí [tree] "three" (Lesson 48)

trí déag [tree jayug] "thirteen" (Lesson

tríocha [tree-khuh] "thirty" (Lesson 48)

triúr [troo-ihr] "three people" (Lesson 6

tú [too] "you (singular)" (Lesson 1)

tuirse [teer-shuh] "tiredness" (feminine) sson 139)

tusa [tuh-suh] *"you (emphatic)"* (Lesson 1

uaibh [wev] "from y'all" (Lesson 157)

uaidh [wy] "from him" (Lesson 157)

uaim [wem] "from me" (Lesson 157)

uainn [weng] "from us" (Lesson 157)

uaireanta [oor-en-tuh] "sometimes" (Lesson 0)

uait [wet] "from you" (Lesson 157)

uaithi [wuh-hee] "from her" (Lesson 157)

uathu [wuh-huh] "from them" (Lesson 157)

uirthi [ur-hee] "on her" (Lesson 137)

uisce [ish-kuh] "water" (masculine) (Lesson 19)

úll [ool] "apple" (masculine) (Lesson 26)

úlla [ool-uh] "apples" (masculine) (Lesson 15)

urláir [oor-lawyer] "floors" (masculine) (Lesson 19)

urlár [oor-lawr] "floor" (masculine) (Lesson 16)

urú [uh-roo] "eclipse" (masculine) (Lesson 24)

Printed by Amazon Italia Logistica S.r.l.
Torrazza Piemonte (TO), Italy